THE PASTORAL EPISTLES
OF ST. PAUL

THE PASTORAL EPISTLES
OF ST. PAUL

THE GREEK TEXT

WITH COMMENTARY BY THE

REV. A. E. HILLARD, D.D.

HIGH MASTER OF ST. PAUL'S SCHOOL
AND EXAMINING CHAPLAIN TO
THE LORD BISHOP OF CHICHESTER
1908-1919

WIPF & STOCK · Eugene, Oregon

Wipf and Stock Publishers
199 W 8th Ave, Suite 3
Eugene, OR 97401

The Pastoral Epistles of St. Paul
The Greek Text With Commentary
By Hillard, A E
Softcover ISBN-13: 978-1-7252-7402-0
Publication date 3/18/2020
Previously published by Rivingtons, 1919

PREFACE

I was led to attempt this edition of the Pastoral Epistles by my experience of the difficulties of candidates for Holy Orders. It is for them that I have been writing my notes and, though I shall be glad if they are useful to others, I shall be amply rewarded if they are found useful from this one point of view.

Candidates for Holy Orders usually study these Epistles during their Diaconate. It is a period during which their new work makes it difficult for them to give more than a margin of time to study. For this reason I have not hesitated to leave out from my notes points which might be expected in a commentary written for other purposes, and on the other hand to include in my notes any suggestions which seemed to me to be useful at this stage—suggestions for work, personal conduct, even for sermons; and while I hope that there is adequate treatment of points of scholarship and history I am much more concerned that the book should be what St. Paul would wish it to be, viz. a useful message to a young man in the early stages of his ministry.

By kind permission of the Delegates of the Oxford University Press and the Syndics of the Cambridge University Press I have used a Greek text incorporating the readings underlying the Revised Version. Where it seemed useful I have drawn attention in the notes to variations from the Received Text and also to the readings of Westcott and Hort's Text.

I desire to thank many friends, and especially the Rev. H. N. Bate, for valuable suggestions on various points in my notes.

A. E. HILLARD.

St. Paul's School,
May 1919.

TABLE OF CONTENTS

INTRODUCTION—
                                                          PAGE

  I. THE PLACE OF THE PASTORAL EPISTLES IN ST. PAUL'S LIFE ix

  II. TIMOTHY AND ST. PAUL—EPHESUS . . . xiii

  III. TITUS AND ST. PAUL—CRETE xxi

  IV. AUTHORSHIP OF THE PASTORAL EPISTLES . . xxiv

THE FIRST EPISTLE TO TIMOTHY 1

THE SECOND EPISTLE TO TIMOTHY . . . 69

THE EPISTLE TO TITUS 111

INDEX TO INTRODUCTION AND NOTES—
  GREEK 131
  ENGLISH 137

INTRODUCTION

I

The place of the Pastoral Epistles in St Paul's life

THE Acts of the Apostles leave St. Paul in *libera custodia* at Rome, dwelling for 'two whole years in his own hired dwelling,' freely receiving and teaching all who cared to come to him. These two years were most probably 60-61 A.D. The abrupt ending of the book may be accounted for either by its being written shortly after these two years or by the supposition that a climax had been reached in the arrival of the Apostle at Rome and that a continuation was intended. But it has made it possible to maintain that St. Paul never was released and was kept a prisoner at Rome until he suffered martyrdom in the Neronian persecution which followed the great fire at Rome (July 64 A.D.).

This supposition is contrary to the traditional history. The Pastoral Epistles themselves imply a period of ministry which cannot be fitted into the period covered by the Acts, and if we accept them as the writing of St. Paul they would decide the question. But apart from them we have two references which seem to imply a journey of St. Paul to Spain, and if this be established it is equally decisive, since no such journey can find a place in the period of the Acts. The first reference is in St. Clement's Epistle to the Corinthians (v.), where he says that St. Paul went to the furthest west, ἐπὶ τὸ τέρμα τῆς δύσεως ἐλθών. St. Clement's letter was written from Rome (of which Church he is reputed the fourth bishop) about 96 A.D., and though a Greek might doubtless speak of Italy vaguely by such a phrase this interpretation is very unnatural in a letter written from Rome. The other reference is in the Muratorian fragment, about 180 A.D. (see below, p. xxiv), which describing the contents of the Acts remarks that the book does not describe the martyrdom of Peter or the departure of Paul from Rome to Spain.[1] The writer therefore seems to take that journey as a known fact of the Apostle's life.

Therefore in spite of the fact that there is no Spanish tradition of such a visit our scanty evidence makes it probable that St. Paul was able to fulfil the wish expressed in Romans xv. 24, and we are justified in believing the tradition recorded by later authorities that he was released from the first imprisonment and had a further period of ministry. It is in this further period that the Pastoral Epistles find their natural place. The allusions in them are all accounted for by this supposition, and the special characteristics of these epistles are naturally accounted for by the interval of time which such a supposition involves.

The first Epistle to Timothy implies (i. 3) a recent journey in Asia in which the Apostle, on proceeding to Macedonia, had left Timothy behind in Ephesus.

The second Epistle to Timothy shows incidentally that he had been in Miletus (iv. 20), Troas (iv. 13), and Corinth (iv. 20).

The Epistle to Titus implies a visit to Crete (i. 5) and an intention to spend the winter at Nicopolis in Epirus (iii. 12).

The most probable hypothesis is that St. Paul on his release first visited Spain, then Crete, then fulfilled the intention expressed in Philemon 22, Philippians i. 25, ii. 24, of revisiting some of the churches of Asia and Macedonia,

[1] Sicute et semote passionem petri evidenter declarat sed profectionem pauli ab urbe ad spaniam proficescentis. The passage is corrupt but justifies the inference drawn above. See Westcott's *Canon of the New Testament,* Appendix C.

INTRODUCTION

and thence went on to Corinth. It is impossible to say whether St. Paul ever reached Nicopolis or where he was again arrested.

It is probable, then, that the first Epistle to Timothy and the Epistle to Titus were written during this journey in Macedonia and Greece. Resemblances in subject and diction make it fairly certain (if both are genuine) that they were written at no great interval, though the differences of language are greater than would be likely if they were written at the same time. (See *e.g.* note on Titus i. 6.)

The historical situation of 2 Timothy is clearly indicated. Timothy is probably still at Ephesus, though such verses as iv. 12 ('Tychicus I sent to Ephesus'), 20 ('Trophimus I left at Miletus sick'), i. 15 ('All that are in Asia turned away from me') require some explanation if this was the case. St. Paul himself is in prison at Rome. The Roman tradition which represents him as in the Mamertine prison is probably incorrect, but we may safely assume that the imprisonment, though of the kind that befitted a Roman citizen, was more rigorous than the earlier one. It was dangerous to stand by him (iv. 16, οὐδείς μοι παρεγένετο, and iv. 10) or even to visit him (as seems implied in i. 16, 17), and he speaks of his sufferings as being μέχρι δεσμῶν ὡς κακοῦργος (ii. 9). The last word expresses the changed attitude of the Roman government. To be a Christian was now for the first time to come under suspicion of being a criminal. We are not bound to accept the belief of Tacitus that Nero deliberately turned suspicion on to the Christians (*Ann.*, xv. 44), but the public excitement demanded a scapegoat. Every disaster in Roman history had led to a temporary revival of religious rites in honour of the Roman gods, and this case was no exception; nor need we seek other cause than this superstition bred of calamity for the attack upon what Tacitus calls the *exitiabilis superstitio* of Christianity. It was doubtless helped by the general opinion that the Church was a secret society with secret rites. At what stage of the persecution St. Paul was arrested we do not know, but the remark of Tacitus that the later victims suffered not so much for complicity in the fire as for *odium humani generis* justifies us in thinking that the persecution lasted for some time, and the most probable chronology of St. Paul's life places his death as late as 67 A.D. When he wrote the second Epistle to Timothy he had already been tried on one charge and acquitted (iv. 16) ;[1] but he was awaiting a further trial in which he expected to be condemned. This expectation was fulfilled and he suffered death, according to tradition, on the Ostian Road, at the spot named Tre Fontane from the three springs which according to the legend burst from the earth at the moment of his death.

[1] See the note on this verse. One interpretation refers ἐν τῇ πρώτῃ μου ἀπολογίᾳ to the first imprisonment; but apart from other reasons against this the οὐδείς μοι παρεγένετο is extremely improbable of that occasion, when there was no capital charge against the Apostle and the Roman authority had received no bias against Christianity.

II

Timothy and St. Paul—Ephesus

The first mention of Timothy is in Acts xvi. 1, from which passage it is presumed that Lystra was his original home. Lystra was situated on a hill-side where the Isaurian hills verge into the Lycaonian plain. It was on the north side of a stream which flows on to that plain, and the district was and is fertile. It was therefore the centre of an agricultural district rather than a centre of trade, and the road (called the Imperial Road) which connected it with Pisidian Antioch westwards and with Derbe south-eastwards had been constructed mainly for military purposes as the Romans pushed their administration into the Isaurian district. Lystra lay in the Roman part of Lycaonia and therefore belonged to the province of Galatia. But it had been made a Roman colony about B.C. 6. Its ruling class would therefore be the 'colonists,' but these would be a small minority. There may have been a few real Greeks, but the bulk of the population would have been the primitive people of the district, oriental in their affinities, though we cannot assign them to any definite race. Their natural language is referred to as Lycaonian in Acts xiv. 11, but the culture of the town was Greek and the better class of inhabitants would speak Greek. These would also be called Greeks by contrast with the less civilised natives, and when Timothy's father is called a Greek (Acts xvi. 1) we cannot infer that he was a real Greek by race but only that he belonged to the more enlightened class of the native community. His mother Eunice was a Jewess. We have no other intimation of the presence of other Jews at Lystra, but, besides the Jewish garrisons planted in Asia Minor in the times of the Syrian kings, many Jews had settled there for purposes of trade, and the harvests of the districts round Lystra gave plenty of scope for the kind of commerce at which the Jews were adepts.

We are not told anything more of Timothy's father. But as Eunice was allowed to bring her son up from earliest childhood in a knowledge of the Jewish scriptures, we may assume that he shared the feeling with regard to Judaism of most thoughtful Greeks and Romans, who, much as they disliked the race, respected the religion on account of its monotheism and purer morality. But of course Timothy was not a Jew in the eyes of the civil law, and he could not be so recognised by the Jews themselves because he had not been circumcised. All these circumstances would have rendered him more ready to receive with open mind the Apostle's teaching. He was probably a witness of the events recorded in Acts xiv. 6-21 on St. Paul's first journey, and one of the converts then made. When St. Paul revisited Lystra at the beginning of his second journey (xvi. 1) Timothy was recommended to him by the good opinion of the brethren both at Lystra and at Iconium, and was taken by him as his assistant. It is probable that we must refer to this time those passages in the Epistles to Timothy which imply a definite 'setting apart' of Timothy for the ministry. In this case we must assume that he was not pointed out only by the general good opinion of the brethren but also by prophetic utterances in the Church, and that his 'setting apart' was a definite ceremony in which the Apostle and the πρεσβύτεροι laid their hands upon him. It is not necessary to assume that this ordination was to any specially defined function in the ministry of the Church—and indeed

INTRODUCTION xv

it is not likely that organisation had yet reached that point. But if any name was used it was probably εὐαγγελιστής, to which there might be an allusion in 2 Timothy iv. 5.

But the fact that Timothy was not circumcised would have made his ministry as an evangelist with St. Paul almost impossible. Doubtless the words of St. Paul at Antioch quoted in Acts xiii. 46 marked a decided change in his conviction as to the advisability of always trying to approach the Gentiles through the Jewish community. But it is clear that he continued to follow this method wherever possible, and even when he reached Rome (Acts xxviii. 17) his first act was to call together 'the chief of the Jews.' Whether Timothy claimed to be a Jew because of his mother, or a Gentile because of his father, the difficulty was equal. As a Jew he would be looked on as a renegade because of his want of circumcision. As a Gentile he would have no *locus standi* in the synagogue except as an adherent and listener. St. Paul therefore caused him to be circumcised. The Council at Jerusalem had just decided that Gentile converts need not be circumcised (Acts xv. 28), and he was probably anxious above all things at the moment to give no handle to those who would say that he was treating this decision as the 'thin edge of the wedge' and was now teaching against the circumcision even of Jews, since Timothy was partly of Jewish blood. He therefore preferred to risk the contrary charge of inconsistency. To him the rite was not essential either for Jew or for Gentile. But Timothy's submission to it would not prejudice him with the Gentiles, his refusal of it would prejudice him with the Jews. In order therefore to make his ministry acceptable to those who had not reached the same standpoint he acquiesced in what to him was non-essential.

From this time onwards Timothy became (with the exception perhaps of St. Luke) the most constant of St. Paul's companions and ministers. He accompanied him now as far as Beroea, joined him again at Athens, and was thence sent back to Thessalonica to convey the Apostle's encouragement to the Church there (1 Thessalonians iii. 1). After joining the Apostle again at Corinth he helped the preaching there (2 Corinthians i. 19).

The next mention of Timothy is in Acts xix. 22, where the Apostle, now being at Ephesus in the course of his third missionary journey, sends forward Timothy and Erastus to Macedonia. Timothy was to continue his journey to Corinth, since this appears to be the mission referred to in 1 Corinthians iv. 17: "For this cause have I sent unto you Timothy, who is my beloved and faithful child in the Lord, who shall put you in remembrance of my ways which be in Christ.' The first Epistle to the Corinthians was sent (direct to Corinth across the Aegean) while Timothy was on his way. That epistle shows that the mission of Timothy was a difficult one, and the Apostle is in some doubt as to his reception. For he writes (xvi. 10) 'If Timothy come, see that he be with you without fear; for he worketh the work of the Lord, as I also do: let no man therefore despise him. But set him forward on his journey in peace that he may come unto me: for I expect him with the brethren.' Timothy returned to St. Paul at Ephesus, and we gather from passages in 2 Corinthians that his mission at Corinth had not been successful. Further, it seems likely that he had been treated with contumely and that he is the person referred to as ὁ ἀδικηθείς in 2 Corinthians vii. 12. On Timothy's arrival at Ephesus it seems that St. Paul wrote to Corinth the lost letter referred to in 2 Corinthians (cf. ii. 4, 'I wrote unto you with many tears'), and that this letter was partly a protest against the treatment of Timothy.

INTRODUCTION xvii

The lost letter was conveyed by Titus, and it was on his return with better news that the Apostle (then in Macedonia, 2 Corinthians ii. 12) wrote the second Epistle to the Corinthians.

From the greetings in 2 Corinthians i. 1, Romans xvi. 21, we may assume that Timothy continued with St. Paul in the journeys through Macedonia and Greece referred to in Acts xx. 1-3, and it is stated (v. 4) that he accompanied him back to Asia. He is not mentioned again in the Acts, but the greetings in Philippians, Colossians, Philemon show that he was with St. Paul during part of his first imprisonment at Rome. The next intimation we have is from the Epistles to Timothy, which show that at some time subsequent to his release St. Paul left him at Ephesus to order the Church there. (See above, p. x.)

No place was so important as Ephesus for the purpose of St. Paul's work—so much so that when he was on his third missionary journey he had stayed there a year and three months. Originally an Athenian colony, Ephesus had succeeded to the importance of Miletus when the harbour of that port had become silted up. It had been made the capital of the Roman province of Asia, and was at this time in some respects the capital of the East. The chief trade route by sea between Italy and the East lay through Corinth and Ephesus. From Ephesus it followed one of two routes —either the ship coasted along the south of Asia Minor to Syria, or the cargo and passengers went by the great road which led from Ephesus across Asia Minor to the Cilician Gates. From this trade the town became very wealthy and as cosmopolitan as Rome itself. It was therefore a centre from which St. Paul's teaching would spread naturally both East and West, but especially to the inland towns of the Asian province, and it was doubtless while St. Paul was

b

still at Ephesus that churches began to grow at places like Colossae and Laodicea. These towns would look to Ephesus as their head, and the Apostle's representative there would exercise control over them as over Ephesus itself.

The cosmopolitanism of Ephesus extended to religion and philosophy—practically every religion and philosophy of East or West was represented there. The official Roman worship of the Augusti was of course established there, and the city was dignified with the title of Neocoros or Warden of this worship. It is noteworthy as one sign of the Roman attitude at the time that the Asiarchs (*i.e.* the provincial Presidents charged with the maintenance of this Roman worship in its various centres) were friendly to St. Paul. But while all religions were represented at Ephesus, its chief and traditional religion was the worship of the Asiatic goddess of fertility whom the Greeks identified with Artemis, the Romans with Diana, though her worship was thoroughly oriental in character. Her temple lay some distance outside the city, was crowded with priests and priestesses, and attracted multitudes of pilgrims whose concourse added much to the business of the city, and whose gifts (often in the shape of shrines with an image of the goddess) added much to the wealth of the temple. It was probably due to the worship of this goddess that Ephesus had become the home of magic and did a thriving trade in the formulae for incantations of all kinds, known as 'Ephesian letters.' The use of these formulae is illustrated in Acts xix. 13-19. In addition to these pagan influences the Church at Ephesus had to reckon with a strong Jewish element and with all forms of current philosophy, oriental as well as Greek.

This cosmopolitanism was in one sense an advantage to the teaching of Christianity. To add one more kind of teaching or one more kind of worship to those already in vogue would not appear to the authorities a matter of very great moment, and besides the Asiarchs we find the Secretary of the Assembly (an important man in the city—called the 'town-clerk' in Acts xix. 35) inclined to take a favourable view of the Christian teachers. But a much more important consequence—and the one with which we are concerned in the Epistles to Timothy—is that which is common to all cosmopolitan centres. On the one hand, the very tolerance accorded to a new teaching tends to breed corrupt forms of it. Those who see something in the new teaching but do not accept it in its entirety proceed to make a compromise, and so produce and present to the public a form of it which intellectually and morally demands less, and therefore attracts more the indolent, the half-hearted, and the eclectic. The various phases of Gnosticism are a good illustration of this process. Oriental thought, Greek thought, Jewish thought, and Christian thought were all necessary to produce this group of heresies as we know them in history, and all these were present and flourishing at Ephesus.[1] On the other hand, the reaction of tolerance on a new teaching is equally dangerous. The compromise may not be all on one side. The pleasure of finding partial acceptance where one expected outright opposition is so great that one is tempted to make the most of points of agreement and lay less stress on what is perhaps the essential message of the new teaching to the world.

That these were the dangers which St. Paul feared at Ephesus is apparent from various passages in the Epistles to Timothy. St. Paul has therefore been criticised for appointing to what was likely to be one of the most important positions in the Church a man who had such limitations

[1] The nature of the heresies at Ephesus is dealt with in the notes on 1 Tim. iv. 3.

as seem to be implied by St. Paul's own words of Timothy in one or two places. That he was shrinking and timid by nature may be reasonably inferred from such a passage as 1 Corinthians xvi. 10, 'If Timothy come, see that he be with you without fear ($ἀφόβως$). . . . Let no man despise him'; and this is supported by such incidental warnings as 1 Timothy iv. 12, 'Let no one despise thy youth'; 2 Timothy i. 8, 'Be not ashamed of the testimony of our Lord.' But the reference in 1 Timothy v. 23 ('thy often infirmities') makes it likely that this point in Timothy's character was due to physical weakness, and though such weakness needs constant precaution, St. Paul knew from his own experience that it need not weaken one's work. That he had great confidence in Timothy's devoted loyalty is shown not only in these epistles but by such passages as 1 Corinthians iv. 17, 'my beloved and faithful child in the Lord'; Philippians ii. 20, 'I have no man like-minded, who will care truly for your state.' There is no one of whom St. Paul uses such frequent expressions of affection, and that this affection was reciprocated is shown by 2 Timothy i. 4.

The only later reference to Timothy which we have is by the writer of the Epistle to the Hebrews xiii. 23, 'Know ye that our brother Timothy hath been set at liberty.' But the doubt as to the date of that epistle makes it impossible to conjecture the occasion of the imprisonment referred to. Tradition represents him as Bishop of Ephesus until his death. He is said to have suffered martyrdom through attempting to repress a popular pagan festival, and his remains are said to have been conveyed to Constantinople by Constantius.

III

Titus and St. Paul—Crete

Titus is not mentioned in the Acts, and our knowledge of him is derived from incidental allusions in the Epistles and from the Epistle written to him by St. Paul.

The earliest mention of him is in Galatians ii. 1-5, from which we learn that he was a Gentile, that he went up with St. Paul from Antioch to Jerusalem on the mission recorded in Acts xv., and that every effort was made by the Jewish element in the Church to compel him to be circumcised. The meaning of Galatians ii. 3 has been disputed on the assumption that the emphasis there is on ἠναγκάσθη and in v. 5 on τῇ ὑποταγῇ; from which it is inferred that St. Paul means that Titus was circumcised, but by way of concession, not through any compulsion or submission. This however does not seem likely. The emphasis on these Greek words is not natural, the decision of the Council (Acts xv.) was that Gentiles need not be circumcised, and St. Paul could hardly have used the strong expression οὐδὲ πρὸς ὥραν εἴξαμεν τῇ ὑποταγῇ if he had acquiesced in a case that was obviously treated as a test. We may therefore conclude that Titus was not circumcised.

That he continued with St. Paul is likely, but we have no further reference to him till about ten years later, when he is mentioned prominently in 2 Corinthians. From this epistle we gather that St. Paul sent him three times to Corinth during the time that he himself was at Ephesus (Acts xix.) or journeying from Ephesus to Macedonia and Greece. The first of these visits was to arrange the collection for the Judaean brethren about which St. Paul was anxious.

The second followed the return of Timothy with the distressing news of the disaffection and disorder at Corinth, and on this occasion Titus conveyed the now lost epistle (see above, p. xvi). Titus threw himself into the task with zeal (2 Corinthians viii. 17), was well received and was successful in his efforts (vii. 7). We may gather that he was a man capable of administrative work, firm but conciliatory in temper. On the third occasion Titus conveyed the second of our Epistles to the Corinthians and proceeded with the arrangements for the collection (2 Corinthians viii. 16-24).

Again for about eight years we have no mention of him. Then we have the present epistle, for the circumstances of which see above, p. xi. The only other mention is in 2 Timothy iv. 10, 'Titus went to Dalmatia.' This may imply, but does not necessarily imply, that Titus had been with St. Paul during part of the second imprisonment at Rome.

But the work with which Titus is associated by all tradition (as recorded in Eusebius and elsewhere) is that on which he was engaged in Crete when this epistle was written to him. He is represented as having been Bishop of Crete. Churches in Crete still bear his name. He is said to have been buried there, and it is said that his head was carried off by the Venetians in the Middle Ages and placed in St. Mark's at Venice.

We do not know when or by whom Christianity was founded in Crete. St. Paul's only recorded visit there was on the voyage to Rome (Acts xxvii.), and it is not likely that his circumstances then permitted him to do any evangelising work. Titus i. 5 implies that he had been in Crete recently, and a visit between the first and second imprisonment is most likely. But an earlier visit, *e.g.* during his stay at Ephesus, is quite possible and is rather pointed to by the evidence of the epistle as to the spread of Christianity in several cities of the island (i. 5). There was a considerable

INTRODUCTION xxiii

Jewish element in Crete (Cretan Jews are represented in the multitude at Jerusalem on the day of Pentecost, Acts ii. 11), and it is therefore likely that Christianity came there independently of the Apostle. The influence of the Jews was considerable and dangerous, as we see from the warning in Titus i. 10-11, 14. We have no information as to the history of the Church in the island after St. Paul's time; but the two churches of Gortyna and Cnossus are mentioned in letters of Dionysius of Corinth who (about the middle of the second century) wrote to the Bishop of the former with warnings against heresy and to the Bishop of the latter (Pinytus by name) urging him not to demand too great an asceticism among his flock but to consider the weakness of human nature. (Eusebius iv. 23, 25.)

Of the population of Crete we can say little. The greatness of Crete is prehistoric, connected with the Minoan period of pre-Hellenic culture, and doubtless the bulk of the population continued to be of the same stock, already mixed. (See Bury's *History of Greece*, chap. i.). To the Biblical student there is special interest in the fact that the Philistines (with David's Cherethites and Pelethites) probably came from this stock. But the island had been settled by Dorians, and its civilisation was gradually assimilated to the ordinary Hellenic type. It held a favourable position 'between three continents' for commerce; the plains along its northern coast were fertile and populous, and in ancient times its mountains were covered with forests. It had been made a Roman province (joined with Cyrene) in B.C. 67. What St Paul says of the avarice and untrustworthiness of its people (i. 12, 13) was almost proverbial, and is confirmed by Livy, Plutarch, and other authors. This character probably continued through all political changes, since, when the Turks conquered the island in 1645, the majority of its population accepted Mohammedanism.

IV

Authorship of the Pastoral Epistles

In the second century there was a great deal of Christian literature which was read in the churches for purposes of edification besides those books which have come to be included in the New Testament. Such books were the Epistle of Clement to the Corinthians (about 96 A.D.), the Epistle of Barnabas (about 75 A.D.), and the *Pastor* of Hermas (about 156 A.D.). It is not possible to trace exactly the steps by which a distinction was made, and some books were recognised as canonical in our sense and authoritative, while others were regarded as only ecclesiastical and useful. For a long time different parts of the Church differed in their use of the books, and *e.g.* the Western part of the Church seems to have been without the Epistles of St. Peter until comparatively late. It is not therefore a matter of surprise that we have no statement or list of recognised books in the first half of the second century. When a distinction began to be drawn it is important to notice that it was drawn, not on any internal evidence of inspiration or even usefulness, but on the basis of authorship. The *apostolic* writings came to be classed by themselves.

The earliest list which professes to give the apostolic writings recognised by the Catholic Church [1] is that contained in what is called the Muratorian fragment. This is a manuscript found about 1740 by the Italian scholar Muratori in the Ambrosian Library at Milan. It was written in the eighth century, but purports to be a copy of a document

---

[1] For Marcion's list see below, p. xxvii.

written not long after the *Pastor* of Hermas had become generally accepted. Its probable date is therefore about 180 A.D. It gives a list of the books which the Catholic Church at that time acknowledged as apostolic by its usage —the writer is of course not giving an official ' canon ' of Scripture. The Latin of the document is very barbarous, but the sentence which concerns us in the list of St. Paul's epistles reads thus : ' ad filemonem una et ad titum una et ad tymotheum duas pro affecto et dilectione in honore tamen ecclesiae catholice in ordinatione ecclesiastice descepline sanctificate sunt,' *i.e.* the one letter to Philemon, one to Titus and two to Timothy, written from motives of affection and love, were treated as sacred in the ordering of ecclesiastical discipline. That discrimination was used in compiling the list is shown by the sentence with which the author continues, in which he asserts that there are other alleged letters composed in the name of St. Paul—to the Laodiceans, to Alexandria, and several others which cannot be admitted into the Catholic Church ('fertur etiam ad laudecenses alia ad alexandrinos pauli nomine fincte ad haeresem marcionis et alia plura quae in catholicam eclesiam recepi non potest ').

It is safe therefore to assert that about 180 A.D. in the author's part of the Church (possibly Africa) there was a recognised list of authentic apostolic writings, that the three Pastoral Epistles are included in these under the name of St. Paul, and that their authenticity is apparently undoubted, so that the tradition which assigned them to him must have been already long established.

The authority of Irenaeus about the same period (120-202 A.D.) adds the testimony of other parts of the Church, since he was brought up in Asia Minor, where he was under the influence of Polycarp, and from 177 was bishop of

Lugdunum in Gaul. He quotes 1 Timothy i. 4 with the addition 'as the Apostle says'; quotes 2 Timothy iv. 10, 11 as the statement of St. Paul and Titus iii. 10 with ὁ Παῦλος ἐγκελεύεται ἡμῖν—besides other passages.

Similar evidence is forthcoming from Tertullian of the African Church (160-230 A.D.), who besides other passages quotes as words of St. Paul 1 Timothy vi. 20, 2 Timothy i. 14, Titus iii. 10, 11.

Representing another branch of the Church we have Clement of Alexandria (died 220 A.D.), who with other passages quotes as words of St. Paul 1 Timothy vi. 20, Titus i. 12.

These are the earliest quotations from these epistles with the name of St. Paul attached. In earlier writers there are many phrases which seem to be due to familiarity with their language, and taken cumulatively they help to a conclusion. But each one taken by itself might be attributed to a common phraseology in the Church's teaching. There are two, however, in which it is hardly possible not to assume quotation, viz. (1) Polycarp, Epistle to the Philippians 4, εἰδότες οὖν ὅτι οὐδὲν εἰσηνέγκαμεν εἰς τὸν κόσμον, ἀλλ' οὐδὲ ἐξενεγκεῖν τι ἔχομεν (1 Timothy vi. 7); (2) Justin Martyr, Dialogue with Trypho, 47 ἡ χρηστότης καὶ ἡ φιλανθρωπία τοῦ θεοῦ (Titus iii. 4). Polycarp's life covered about the period 70-155 A.D., Justin Martyr's about 100-148 A.D.

The inclusion of the epistles in the Peshitto-Syriac and Latin versions supports the view of authenticity. The former, though of the fourth century, is probably based on translations going back to the second century.

All the testimony which the second century has left us against the authenticity of the Pastoral Epistles depends on their treatment by certain men of heretical views— Basilides, who lived early in the century, 'near the time of the Apostles'; Marcion, who was teaching in Rome about 140 A.D.; and Tatian, who was a pupil of Justin and was probably at the height of his activity about 160 A.D. Of these the most important is Marcion, because we have a list of the books which he recognised—and indeed it is from this heretic that we have our earliest list of apostolic writings. But the list is based only on his personal judgment, and we have no reason to suppose that in leaving a book out of his list he meant to stamp it as unauthentic. For the purpose of his teaching he recognised only one Gospel (that of St. Luke very much altered) and ten epistles of St. Paul. To him St. Paul was the only Apostle whose teaching was sound and he regarded no apostolic authority as final, so that Tertullian says (though it is not proved) that even in the epistles which he accepted he made alterations to suit his own teaching. That teaching was Gnostic, and included abstinence from wine, flesh, and marriage. Therefore, though we are not given any reason for his omission of the Pastoral Epistles, it is probable that he omitted them simply on account of what he regarded as wrong teaching on these subjects. Tatian's teaching was similar to that of Marcion, but he accepted the Epistle to Titus.

It has been necessary to record this external evidence as to the authenticity of the Pastoral Epistles in order to show the strength of the position which those who doubt it in modern times have set themselves to attack. All evidence that could be produced and the universal tradition of the Church marked them as authentic till the nineteenth century. But then their authenticity came to be questioned on several grounds of internal evidence, and on these grounds it has been argued that these epistles (one or all) were written by a second-century imitator who wrote as in the name of St. Paul for the sake of authority, had some purpose of his own to serve by the forgery, and perhaps used some genuine fragments of St. Paul's writings. That this was possible cannot be denied. In the second century there appeared a considerable number of writings falsely attributed to authors of the first century, especially 'Acts' of various apostles but also Gospels. They were largely of Gnostic origin, but in expurgated copies they long continued to be used in the churches, especially on saints' days and on the days of the apostles, and they are responsible for many of the legends which have come down to modern times—much in fact of what is contained in the *Golden Legend*. That an epistle also could be thus fabricated is shown by the instance of the spurious Epistle to the Laodiceans. Even if it is not this which is referred to in the Muratorian fragment (see above, p. xxv) it is referred to by St. Jerome as having been widely circulated, and the Second Council of Nicaea (787 A.D.) found it necessary to issue a warning against it.

But though such fabrications were possible, the external evidence for the Pastoral Epistles is so good that very clear internal evidence must be required before their genuineness can be doubted. The chief points which have been raised against genuineness are common to all three epistles and can in the main be dealt with for all three together. They are as follows :

(1) *The historical difficulty.*—The circumstances implied in these epistles cannot be made to tally with any part of St. Paul's life as recorded elsewhere. This is admitted; but (*a*) the Acts have important omissions even in the ground which they cover, as is shown conclusively by the Epistles to the Corinthians and the Galatians; (*b*) the Acts end without any account of St. Paul's trial or death, and all tradition asserts that he was acquitted and had a further period of ministry. It is in this later ministry that the

Pastoral Epistles have their natural place. This is further dealt with on p. x.

(2) *The difficulty of stereotyped phraseology.*—There are certain phrases which seem to have become stereotyped, almost technical theological expressions, as if every one would by this time know what they meant without explanation. For this, it is argued, there was not sufficient time during St. Paul's life. The most striking and characteristic of such phrases are perhaps the use of the word ὑγιαίνω (1 Timothy i. 10 and seven other passages—nowhere else in St. Paul); πιστὸς ὁ λόγος (1 Timothy i. 15 and four other passages); the use of the word μυστήριον in such phrases as τὸ τῆς εὐσεβείας μυστήριον (1 Timothy iii. 16), τὸ μυστήριον τῆς πίστεως (1 Timothy iii. 9); the use of εὐσέβεια itself for the religious life (1 Timothy ii. 2 and nine other passages —not elsewhere in St. Paul); the use of the word καλός in such phrases as τὴν καλὴν στρατείαν (1 Timothy i. 19), ἡ καλὴ διδασκαλία (1 Timothy iv. 6); the use of the word παραθήκη (1 Timothy vi. 20). These are all dealt with in the notes on the passages referred to. But the most striking consideration is that most of these words (and others that are quoted like ἐπίγνωσις ἀληθείας) have a special naturalness if we once accept the fact (abundantly proved apart from these epistles) that already in St. Paul's lifetime false doctrines were making dangerous assaults on the Church. In such circumstances St. Paul and those who held with him would naturally have come to use frequently new phrases for sound teaching as opposed to the false, and it will be seen that most of the phrases quoted above are apposite to this line of thought. And as to their 'stereotyped' character, it is inevitable that a man who has to preach and teach the same thing over and over again, especially if it is a truth new to the world, develops a phrase-

ology of his own which his followers come to recognise, and there is no need for him to explain every time a phrase which a few years earlier would have been so strange as to require explanation. A good instance of this is probably παραθήκη, which only those accustomed to St. Paul's way of speaking would have understood as he uses it.

(3) *The difficulty of* ἅπαξ λεγόμενα.—A third argument is the number of words used in these epistles which are not to be found in the rest of the New Testament. It is summed up thus : ' seventy-two words are found in 1 Timothy only, forty-four in 2 Timothy only, twenty-six in Titus ; ten are peculiar to 1 Timothy and Titus ; eight to 1 and 2 Timothy ; three to 2 Timothy and Titus.' [1] In the Pastoral Epistles together there is one ἅπαξ λεγόμενον for 1·55 verses. But this fact appears less striking upon an analysis of the vocabulary of other epistles. In 1 Corinthians the number of ἅπαξ λεγόμενα is one for 5·53 verses, in 2 Corinthians it is one for 3·66 verses—in other words, there is nearly as great a difference in vocabulary between two epistles written to the same people in the same year as there is between the Pastoral Epistles and epistles written five or six years before.

The weakness of any argument against genuineness based on the number of ἅπαξ λεγόμενα is still more apparent if we analyse the list of such words. Taking the forty-four in 2 Timothy, we find that twenty-one of these are words so common in Greek of all periods that their occurring or not occurring in a particular book can only be a matter of accident. Of the rest, ten occur in Plutarch, who was a contemporary of St. Paul, three occur in Aristotle, two occur in the LXX (which alone would account for St. Paul's use of them), and two are Latin words (μεμβράνα and φαιλόνης) the use of which was natural in St. Paul's circumstances. The remaining

---

[1] See Hastings' *Dictionary of the Bible* articles on these Epistles.

INTRODUCTION   xxxi

rarer words are ἀνεπαίσχυντος, ἀντιδιατίθεσθαι (the Act. of which occurs in Diodorus, c. B.C. 8), ἀφιλάγαθος (Aristotle and Plutarch use φιλάγαθος), γυναικάριον (a form found in early comedy), λογομαχεῖν, συνκακοπαθεῖν (both of which may have been very happily coined by St. Paul to express his thought forcibly). It is obvious that no serious argument can be built on this vocabulary. There is no word in any of the three epistles which is demonstrably of later date.

(4) *The argument from developed institutions.*—It is urged that there is in the Pastoral Epistles evidence of more developed Church institutions than one would expect in the life of St. Paul. More is certainly said here about the organisation of the Church ministry, because directions to Timothy and Titus on this form one of the professed objects of the epistles. But there is no clear addition to what we should gather from other places except perhaps on (*a*) deaconesses and the roll of widows, and (*b*) the suggestion of 1 Timothy v. 17, 18, that in some way πρεσβύτεροι were paid; and with regard to (*a*) it is to be observed that the service of women as assistants to deacons in their work of visiting was necessitated by the conditions of society and may be assumed from the start, that the word διάκονος (though in its general sense) is applied to a woman in Romans xvi. 1, and that the difficulty of providing for widows had been one of the earliest difficulties of the Church. See further notes on 1 Tim. iii. 11, v. 3, 9. It is impossible to point with certainty to any detail in these epistles which is beyond the range of possible development in St. Paul's time. On the other hand, the absence of any distinction between the terms ἐπίσκοπος and πρεσβύτερος and the references to prophecy would not be natural to a second-century writer, though of course they could be accounted for on the theory of an imitative reproduction of a past age.

In estimating at their true value criticisms based like the above on internal evidence we must take into account one or two general considerations.

(1) Such criticisms are of necessity based on a comparison with St. Paul's other writings—on resemblances or want of resemblance. From either resemblance or want of resemblance contrary inferences may be drawn. If a writer is convinced on other grounds that the letters are not genuine, he sees in resemblances the cleverness of the imitator, in want of resemblance something so unlike St. Paul that it cannot be his writing. If on the other hand he is convinced on other grounds that the letters are genuine, he sees in resemblance a sign of Pauline writing, in want of resemblance something that no imitator could have invented. It is obvious therefore that such considerations want corroboration on other grounds and, though they might add some force to another argument, can hardly stand alone.

(2) In making such a comparison we ought to make full allowance for (a) lapse of time, the author's age and new experiences; (b) different circumstances, purposes and needs; and even (c) the author's own reading, study and thought—since no active mind, and least of all men's St. Paul's, could stand still. The Epistles of St. Paul cover a period of about twelve years, and the nearest to the Pastoral Epistles (viz. those of the first imprisonment) are on the usual reckoning separated from them by an interval of about four years. Those years had been crowded with new experiences in Rome, Crete, and probably Spain; and (probably most important of all from this point of view) St. Paul had been able to see by personal observation what developments there had been during the absence of his personal influence in the churches of his earlier foundation. In the Pastoral

Epistles we find what we should have expected. In the absence of the Apostle there had been at Ephesus some tendency on the part of imperfectly grounded Christians to listen to clever thinkers who aimed at philosophising and 'Hellenising' some important facts of the Gospel. But still more than this there was the fear, which breaks out in every part of all three epistles, of a compromise with the pagan standard of life. St. Paul fears this even in those who are set to rule in the Church, and for them, as for all others, we find him emphasising more than he formerly thought necessary things which we should regard as ordinary points of good character—the καλὰ ἔργα that must prove the faith, the whole life ordered κατὰ τὴν εὐσέβειαν. So also we find what we should have expected in the somewhat greater attention given to the organisation of the Church. It may have been borne in on the Apostle that arrangements must be made to last longer than he had at first anticipated, and that the checking of evils, whether in doctrine or in life, would depend on the local officers of the Church. If therefore the tone and subject matter of the Pastoral Epistles in these and other respects show a difference from his earlier epistles, it is a difference to be expected if the traditional view of the circumstances and time of the Pastoral Epistles be the correct view.

But though circumstances may change and may bring about a certain change in a writer's style, tone, and the stress he lays on particular points, there are certain things in character and teaching which we should not expect to find essentially changed, and a consideration of these supports all that is said above. (*a*) There is no point of doctrine in the Pastoral Epistles which does not correspond with St. Paul's earlier teaching or cannot be paralleled from it. (*b*) The character of St. Paul which we should deduce if we had no other source for it than these epistles agrees in numerous ways with the St. Paul of his other writings, *e.g.* the way in which he depreciates himself as he once was without Christ (Titus iii. 3), and the confidence with which he asserts himself as a minister of Christ, appealing to his own teaching and sufferings as an example ; the impatience with which he brushes aside trivial arguments ; his respect for the religion of his fathers and for the O.T. scriptures ; his feelings towards companions in labour, kind friends, deserters — in all these things there are parallels, though without any copying of phrases, to such an extent that the idea of imitation is almost incredible. (c) The characters of Timothy and Titus (especially the former, because of him we know rather more) agree entirely with what we gather of them elsewhere — *e.g.* the affection and timidity of Timothy. (d) The style of the writing resembles closely at any rate the more personal and practical parts of other epistles, *e.g.* in sudden transitions from one thought to another or from a general teaching to a personal remark, or the way in which he lets a word suggest the next thought. All these things taken together would seem beyond the skill of an imitator—in some way or another he would betray himself.

(3) If an epistle is to be regarded as spurious, a motive for the fabrication must be found. For the invention of such a document as the Epistle to the Laodiceans we have the almost childish desire to satisfy the supposed meaning of Colossians iv. 16. But what can we find for the Pastoral Epistles ? The most likely purpose of a fabrication would be to support some point of doctrine or of Church organisation. There is little that is doctrinal in them, and the passages which are anti-Gnostic or anti-Jewish in them (which might suggest the work of a Catholic apologist)

are too brief to bear the conclusion that they are more than incidental (though an important part) in the personal and pastoral advice which the Apostle is giving to his disciples. Nor does the reading of the epistles suggest that they might have been fabricated to support some view of Church institutions — they show more concern for the character of the ministers than for the nature of the ministry, and the institutions dealt with do not correspond entirely with what we know to have been developing in the second century. In fact the purely personal and hortatory character of all three epistles is a strong argument against fabrication— they show mostly concern for the steadfastness and character of those to whom they are written and others who may hold commissions in the Church. Against all tradition and such evidence as does exist there is no sufficient reason for imagining that any one composed letters in this form for the sole purpose of clothing his own exhortations with apostolic authority.

It is beyond the scope of this work to recount the theories which have accepted parts of these epistles as genuine but have rejected other parts, or which have treated them as fragmentary in one part or another. No theory has produced substantial grounds for doubting the integrity of the epistles as a whole. A summary of such theories will be found in Hastings' *Dictionary of the Bible* and full treatment of them in the authors there referred to.

Η ΠΡΟΣ ΤΙΜΟΘΕΟΝ

ΕΠΙΣΤΟΛΗ ΠΡΩΤΗ

CHAPTER I

1. Παῦλος ἀπόστολος Χριστοῦ Ἰησοῦ κατ' ἐπιταγὴν

1-2. The greeting. In this, as in most of St. Paul's Epistles, there is a declaration of his authority as given to him by God. The exceptions are 1 and 2 Thessalonians (written before his authority had been subject of dispute, and written in the name of Silvanus and Timothy, as well as his own name), Philippians (where in like manner Timothy's name is coupled with his in the greeting), and Philemon (a purely personal letter in which St. Paul is purposely avoiding an appeal to his authority and prefers δέσμιος Χριστοῦ Ἰησοῦ).

The points peculiar to this greeting are γνησίῳ τέκνῳ and ἔλεος. See notes below.

An expanded greeting of the kind used by St. Paul is rather Oriental than Western, and is not in accordance with Greek or Roman style. For the ordinary letter style see Acts xxiii. 26, 'Claudius Lysias unto the most excellent governor Felix, greeting (χαίρειν).'

1. **Παῦλος.** It may be taken for certain that the Apostle bore this Latin cognomen from his birth as well as the Aramaic name *Saul*. As a Roman citizen ('born a Roman citizen,' Acts xxii. 28) he would naturally have a full Latin name; but even apart from this it was customary for Jews, whose Aramaic names did not lend themselves naturally to a Greek or Latin form, to adopt some other in their dealings with Gentiles. Sometimes they took a name of somewhat similar sound (*e.g.* perhaps Jesus Justus in Col. iv. 11). Sometimes they translated their names (*e.g.* probably Thomas was called Didymus because both names meant *twin*). Sometimes they seem to have followed merely caprice (*e.g.* apparently John Mark in choosing the name of Marcus). We may compare the practice of modern Jews who do not always bear in the synagogue the name by which they are known to the world. It is to be noted that Σαῦλος was an impossible name in Greek, as meaning *waddling*.

ἀπόστολος. This word had meant *envoy* or *ambassador* as far back as Herodotus. The ἀπόστολος was more than a messenger—he represented with authority the person who

A

sent him. The name seems to have been applied by the Jews to those who were sent from Jerusalem by the Sanhedrin to convey the decrees of that council to synagogues which did not lie within their more direct jurisdiction; and in this sense St. Paul was probably an apostle of the Sanhedrin when he went to Damascus (Acts ix. 2) with power to 'bring men and women bound to Jerusalem.' When, therefore, our Lord named the Twelve 'apostles' (St. Luke vi. 13) He used a word which implied that He sent them out as His representatives with authority. St. Mark (iii. 14) expresses it thus:—'He appointed twelve, that they might be with Him, and that He might send them forth to preach and to have authority to cast out devils.'

For the subsequent application of the name the student must consider the following passages:—

(1) Acts i. 21-26. 'Of the men, therefore, which have companied with us all the time that the Lord Jesus went in and out among us ... of these must one become a witness with us of his resurrection.' The Eleven selected two, and after prayer to our Lord ('Shew of these two the one whom thou hast chosen to take the place in this ministry and apostleship') the lot fell upon Matthias, 'and he was numbered with the eleven apostles.'

(2) The name is subsequently applied to others. It was certainly applied to Paul and Barnabas (Acts xiv. 14). The natural interpretation of Gal. i. 19 ('Other of the apostles saw I none, save [εἰ μή] James, the Lord's brother') and 1 Cor. xv. 7 ('Then he appeared to James; then to all the apostles') would imply that James, the brother of the Lord, was also an apostle, though εἰ μή in the former passage has been explained by some as 'but only.' The same is true of Andronicus and Junias (Rom. xvi. 7), who are spoken of as 'of note among the apostles,' ἐπίσημοι ἐν τοῖς ἀποστόλοις, though here again the meaning of ἐν has been disputed.

(3) The most important passages relating to the conditions of apostleship, apart from Acts i. referred to above, are those in which St. Paul refers to his own claim. 1 Cor. ix 1, 'Am I not free? am I not an apostle? have I not seen Jesus our Lord? are not ye my work in the Lord? If to others I am not an apostle, yet at least I am to you: for the seal of mine apostleship are ye in the Lord.' 2 Cor. xii. 11, 'In nothing am I behind the very chiefest apostles, though I be nothing. Truly the signs of an apostle were wrought among you in all patience, in signs, and wonders, and mighty deeds.' Gal. i. 12, 'Neither did I receive it' (the gospel) 'from man, nor was I taught it, but it came to me through revelation of Jesus Christ.'

(4) We have the following passage in the *Teaching of the XII Apostles*, which was probably written in its present form for the use of the Church in Palestine about the end of the first century:—'In regard to the apostles and prophets, according to the ordinance of the gospel, so do ye. And every apostle who cometh to you let him be received as the Lord; but he shall not remain more than one day; if, however, there be need, then the next day; but if

Θεοῦ σωτῆρος ἡμῶν καὶ Χριστοῦ Ἰησοῦ τῆς ἐλπίδος

he remain three days, he is a false prophet. But when the apostle departeth, let him take nothing except bread enough till he lodge again; but if he ask money, he is a false prophet.'

From the above quotations we can draw certain conclusions:—

(1) The most prominent thought in the original apostles' conception of their office was that they were commissioned by Christ to bear witness of His teaching, and especially of the Resurrection. At first they seem to have thought that the number twelve was to be preserved, and it is probable that the name Apostles continued to be used in a special and limited sense of them.

(2) When the name was applied to others the evidence goes to show that its use was limited by the two conditions implied above, viz. (a) the person so named must be able to testify by personal experience of the risen Christ; (b) he must have received his commission from Christ. These two conditions were fulfilled in the case of Matthias—the words 'the one whom thou hast chosen' (ὃν ἐξελέξω) show that the Eleven thought of Christ as making the choice. St. Paul's words also show that for himself he recognised these two tests.

(3) The evidence also goes to show that the name was at no time used in a vague way simply for those who had supreme authority in the Church. For, in addition to what is implied in the quotations already given, we must consider (a) that some to whom we should in that case have expected the name to apply are never called apostles, e.g. Timothy, in whose case the greetings of 2 Cor. i. 1 and Col. i. 1 show decisively that the name was for some reason not applicable to him; (b) the quotation given from the *Teaching* shows clearly that at the time when that was written *authority* was not the mark of an apostle; (c) if the name had been applied simply in virtue of the exercise of pre-eminent authority or control in the Church, it is inconceivable that the use of it would have died out as soon as it did.

(4) As to the actual position of the apostles at the time of the *Teaching* we must conclude that they were travelling evangelists, whose visit to a church must have been important, perhaps as bringing home to the members the testimony of eyewitnesses. Thus they formed part of the non-local ministry of the Church. The limitation of their visit to two days shows clearly that they had no authority to order the local affairs of a particular church.

Χριστοῦ Ἰησοῦ. Note the order. Where Χριστός stands first it is felt more as a proper name, when it stands second it is felt more as a title, 'the Christ.' Hence we find the order *Christ Jesus* more prevalent in St. Paul's later epistles than in the earlier ones.

κατ' ἐπιταγήν, by command of. Cf. 1 Cor. vii. 6, where it is directly opposed to κατὰ συγγνώμην ('by permission,' 'by way of concession').

τῆς ἐλπίδος ἡμῶν, the ground of our confidence, that on which we rely, as in Thuc. 3. 57, ὑμεῖς ἡ μόνη

ἡμῶν 2. Τιμοθέῳ γνησίῳ τέκνῳ ἐν πίστει· χάρις, ἔλεος, εἰρήνη ἀπὸ Θεοῦ πατρὸς καὶ Χριστοῦ Ἰησοῦ τοῦ Κυρίου ἡμῶν.

3. Καθὼς παρεκάλεσά σε προσμεῖναι ἐν Ἐφέσῳ πορευόμενος εἰς Μακεδονίαν, ἵνα παραγγείλῃς τισὶ μὴ ἑτεροδι-

ἐλπίς. So Col. i. 27, 'Christ in you, the hope of glory.'

2. γνησίῳ τέκνῳ ἐν πίστει, my own child in (the) faith. Whereas υἱός indicates only the legal relationship, τέκνον adds the idea of affection. γνήσιον τέκνον means a man's own real son as opposed to, *e.g.*, an adopted son—it was through St. Paul himself that Timothy was converted. The personal affection of St. Paul is apparent throughout these two epistles, and Timothy obviously reciprocated it. Cf. Phil. ii. 22, 'As a child serveth a father, so he served with me in furtherance of the gospel.'

χάρις, ἔλεος, εἰρήνη. It is only in the two epistles to Timothy that St. Paul adds ἔλεος to the greeting. An early commentator suggests that it was because Timothy had to teach, and a teacher most needs God's ἔλεος in his hard task. We must apply it more widely. Timothy's position was extremely difficult (see Introd., p. xix.), and for errors of judgment, perhaps failures of courage, he needed the consciousness of God's compassion.

χάρις, the divine favour in the fullest sense. The word often has the sense of favour or goodwill in ordinary relationships in Classical Greek, and is used in the LXX in the common expression χάριν εὑρεῖν, 'find favour.' In its religious use, like our equivalent *grace*, it came to mean every form of divine help in

spiritual life—'the might of the everlasting Spirit renovating man' (Liddon).

εἰρήνη, a religious deepening of the ordinary Hebrew and Arabic greeting, 'Peace.' In the Christian greeting it means the peace of the soul in harmony with God.

3-11. A reminder to Timothy of his duty in view of the growth of unsound doctrine in Ephesus.

3-4. The sentence begun is not finished. At the end of v. 4 the A.V. understands the conclusion 'so do,' the R.V. 'so do I now,' *i.e.* I repeat the request. For a similar break in St. Paul's sentence, cf. Rom. ix. 24. It is doubtless due partly to his dictating his letters, but primarily to the rapidity with which his mind, often on the suggestion of some word, passed on to a new thought.

3. For the occasion of Timothy's being at Ephesus, see Introd., p. x. It is impossible to be certain of St. Paul's course after his release from the first imprisonment, but it is probable that this visit to Macedonia belonged to the last stage of it, and that from Macedonia he passed on to Corinth and Nicopolis.

ἑτεροδιδασκαλεῖν, to teach doctrine different from St. Paul's. Cf. Gal. i. 8. The word is St. Paul's invention.

FIRST EPISTLE TO TIMOTHY

δασκαλεῖν, 4. μηδὲ προσέχειν μύθοις καὶ γενεαλογίαις ἀπεράντοις, αἵτινες ἐκζητήσεις παρέχουσι μᾶλλον ἢ οἰκονομίαν Θεοῦ τὴν ἐν πίστει,—5. τὸ δὲ τέλος τῆς παραγ-

4. μύθοις καὶ γενεαλογίαις ἀπεράντοις. Besides the present passage the following are important in any consideration of the false doctrine with which Timothy had to cope at Ephesus, viz. 1 Tim. iv. 1-5, vi. 20, 2 Tim. ii. 18. The most precise intimation of its nature is given in ch. iv., and in connection with that passage it will be considered how far St. Paul's words refer to incipient Gnosticism. It is not necessary to assume that he is referring to the same teaching in all the passages; and that the present passage refers to some Jewish influence in the Church seems certain from θέλοντες εἶναι νομοδιδάσκαλοι in v. 7. In support of this reference we may compare the phrase Ἰουδαικοῖς μύθοις in Titus i. 14. It is observable also that ἐκζητήσεις, 'curious speculations,' would be a remarkably mild word to apply to the characteristic Gnostic doctrines. Nevertheless the present passage is applied to Gnosticism by Irenaeus (180 A.D.) and later writers, interpreting the γενεαλογίαι of the series of aeons and angels. (See n. on ch. iv.)

The probable meaning of μῦθοι καὶ γενεαλογίαι will be best understood by reading such a work as the Book of Jubilees. The object of this book (written before B.C. 100) was to glorify the law by proving that it was not for one age or dispensation only, but for all time; and for this purpose the author rewrote from the standpoint of the law all the history contained in Genesis and Exodus.

There was much literature of this kind, containing many legends about the patriarchs and others, legends which are here represented as narrated to Moses by an angel. Apart from their purpose such legends might have been harmless, but their purpose was to reinforce the claims of all the institutions of the law, for which reason the chief feasts (*e.g.* the Passover, the Feast of Weeks, the Feast of Tabernacles) are all represented as established in the patriarchal times, and even the sun was created with a view to fixing the feasts. This sort of development of the written narrative formed a considerable part of rabbinical teaching. There is nothing in the present passage (as there may be in ch. iv.) to suggest a special reference to Essenism.

ἐκζητήσεις. The compound (not given in L. and S.) emphasises the elaborateness of the speculation—'curious questionings.'

οἰκονομίαν Θεοῦ τὴν ἐν πίστει. The R.V. 'a dispensation of God which is in faith' is poor as a representation of the Greek. The word οἰκονομία meant first the management of a household, and so especially the proper providing of that which the members of a household needed. Hence the meaning here is the making available those blessings of God which are given as a consequence of faith. It is not the falseness of such speculations that is here emphasised, but rather their unproductiveness. 'Non in dialectica

γελίας ἐστὶν ἀγάπη ἐκ καθαρᾶς καρδίας καὶ συνειδήσεως

complacuit Deo salvum facere populum suum' (St. Ambrose). Even if we could discover the number and the names of the angels it would add no power or resource to those who are living the life of faith—such questions are subtleties on the discovery of which no reality is dependent. The wrong reading of the T.R. οἰκοδομίαν gives the sense—such things do not build up, but upset—they are ἐπὶ καταστροφῇ τῶν ἀκουόντων (2 Tim. ii. 14).

5. παραγγελίας. Though this word (and παραγγέλλω, v. 3) had come to mean simply *command*, its earlier use of the command or watchword passed on from one man to another made it particularly applicable to the passing on of the gospel message in its truth and entirety from man to man, and from one generation to another.

τὸ τέλος, 'the end,' in the sense in which it is common in Greek philosophy, 'the end aimed at,' 'the supreme object.' τὸ τέλος ἀγάπη is the true opposite of τὸ τέλος ἡδονή.

ἀγάπη. This word suffers through having no English equivalent, as the translations of 1 Cor. xiii. make manifest. At one time, perhaps, *charity* came near it, or Wyclif could hardly have written for Rom. viii. 39, 'Neither death, neither lyfe, neither noon other creature may departe us fro the charitie of God'; but now the word is narrowed down and only represents ἀγάπη by a kind of convention. The word *love* also requires a convention to represent it, for it properly implies affection (φιλία), whereas you can have ἀγάπη for a person you have never met. ἀγάπη is essentially a Christian conception based on the common brotherhood in Christ and the consciousness of sharing the same great object of life. It implies, therefore, all the consideration and sympathy that the consciousness of this bond creates. If a stranger wrote to you from the ends of the earth because he was in a difficulty and had no one to trust, having picked your name at random out of a list, you might take great pains in answering him, δι' ἀγάπην, but not out of love or out of charity.

ἐκ καθαρᾶς καρδίας, κ.τ.λ. The ἀγάπη is not a forced product, but the natural outcome in our dealings with others of certain qualities in ourselves—the possession of 'a pure heart,' 'a good conscience,' 'unfeigned faith.' The word καθαρός was very early used in Greek in the metaphorical sense of 'free from moral stain,' *e.g.* καθαρός νοῦς; and the phrase *a pure heart* was more natural to Hebrew writers than *a pure mind*, because they thought of the heart as being the seat of the thought. [Cf. Ps. xix. 14, 'Let the words of my mouth and the meditation of my heart be acceptable in thy sight.'] To have 'a pure heart,' therefore, meant to be free from all evil motives, to be singleminded in one's pursuit of good. Hence to them is promised the vision of God—'Blessed are the pure in heart: for they shall see God' (Matt. v. 8). A 'good conscience' adds something to this—not only are we purified from evil motives, but the consciousness of guilt has gone also with all the weakness that an ever-present fear of doing evil entails. The word συνείδησις meant

literally the being conscious of one's own thoughts, and then the being conscious of rightness or wrongness. The phrase 'good conscience' shows how the one meaning passes into the other. πίστις ἀνυπόκριτος means faith that is not acting a part, 'unfeigned faith'—it implies such complete confidence in our Lord that the ἀγάπη is its *natural* outcome. It is possible to be 'feigning' faith without being conscious of it—one wants to believe and therefore adopts belief as one's attitude, but one wants it at little cost; its unreal and unspontaneous character is tested by its failure to produce works of ἀγάπη. The word ἀνυπόκριτος occurs first in the LXX.

By conscience we mean that power or voice within us which judges our actions (and by inference the actions of others) as morally good or morally bad. The conception of conscience as an independent faculty may be said to be peculiar to Christian teaching. Greek philosophy was concerned to determine what was the 'highest good' for man, and what was the best means to that 'highest good'; but the choice both of end and of means fell within the province of the same 'reason' which dealt with other problems, and led to no analysis of 'moral obligation' as we understand it. The idea of a conscience does not occur in Aristotle; and the Stoic philosophy differs from the rest rather in its results (because of its exalted standpoint with regard to things of sense and material pleasure) than in any original psychological basis.

It is in St. Paul's writings that we first find what we may call a doctrine of conscience as an independent power in us, able to pass an authoritative verdict on right or wrong in our actions—a verdict followed by the consciousness of 'I ought' regardless of consequences to oneself. To say that St. Paul analysed this psychologically would be probably incorrect—it is better to say that his way of expressing it is the result of his own experience and introspection. He felt so intensely the conflict of the 'two selves' (as expressed in the Epistle to the Romans), that he could only express what he meant by regarding the higher self as a separate faculty or power with a voice of its own, able to issue its commands to the whole personality of the man. Cf. Rom. ii. 15, συμμαρτυρούσης αὐτῶν τῆς συνειδήσεως; Rom. ix. 1, συμμαρτυρούσης μοι τῆς συνειδήσεώς μου ἐν Πνεύματι Ἁγίῳ. The former of these passages especially illustrates his conception of conscience as a faculty possessed by all men, because he is there speaking of Gentiles who, without any special revelation, 'are a law unto themselves; in that they shew the work of the law written in their hearts.'

Since the time of St. Paul an attempt to analyse the nature of this 'I ought' in the consciousness of every man has formed a necessary part of every system of ethics. On the one extreme it has been explained as a habit of the reason based on long-continued utilitarian considerations in the individual, or on the same considerations developed by evolution and inherited in the race. On the other extreme it has been regarded as in every sense an independent faculty planted in man by God, capable of guiding him always right, though capable of weakening

ἀγαθῆς καὶ πίστεως ἀνυποκρίτου· 6. ὧν τινὲς ἀστοχήσαντες ἐξετράπησαν εἰς ματαιολογίαν, 7. θέλοντες εἶναι νομοδιδάσκαλοι, μὴ νοοῦντες μήτε ἃ λέγουσι μήτε περὶ τίνων διαβεβαιοῦνται. 8. οἴδαμεν δὲ ὅτι καλὸς ὁ νόμος,

and even extinction through neglect and opposition. Better than this is the thought which, starting from the conception of man as a spiritual being made 'in the likeness of God' and therefore able to apprehend moral good, regards conscience as the man himself or his self-consciousness rather than as a separate 'faculty'—the man himself uttering as his own will the will of God, imposing upon all the impulses of his composite nature what he knows and wills as a spiritual being. He is not accepting the will of God as a thing from outside, but exercising and expressing that will in his own right.

6. ὧν. The antecedent is τισί in v. 3. St. Paul resumes his sentence irregularly.

ἀστοχήσαντες. Literally 'having missed their aim.' Possibly St. Paul does not wish to suggest that their original aim was wrong. Men may start out with an honest intention to establish the truth, but become so fascinated by their own intellectual subtleties that they can no longer exercise sound judgment over their own conclusions.

ματαιολογίαν. The word μάταιος generally implies more than 'resultless' (κενός)—that is μάταιος which is purposeless and frivolous in its essence. The discourse of the men referred to here is not only useless, it is a mere playing with words.

7. νομοδιδάσκαλοι. Naturally an honourable title, cf. St. Luke v. 17,

but here carrying with it the implication of exalting too much the place of the law. These men professed to be authorities on the interpretation of the Old Testament, and doubtless were often quoting texts in proof of fantastic theories. See note on verse 4. In this work they had failed to realise the limited purpose of the law (v. 8), and were imparting into Christian teaching much that was erroneous in the methods and conclusions of the great Jewish teachers.

μὴ νοοῦντες κ.τ.λ., 'without understanding their own statements on the subjects on which [concerning what subjects] they make confident affirmations.' It is perhaps natural to take τίνων here for the relative, though this use of τίς for ὅστις is not clearly established in N.T. writers. [See, however, St. Mark xiv. 36, ἀλλ' οὐ τί ἐγὼ θέλω ἀλλὰ τί σύ.]

μή. The student will observe that the regular negative of Participles in N.T. Greek is μή, without the limitation that he has been accustomed to in the Grammar of Attic Greek.

διαβεβαιοῦνται, assert positively.

8-11. 'These teachers of error have forgotten the limited purpose of the law, viz. that it was for men in a state of sin.' To them it supplied the necessary imperative. 'Thou shalt not' awoke in them the consciousness of sin, and was meant to make them

CH. I. 8-10.]   FIRST EPISTLE TO TIMOTHY   9

ἐάν τις αὐτῷ νομίμως χρῆται   9. εἰδὼς τοῦτο, ὅτι δικαίῳ νόμος οὐ κεῖται, ἀνόμοις δὲ καὶ ἀνυποτάκτοις, ἀσεβέσι καὶ ἁμαρτωλοῖς, ἀνοσίοις καὶ βεβήλοις, πατραλῴαις καὶ μητραλῴαις, ἀνδροφόνοις,   10. πόρνοις, ἀρσενοκοίταις,

feel the need of divine grace. But it did not by itself convey the means which would enable a man to fulfil it. To those whose heart and will had come into a new relation towards God by union with Christ, the law occupied a different position. This is St. Paul's subject in Rom. vii.

8. **οἴδαμεν**, for the Attic ἴσμεν. An Ionic form.

ἐάν τις αὐτῷ νομίμως χρῆται, *i.e.* if a man use it for its natural purpose. νόμιμος means in accordance with custom, regular, natural. The R.V. translation 'lawfully' is not good, and the only way in which we can keep the play on the word is by translating 'The law is good if a man use it as a law.' With the use of the adverb we may perhaps compare νομίμως ἀποθανεῖν, to die a natural death.

9. From ἀνόμοις to βεβήλοις we have words describing in a general sense the arrogant rejection of all external control or external standard of living, whether that approved by God or that set up by man. From πατραλῴαις to ἐπιόρκοις we have eight sins specified that may result from this rejection.

ἄνομος, refusing to recognise the claims of law and custom among men.

ἀνυπότακτος, refusing all control, unruly.

ἀσεβής, rejecting the authority of God and religion.

ἁμαρτωλός, carrying this irreligion into conduct, sinful.

ἀνόσιος. The word ὅσιος was primarily applied to things approved by the law of God or nature, and so to men who lived according to this law. ἀνόσιος here therefore means 'rejecting the law of God,' and differs from ἀσεβής only in that it refers more to outward acts, while ἀσεβής describes the attitude of the mind.

βέβηλος (from the root of βαίνω) was originally applied to ground that might be trodden, as opposed to ground that was consecrated (ἱερός) and so meant 'unhallowed.' Applied to persons it naturally meant those who had no right to approach the sanctuary and so 'unholy,' 'separated from God.' The Latin *profanus* expressed the same idea (*pro fano*, in front of or outside the sanctuary). Cf. *Aen.* vi. 258, *Procul este, profani*, addressed to those who may not approach the holy place. The word βέβηλος to a Jew would mean one who by reason of uncleanness was banished from all religious observances.

10. **ἀνδραποδιστής**. This meant one who reduced a free person to slavery, or stole slaves from their lawful owners. The penalty in Athenian law was death. We have no means of knowing how far this crime was prevalent in St. Paul's days. He is probably only meaning to suggest by his words the worst crimes possible; indeed he happened

ἀνδραποδισταῖς, ψεύσταις, ἐπιόρκοις, καὶ εἴ τι ἕτερον τῇ ὑγιαινούσῃ διδασκαλίᾳ ἀντίκειται, 11. κατὰ τὸ εὐαγγέλιον τῆς δόξης τοῦ μακαρίου Θεοῦ, ὃ ἐπιστεύθην ἐγώ.

to use four (πατραλοίας, μητραλοίας, ἀνδροφόνος, ἀνδραποδιστής) which when merely used as abusive epithets incurred a fine of five hundred drachmae at Athens.

ψεύσταις. We are almost surprised to find this coupled with the gross crimes just mentioned. But it was characteristic of St. Paul to go beneath the popular estimate of crimes, and he counts as a gross crime that which destroys the possibility of men's living together in confidence. Cf. the list in Gal. v. 19-20, where 'enmities, strife, jealousies' come between grosser sins. Cf. n. on διλόγους, iii. 8.

ὑγιαινούσῃ, healthy, sound. The use of this word in this metaphorical sense, several times in the Pastoral Epistles and in no other, is used as an argument against their authenticity. See Introd., p. xxix. But circumstances and age change vocabulary, and the idea expressed by this word—the need of healthy teaching as opposed to morbid speculations—is one of the most prominent ideas in the Pastoral Epistles.

11. κατὰ τὸ εὐαγγέλιον goes with the whole preceding statement about the law. On St. Paul's claim to have been entrusted with a special message as to this part of the 'good tidings,' cf. Gal. ii. 7, 'When they saw that I had been entrusted with the gospel of the uncircumcision, even as Peter with the gospel of the circumcision.'

The word εὐαγγέλιον in Classical Greek meant a reward for good tidings, or thank-offering for good tidings, but later writers used it for good tidings. The verb εὐαγγελίζεσθαι, 'to announce good tidings,' was used from the start for 'to announce the good tidings of the gospel' (cf. St. Luke ii. 10, εὐαγγελίζομαι ὑμῖν χαρὰν μεγάλην, κ.τ.λ.), and the noun gradually acquired the specific meaning of 'the gospel message' and eventually a written 'gospel.'

τῆς δόξης must not be taken as the equivalent of an adjective, as A.V.; rather the whole phrase means 'the gospel of the manifestation of God's glory in Christ.' In interpreting phrases containing the word δόξα, we must remember that this word was used in LXX Greek to express the visible Divine Presence. See Mayor's note on James ii. 1, where he shows good reason for translating the verse, 'the faith of our Lord Jesus Christ who is the glory.'

τοῦ μακαρίου Θεοῦ. As used of God here and in vi. 15, the adjective is one of the peculiarities noticed in the vocabulary of the Epistle. See Introd., p. xxix.

12-17. The contrast of those who had 'missed their aim' (v. 6), and the thought of the wonderful work entrusted to himself (v. 11), occasion an outburst of thanksgiving for his own experience.

CH. I. 12-14.] FIRST EPISTLE TO TIMOTHY 11

12. Χάριν ἔχω τῷ ἐνδυναμώσαντί[a] με Χριστῷ Ἰησοῦ τῷ Κυρίῳ ἡμῶν, ὅτι πιστόν με ἡγήσατο, θέμενος εἰς διακονίαν, 13. τὸ πρότερον ὄντα βλάσφημον καὶ διώκτην καὶ ὑβριστήν· ἀλλ' ἠλεήθην ὅτι ἀγνοῶν ἐποίησα ἐν ἀπιστίᾳ, 14. ὑπερεπλεόνασε δὲ ἡ χάρις τοῦ Κυρίου ἡμῶν μετὰ πίστεως καὶ ἀγάπης τῆς ἐν Χριστῷ Ἰησοῦ.

[a] ἐνδυναμοῦντι.

12. Whether we read ἐνδυναμώσαντι (gave me strength) or ἐνδυναμοῦντι (giveth me strength), the reference is to the strength given to fulfil the trust expressed in ὁ ἐπιστεύθην ἐγώ.

πιστόν με ἡγήσατο θέμενος εἰς διακονίαν, 'showed that he counted me faithful by appointing me to a service.' The word διακονία is used here in a general sense, any function in the Christian ministry.

13. βλάσφημον. Though this word in Classical Greek is used generally of slander, its religious application was the original one. βλασφημία was the utterance of ill-omened words at a sacrifice, hence speaking lightly of the gods or sacred things. St. Paul had spoken evil of Christ and compelled timid Christians to do the same (Acts xxvi. 11).

ὑβριστήν. The word implies insulting violence due to arrogant self-confidence. Cf. St. Paul's own words in Acts xxvi. 9-11, περισσῶς ἐμμαινόμενος αὐτοῖς ἐδίωκον, etc. Also viii. 3, ἐλυμαίνετο τὴν ἐκκλησίαν (made havoc of the Church).

ἠλεήθην ὅτι ἀγνοῶν ἐποίησα. St. Paul is not claiming that his ignorance made him guiltless. It is too readily assumed that ignorance is not culpable, error is often the result of shutting the doors of the mind. We may compare our Lord's words, 'Father, forgive them, for they know not what they do': ignorance may be perhaps an excuse for a present action but the fruit of past sin and therefore in need of forgiveness.

It would be contrary to St. Paul's own teaching (Rom. ix.) to inquire why God chose him ὄντα βλάσφημον καὶ διώκτην καὶ ὑβριστήν to be an apostle. But, humanly speaking, we can believe that he was sincere in his ignorance. From the words, 'It is hard for thee to kick against the goad,' we must assume that a struggle had already been going on in him; the very doubts in his mind perhaps made him more bitter in his persecution, as men will sometimes try to smother doubts of their own rightness by more active assertion of it.

14. ὑπερεπλεόνασε, abounded exceedingly. The word occurs only here and in later ecclesiastical writers. Cf. ὑπερεπερίσσευσεν ἡ χάρις in Rom. v. 20.

μετὰ πίστεως καὶ ἀγάπης, the results accompanying the work of the divine χάρις in him. For this word, see n. on v. 2, and for ἀγάπη, v. 5.

15. πιστὸς ὁ λόγος καὶ πάσης ἀποδοχῆς ἄξιος, ὅτι Χριστὸς Ἰησοῦς ἦλθεν εἰς τὸν κόσμον ἁμαρτωλοὺς σῶσαι· ὧν πρῶτός εἰμι ἐγώ· 16. ἀλλὰ διὰ τοῦτο ἠλεήθην, ἵνα ἐν ἐμοὶ πρώτῳ ἐνδείξηται Ἰησοῦς Χριστὸς τὴν ἅπασαν

15. **πιστὸς ὁ λόγος**, the saying is faithful, *i.e.* to be trusted as wholly true. This phrase occurring only in the Pastoral Epistles (cf. iii. 1, iv. 9 ; 2 Tim. ii. 11 ; Titus iii. 8) is held to be an indication of their not being St. Paul's. But see Introd., p. xxix. For a comparison of the places where it occurs, see n. on iii. 1. Of course it implies the general currency and familiarity of certain sayings in the Church, but this may well have come about before the death of St. Paul. There is every reason to believe that the first form of a written gospel was a collection of our Lord's sayings, and such a saying as the present one is only a variant of that quoted in St. Matt. ix. 13, 'I came not to call the righteous but sinners,' which (cf. St. Luke xix. 10) may have been often on our Lord's lips. It is not difficult to understand how often the saying was needed for the encouragement of candidates for baptism, a reason similar to that which prompted its inclusion in the 'comfortable words' of the Office of Holy Communion. Matthew Arnold's sonnet 'The Good Shepherd with the Kid' will illustrate the way in which, from the first, the Church must have treasured and often repeated such a saying :

He saves the sheep, the goats he doth not save.
So rang Tertullian's sentence, on the side
Of that unpitying Phrygian sect which cried:

'Him can no fount of fresh forgiveness lave,
Who sins, once washed by the baptismal wave.'
So spake the fierce Tertullian. But she sighed,
The infant Church ! of love she felt the tide
Stream on her from her Lord's yet recent grave.
And then she smiled; and in the Catacombs,
With eye suffused but heart inspired true,
On those walls subterranean, where she hid
Her head 'mid ignominy, death, and tombs,
She her Good Shepherd's hasty image drew—
And on his shoulders, not a lamb, a kid.

ἀποδοχῆς, another word not found in the N.T. outside the Pastoral Epistles.

σῶσαι. See note on 2 Tim. i. 9.

16. **πρώτῳ** must be taken in the same sense as πρῶτος in the previous sentence. As he feels that he was the chief of sinners, so he is also the most notable example to show the long-suffering of Christ.

It is to be observed that in stating the purpose of his own 'election' here, St. Paul applies to himself the teaching that he explains in the Epistle to the Romans. God's choice of the individual to receive special privileges or a special call must be set down to God's inscrutable will in the furtherance of His eternal

μακροθυμίαν πρὸς ὑποτύπωσιν τῶν μελλόντων πιστεύειν ἐπ' αὐτῷ εἰς ζωὴν αἰώνιον. 17. τῷ δὲ βασιλεῖ τῶν αἰώνων,

purposes, and not to anything in the individual.

τὴν ἅπασαν μακροθυμίαν, the completeness of his long-suffering. μακροθυμία as applied to man in the holding out of the temper under provocation, especially not letting one's treatment of another be affected by the sense of personal wrong. St. Paul's feeling towards our Lord was one of such intense personal devotion that he thinks of his early conduct as not only a sin but a personal injury to a friend, and his phraseology is coloured by this. The word reminds of Psalm vii. 12 (P.B. version), 'God is a righteous judge, strong and patient: and God is provoked every day.'

ὑποτύπωσιν, properly an *outline*, and that is in effect its use in 2 Tim. i. 13. But an outline is meant to suggest the fuller treatment, and so the word came to mean, as here, a suggestive example or type. St. Paul's experience shows what 'all those who hereafter believe' will also realise.

εἰς ζωὴν αἰώνιον, to be taken with πιστεύειν.

ζωὴ αἰώνιος. The word ζωή stands for the principle of life, the being alive as opposed to being dead. Hence zoology is the science of animal life. But the Christian has a spiritual life as well as a physical life, and this spiritual life also is expressed by ζωή. It could not well be expressed by βίος, which meant not the simple fact of living, but a man's way and course of life as a social and moral being, with all that human life as such involves (compare the meaning of Biography with that of Zoology), so that Aristotle even says a slave shares in ζωή but hardly in βίος.

The word αἰώνιος is the adjective of αἰών, and meant *everlasting* in Classical Greek, *e.g.* Plato. But in considering its Biblical use, it is necessary to remember that the Jews would use it as the adjective of αἰών, in the sense in which they regarded time as divided into a succession of αἰῶνες or epochs, *e.g.* the pre-Messianic period and the Messianic period. Especially did they speak of the Messianic period as ὁ αἰών (as in the expansion εἰς τὸν αἰῶνα, *for ever*), and as the adjective of this the word αἰώνιος not only meant *eternal*, but carried with it also some such connotation as *appertaining to the Messianic time and rule*. It was therefore doubly natural that ζωὴ αἰώνιος in Christian language, while it can be spoken of as the life that the Christian is to have in the future (cf. St. Mark, x. 30), can also be spoken of as the life of which he partakes already (cf. St. John v. 24)—it is the participation in the divine life through union with Christ.

17. **τῷ δὲ βασιλεῖ τῶν αἰώνων**, but to the King eternal. See n. on v. 16. The phrase means 'the King of all ages, of all time.' Outside these epistles the title βασιλεύς is only used of God in St. Matt. v. 35 ('the city of the great King'), but the thought of God as King was of course common with the Jews.

ἀφθάρτῳ, ἀοράτῳ, μόνῳ Θεῷ, τιμὴ καὶ δόξα εἰς τοὺς αἰῶνας τῶν αἰώνων. ἀμήν.

18. Ταύτην τὴν παραγγελίαν παρατίθεμαί σοι, τέκνον Τιμόθεε, κατὰ τὰς προαγούσας ἐπὶ σὲ προφητείας, ἵνα

μόνῳ Θεῷ. Notice that the word σοφῷ in the T.R. was introduced here from Rom. xvi. 27.

Some doxology or ascription of praise to God beginning with 'Blessed be God' formed the regular conclusion of the synagogue service, and the use of such expressions naturally spread to every occasion where the speaker was moved by special feelings of gratitude, as St. Paul is here. The doxology with which we conclude the Lord's Prayer is doubtless derived from synagogue usage. Cf. 1 Chron. xxix. 11, 'Thine, O Lord, is the greatness, and the power, and the glory, and the victory, and the majesty.' In the *Didache* viii. it appears in the form, 'For Thine is the power and the glory for ever.'

εἰς τοὺς αἰῶνας τῶν αἰώνων, i.e. for endless ages, an intensified expression of εἰς τὸν αἰῶνα.

ἀμήν. The use of this Hebrew word—a verbal adjective equivalent to '(be it) established'—was customary in the synagogue as the response to the priests' doxology or blessing; and (though in many cases where the T.R. has it in the N.T. it has not good manuscript authority) there is no doubt that the practice passed at once into the Church. Cf. 1 Cor. xiv. 16, 'Else if thou bless with the spirit, how shall he that filleth the place of the unlearned say the Amen at thy giving of thanks, seeing he knoweth not what thou sayest?'

18-20. These verses go back to the thought of 3-5. As Timothy has to charge others, let him see to it that he keeps in all purity the charge committed to him.

18. **παρατίθεμαι,** commit as a thing to be guarded. See n. on vi. 20.

κατὰ τὰς προαγούσας ἐπὶ σὲ προφητείας. The 'prophecy' of the N.T. is best paraphrased as 'an inspired utterance intelligible to all.' It was of course distinct from the 'speaking with tongues,' which was not intelligible without an interpreter. It did not necessarily include any prophesying of the future, but might do so (Acts xi. 28, xxi. 11). Its object was the encouragement and enlightenment of the Church (Acts xv. 32; 1 Cor. xiv. 3). It was an inspiration that might come upon any member of the Church on occasion, but there were some who were called prophets *par excellence*, because, presumably, the gift was often manifested in them, and these quickly assumed an important position in the Church ('Built upon the foundation of the apostles and prophets,' Eph. ii. 20). It is not quite clear how far the prophetic utterance was regarded as independent of the prophet's conscious reasoning powers ('The man speaketh then when God wisheth him to speak,' *Hermas*); but St. Paul states very clearly that the exercise of the gift was subject to the prophet's control—'The spirits

στρατεύῃ ἐν αὐταῖς τὴν καλὴν στρατείαν 19. ἔχων πίστιν καὶ ἀγαθὴν συνείδησιν, ἥν τινες ἀπωσάμενοι περὶ

of the prophets are subject to the prophets' (1 Cor. xiv. 32); and his warnings on the subject show that there was a tendency to regard the gift as beyond human control. This question of the control of the prophetic gift was one of the issues between the Church and Montanism. Montanus claims to be just the lyre on which the Spirit plays, while the orthodox write tracts περὶ τοῦ μὴ δεῖν προφήτην ἐν ἐκστάσει λαλεῖν. As with other χαρίσματα it is not possible to trace its gradual disappearance as a special recognised gift. In the *Didache* the prophets still hold a very prominent position (ch. xi.). The last heard of lived about the time of Hadrian. See for a useful summary on the subject, Rackham's *Acts*, Introd., vi. 2.

When we consider the present verse in connection with iv. 14, it is hardly possible to take the words as referring to anything but special prophetic utterances, preceding and pointing to Timothy's appointment or ordination to special ministry in the Church. See n. on iv. 14.

προαγούσας, 'foregoing,' in the sense of anticipating his work. Cf. ὁ προάγων λόγος (the preceding discourse) in Plato.

ἐν αὐταῖς, R.V. 'by them,' and it is best, perhaps, to take it instrumentally—the prophecies are thought of as assisting the 'warfare' that fulfils them. But it is difficult to discriminate this use of ἐν from its use to denote the *sphere* or 'according to,' *e.g.* περιπατεῖν ἐν ἀγάπῃ (Eph. v. 2).

τὴν καλὴν στρατείαν. R.V. has 'the good warfare,' but the use of the Greek article with these abstracts does not really necessitate the less natural use of the English article, any more than in such an expression as τῇ φιλαδελφίᾳ φιλόστοργοι, τῇ τιμῇ ἀλλήλους προηγούμενοι ('in love of the brethren tenderly affectioned one to another, in honour preferring one another,' Rom. xii. 10).

19. ἔχων, holding, keeping.

συνείδησιν. See n. on v. 5.

ἥν to be taken with συνείδησιν only, as the following words περὶ τὴν πίστιν ἐνανάγησαν show.

ἀπωσάμενοι, having thrust away, suggesting the violent rejection of something after a struggle. The whole sentence implies that these men had begun their declension by moral failure, and then had adapted their faith and teaching to their lowered moral standard. The demand that Christianity made for a change of life was a severe demand upon Gentile converts in the state of their world, and it is evident that many tried to compromise, professing Christ but keeping some of their old life. (We may compare the difficulty still found by missionaries with converts in polygamous countries.) Some, to justify themselves, went so far as to teach that what was done to the body did not matter—and this naturally involved denial of all doctrine of the resurrection of the body. Nor would it be difficult to find modern instances where a man first succumbs to a moral weakness, then tries to defend it by argument,

τὴν πίστιν ἐναυάγησαν· 20. ὧν ἐστιν Ὑμέναιος καὶ

and finally convinces himself: his faith is altered and his ideal lowered. The maxim 'practise what you preach' is sound, but it is too often interpreted to mean that you must not preach more than you practise—in reality, if a man is weak, it is still something that he should continue to see and admit openly a higher ideal. The words of St. Paul in Rom. i. 32 really contain a fine climax—'men who not only do these things *but also approve of those who practise them*.'

20. Hymenaeus is referred to again in 2 Tim. ii. 17, 18, where the nature of his error is explained. See n. on that passage. Alexander may be the same as the man mentioned in 2 Tim. iv. 14, but the name was very common, and the fact that the Alexander of that passage is there called ὁ χαλκεύς suggests in itself that he needed to be distinguished from another.

οὓς παρέδωκα τῷ Σατανᾷ.

The existence of spirits of evil, as well as angels, probably formed a part of Jewish belief from very early times, as is indicated by expressions in pre-exilic books, *e.g.* 1 Sam. xvi. 14, 'An evil spirit from the Lord troubled him'; Judges ix. 23, 'God sent an evil spirit between Abimelech and the men of Shechem'; 1 Kings xxii. 22, 'I will go forth and will be a lying spirit in the mouth of all his prophets.' But it was in post-exilic times that the doctrine both of angels and of evil spirits was developed, probably under Babylonian and Persian influence. The Jews of this period came to believe in a world of evil spirits, to whom they gave names, ranks, and functions. The chief of these was called Satan, or 'the adversary.' The earliest references to him are Zech. iii. 1, 'He shewed me Joshua, the high priest, standing before the angel of the Lord, and (the) Satan standing at his right hand to be his adversary'; Job i. 6, 'The sons of God came to present themselves before the Lord, and (the) Satan came also among them'; 1 Chron. xxi. 1, 'Satan stood up against Israel, and moved David to number Israel,'—here the word is used as a proper name without the article, and we must contrast the expression used in 2 Sam. xxiv. 1. The functions allotted to the evil spirits by Jewish thought of the time were (1) to accuse men before God; (2) to tempt them to evil; (3) to inflict evil, including physical evil. The main motive in all such speculations was probably to account for the existence of evil without attributing it directly to God. But there was this marked difference from the religions of the East, viz. that orthodox Judaism never accepted a 'dualism' in which the power of evil stood in *independent* opposition to God. It is under His control and permitted by Him for disciplinary purposes.

In the New Testament—both in our Lord's teaching and in the writings of St. Paul—we find the general conception of a world of evil spirits, tempting to evil and inflicting evil, accepted and acted upon. The chief of them is spoken of either as Satan, or by the Greek equivalent ὁ διάβολος (the accuser or false accuser)

Ἀλέξανδρος, οὓς παρέδωκα τῷ Σατανᾷ, ἵνα παιδευθῶσι μὴ βλασφημεῖν.

Our Lord attributed Peter's trial to Satan (St. Luke xxii. 31, 'Satan asked to have you that he might sift you as wheat'), spoke of disease as the work of Satan (St. Luke xiii. 16, 'Whom Satan hath bound, lo, these eighteen years'), and regarded the casting out of devils by His disciples as the overthrow of Satan (St. Luke x. 18, 'I beheld Satan fallen as lightning from heaven'). In St. Paul's writings also Satan is the tempter (1 Cor. vii. 5), and his own 'thorn in the flesh' is a 'messenger of Satan' (2 Cor. xii. 7). His words in Eph. ii. 2 ('the prince of the power of the air') follow the current Jewish phraseology, which implied that the devil and other evil spirits had their abode in the lower atmosphere.

With the present passage we must compare, besides 2 Cor. xii. 7, the words of 1 Cor. v. 4-5. In that passage St. Paul represents himself as in a church assembly handing over an offender to Satan for the destruction of the flesh that the spirit may be saved. It is clear that he thought of Satan's power to inflict physical evil as capable of being used under God's permission for disciplinary purposes, and in this sense we must understand the present passage and that in 1 Cor. It is clear also that he understood the Church to have been entrusted with the power in certain cases of using this method of discipline.

παιδευθῶσι. In the New Testament this word generally, if not always, implies teaching by discipline, or punishment.

βλασφημεῖν. See v. 13.

CHAPTER II

1. Παρακαλῶ οὖν πρῶτον πάντων ποιεῖσθαι δεήσεις, προσευχάς, ἐντεύξεις, εὐχαριστίας, ὑπὲρ πάντων ἀνθρώ-πων· 2. ὑπὲρ βασιλέων καὶ πάντων τῶν ἐν ὑπεροχῇ

1-7. 'Pray for all men; for God's will is that all men should come to the knowledge of the truth—not only the truth that "God is one," but the truth that Jesus is the ransom for all, as I have been sent to proclaim to Gentiles as well as to Jews.'

The emphasis in this passage is clearly on the all. St. Paul's belief in the efficacy of prayer is shown not only by the πρῶτον πάντων, but by the inclusion of Nero in the subjects of the Church's intercession.

1. δεήσεις, προσευχάς, ἐντεύξεις. The words differ somewhat in meaning ('petitions,—prayers,—intercessions'), but the threefold formula is meant to emphasise the one idea. προσευχή was the ordinary word of prayer to God, and could not be used as δέησις could of petition to men. ἔντευξις (not found in the N.T. except in this Epistle) is the noun of ἐντυγχάνω, which meant to meet a person and so to meet with a view to pleading, and is regularly used in the N.T. for interceding for another person (*against* another person in Rom. xi. 2).

εὐχαριστίας. In this *thanksgiving* we must see a reference to the thought of v. 6—the Church gives thanks on behalf of all men because all men are the objects of Christ's atoning sacrifice.

2. ὑπὲρ βασιλέων καὶ πάντων τῶν ἐν ὑπεροχῇ ὄντων. The reference in βασιλεύς is without doubt specially to the Roman emperor, whose natural title this was throughout the East. For the language of such a prayer, see *Clement of Rome*, ch. lxi.: 'Thou, Lord, hast given to our rulers and governors upon the earth the power of their sovereignty, through Thine exceeding and unutterable might, that we, knowing the glory and honour which is given unto them from Thee, may submit ourselves unto them, in no wise resisting Thy will. Give unto them, Lord, health, peace, oneness of mind, stability, that they may order the government which hath been committed to them of Thee without stumbling. For Thou, O Heavenly Lord, King of the ages, givest glory to the sons of men, and honour and power over the things which are upon the earth. Do Thou, O Lord, direct aright their counsel towards that which is good and well-pleasing in Thy sight, that, ordering devoutly in peace and meekness the authority committed to them by Thee, they may obtain Thy mercy.'

ὄντων, ἵνα ἤρεμον καὶ ἡσύχιον βίον διάγωμεν ἐν πάσῃ εὐσεβείᾳ καὶ σεμνότητι. 3. τοῦτο καλὸν καὶ ἀπόδεκτον ἐνώπιον τοῦ σωτῆρος ἡμῶν Θεοῦ, 4. ὃς πάντας ἀνθρώπους θέλει σωθῆναι καὶ εἰς ἐπίγνωσιν ἀληθείας ἐλθεῖν. 5. εἷς γὰρ Θεός, εἷς καὶ μεσίτης Θεοῦ καὶ ἀνθρώπων

St. Paul's words show that he believed in the divine guidance of governments and that prayer could help it. He had always had reason to look upon the Roman power as that which protected Christianity from the violence of opponents. The popular outbreaks at Rome in 64, which were utilised, if not encouraged, by Nero after the great fire, began a change of attitude at the centre of government; but in the provinces the effect of this would have been delayed, and even if this Epistle and that to Titus were written after 64, St. Paul's attitude shows no change. With his words we may compare St. Peter's 'Fear God, honour the king,' written at a time when the Roman power was at least threatening persecution.

ἤρεμον καὶ ἡσύχιον. The word ἤρεμος is late Greek for the Classical ἠρεμαῖος, and signifies tranquillity in every aspect. ἡσύχιος means 'of a quiet disposition.' We may, therefore, translate 'peaceable and quiet.'

ἐν πάσῃ εὐσεβείᾳ would in modern phrase be 'in free practice of our religion.' ἐν σεμνότητι (R.V. *gravity*) adds to this the idea of not being flouted in their serious view of life and duty by the ridicule and active interference of the unbeliever. There was hardly any gaiety of the Greek or Roman world which the Christian could take part in without some sacrifice of principle, because there was hardly any festivity unassociated with religious ceremony, however technical and formal this may have become. The Christian was therefore credited with sourness instead of seriousness, and his very σεμνότης was made a reproach against him. We may compare the treatment of the Puritan, whose seriousness, however exaggerated and affected it became under opposition, was just this σεμνότης and a protest against irreligious and frivolous views of life.

3. τοῦτο, *i.e.* the praying for all men. This is good and acceptable in God's eyes, because it is our best co-operation with His work of saving all men.

σωτῆρος—σωθῆναι. For St. Paul's use of these words, see note on 2 Tim. i. 9.

4-5. ἐπίγνωσις. The preposition in this compound doubtless makes the word more emphatic, and in such a passage as 2 Tim. iii. 7 'full knowledge' is a natural rendering. Perhaps also here, since the following verse states first the chief article of the Jewish creed (εἷς Θεός), and then adds the fuller knowledge that came with Christ.

5. εἷς γάρ. The *oneness* of God and of God's purpose further emphasises the *all* of these verses—His purpose has always been and is in Christ the same for all.

μεσίτης. This word could be used in the widest sense of any one who formed the channel of communication

ἄνθρωπος Χριστὸς Ἰησοῦς, 6. ὁ δοὺς ἑαυτὸν ἀντίλυτρον ὑπὲρ πάντων, τὸ μαρτύριον καιροῖς ἰδίοις, 7. εἰς ὃ ἐτέθην ἐγὼ κῆρυξ καὶ ἀπόστολος (ἀλήθειαν λέγω, οὐ ψεύδομαι), διδάσκαλος ἐθνῶν ἐν πίστει καὶ ἀληθείᾳ.

between two others, but naturally came to mean specially him through whom they are brought together in agreement. It was a regular Jewish title for Moses as him through whom God revealed the law and made the covenant (see Gal. iii. 19 and Lightfoot's note). But in a very special sense it applied to the priest who approached God in sacrifice on behalf of the people, and also pronounced God's blessing on the people. The present passage, with its words ὁ δοὺς ἑαυτὸν ἀντίλυτρον, suggests rather this sacrificial aspect of Christ's mediation. Compare the treatment of the subject in Heb. iv. 14 fol. Our Lord is thrice spoken of as the mediator of a new or better covenant in the Ep. to the Hebrews (viii. 6, ix. 15, xii. 24).

ἄνθρωπος, 'himself man,' as R.V. The reason for this emphatic addition is doubtless that expressed in Heb. iv. 15.

6. ἀντίλυτρον, the price paid for deliverance. This word only occurs here, but cf. St. Matt. xx. 28, δοῦναι τὴν ψυχὴν αὐτοῦ λύτρον ἀντὶ πολλῶν. The sacrifice of Christ is thought of as a price paid to redeem, buy back man from sin and its consequences. See the note on ἀπολύτρωσις in Sanday and Headlam's *Romans*, iii. 24, where a needful warning is given: 'The emphasis is on the *cost* of man's redemption. We need not press the metaphor yet a step further by asking (as the ancients did) to whom the ransom or price was paid. It was required by that ultimate necessity which has made the whole course of things what it has been; but this necessity is far beyond our powers to grasp or gauge.'

τὸ μαρτύριον καιροῖς ἰδίοις, R.V. 'the testimony to be borne in its own times.' μαρτύριον, however, is not 'the thing testified to,' but the evidence, proof, or testimony. Therefore, taking the phrase as in apposition to the clause ὁ δοὺς ἑαυτὸν ἀντίλυτρον ὑπὲρ πάντων, we must understand that Christ's sacrifice is spoken of as the proof, given at the due time, of God's purpose described in the words πάντας θέλει σωθῆναι (v. 4). St. Paul proceeds to describe himself as a herald appointed to proclaim this testimony of God's love.

For the construction of τὸ μαρτύριον, cf. 2 Thess. i. 5, ἔνδειγμα.

7. ἀλήθειαν λέγω, οὐ ψεύδομαι. It is not very easy to see the reason for this strong form of asseveration here, and Alford attributes it to 'the growth of a habit in the apostle's mind, which we already trace in 2 Cor. xi. 31, Rom. ix. 1, till he came to use the phrase with less force and relevance than he had once done.' But if we may take it as referring especially to the following words, διδάσκαλος ἐθνῶν, can it be thought irrelevant? The preceding verses have been asserting that the message is for *all*, he now

CH. II. 8.] FIRST EPISTLE TO TIMOTHY 21

8. Βούλομαι οὖν προσεύχεσθαι τοὺς ἄνδρας ἐν παντὶ τόπῳ, ἐπαίροντας ὁσίους χεῖρας χωρὶς ὀργῆς καὶ διαλο-

asserts, with emphasis, that his own special commission is to all. We should especially compare the same phrase in Rom. ix. 1, where the thought bears some relation to this—the inclusion of both Jews and Gentiles in God's purpose.

ἐν πίστει καὶ ἀληθείᾳ. The preposition ἐν has a very widely extended use in the Greek of the N.T., and the connection indicated by it is often so vague as to be difficult to determine. Through an imitation of Hebrew, it is frequently used to express instrument or even the person through whom a thing is done (1 Cor. vi. 2, ἐν ὑμῖν κρίνεται ὁ κόσμος, the world is judged by you). It expresses also the cause, especially of emotions (Gal. vi. 13, ἵνα ἐν τῇ ὑμετέρᾳ σαρκὶ καυχήσωνται). But much more vaguely still as indicating the *sphere*, literal or metaphorical, of an action it comes to express the *accompanying circumstances* or *manner* (*e.g.* 2 Cor. iv. 2, περιπατοῦντες ἐν πανουργίᾳ, 1 Cor. iv. 21, ἐν ῥάβδῳ ἔλθω, Acts xvii. 31, κρίνειν ἐν δικαιοσύνῃ). Grammatically, therefore, the present passage is vague—ἐν may denote the *sphere*, in which case St. Paul describes himself as a 'teacher of faith and truth'; or the *manner*, in which case he describes himself as 'teaching with faith and truth.' The former is more natural.

8-15. '**I wish then the men to attend to prayer rather than to disputations. And I wish the women to attend to good works rather than outward appearance. Let them learn, not teach. For the Scripture teaches us that woman is to be subject to man.**'

8. τοὺς ἄνδρας, R.V. 'the men,' not τοὺς ἀνθρώπους, which would include women. Clearly the limitation is due to St. Paul's anticipating in thought what he is about to say, and having in mind in this verse rather the public prayers in church than the general practice of prayer (cf. v. 5).

ἐν παντὶ τόπῳ, everywhere, wherever there is a Christian congregation.

ἐπαίροντας χεῖρας. The usual Jewish attitude in prayer was standing, though kneeling was also practised (cf. 1 Kings viii. 54, and for the uplifted hands, viii. 22). The Christian Church doubtless followed the usages of the synagogue at first in both ways, and for some time continued to pray standing on Sundays and on the days between Easter and Whitsunday. (Cf. Justin Martyr's account of the Eucharist: 'Then we all stand up together and offer prayers'; St. Clement's Ep. to the Cor. 29, 'Let us therefore come to Him with holiness of heart, lifting up chaste and undefiled hands unto Him.')

ὁσίους χεῖρας. The word ὅσιος was naturally applied to things, meaning 'right,' or 'permitted by divine law,' so that *e.g.* to bury the dead was ὅσιον, to leave them unburied οὐχ ὅσιον, and a place that might be freely entered would be

22 FIRST EPISTLE TO TIMOTHY [CH. II. 8-11.

γισμοῦ· 9. ὡσαύτως γυναῖκας ἐν καταστολῇ κοσμίῳ μετὰ αἰδοῦς καὶ σωφροσύνης κοσμεῖν ἑαυτάς, μὴ ἐν πλέγμασι καὶ χρυσίῳ ἢ μαργαρίταις ἢ ἱματισμῷ πολυτελεῖ, 10. ἀλλ᾽ (ὃ πρέπει γυναιξὶν ἐπαγγελλομέναις θεοσέβειαν) δι᾽ ἔργων ἀγαθῶν. 11. γυνὴ ἐν ἡσυχίᾳ

ὅσιον as opposed to a consecrated place (ἱερόν). Transferred to persons the word meant *pure* or *sinless*, and this is its meaning as an epithet of χεῖρες here. Cf. Soph. *O.C.*, 470, δι᾽ ὁσίων χειρῶν θιγών, where it means hands made pure by ceremonial washing.

διαλογισμός in Classical Greek meant *reasoning, calculation*. In the N.T. it tends to have the bad sense of *perverse reasoning*, but more from the context in each case than from any inherent change of meaning. It most often means *inward questionings*, and if we take it in this sense here, we have implied two conditions of right prayer as stated in the gospels, viz. the previous forgiveness of others (χωρὶς ὀργῆς), and faith (χωρὶς διαλογισμοῦ); but with such a passage before us as St. Mark viii. 16, διελογίζοντο πρὸς ἀλλήλους λέγοντες, κ.τ.λ., there is no reason for rejecting the meaning *disputing* here.

9. ὡσαύτως may be simply *also*; or it may be in its full sense of *in like manner*, meaning with the same kind of self-repression as is implied in χωρὶς ὀργῆς καὶ διαλογισμοῦ.

ἐν καταστολῇ κοσμίῳ μετὰ αἰδοῦς καὶ σωφροσύνης, in becoming (orderly) apparel with modesty and sobriety. αἰδώς is 'sense of shame,' translated in the A.V. *shamefastness, i.e.* firmness in shame (modesty), which by mistaken spelling became shamefacedness. Cf. Shaks. *Richard III.*, i. 4, 142, '[Conscience] is a blushing shamefast spirit that mutinies in a man's bosom.' σωφροσύνη meant *sound-mindedness, discretion*, and so the temper of *moderation*, especially in pleasure.

πλέγμασιν καὶ χρυσίῳ. L. and S. take πλέγματα here to mean wreaths or chaplets, but it is more natural to take it of the various ways of plaiting the hair for effect (cf. 1 Peter iii. 3). χρυσίῳ will also naturally be taken of a hair ornament—a golden comb or a net of gold thread. R.V. 'with braided hair and gold.'

10. ἐπαγγελλομέναις, *professing*—as quite commonly in Classical Greek.

δι᾽ ἔργων ἀγαθῶν. Cf. Job. xxix. 14, 'I put on righteousness and it clothed me.' So Psalm cxxxii. 9.

11. ἐν ἡσυχίᾳ, quietly, not necessarily in silence (as Alford), but without setting up her opinions against the teaching she receives. But in 1 Cor. xiv. 34-36, St. Paul enjoins very emphatically that in the church women shall keep silence, implying (v. 36) that any contrary usage at Corinth was an innovation peculiar to themselves. It is obvious from xi. 5 (γυνὴ προσευχομένη ἢ προφητεύουσα) that such a usage had begun in Corinth. It does not follow that St. Paul would have forbidden women to speak and teach in our days, but it was contrary both

μανθανέτω ἐν πάσῃ ὑποταγῇ. 12. διδάσκειν δὲ γυναικὶ
οὐκ ἐπιτρέπω, οὐδὲ αὐθεντεῖν ἀνδρός, ἀλλ' εἶναι ἐν ἡσυχίᾳ.
13. Ἀδὰμ γὰρ πρῶτος ἐπλάσθη, εἶτα Εὖα· 14. καὶ
Ἀδὰμ οὐκ ἠπατήθη, ἡ δὲ γυνὴ ἐξαπατηθεῖσα ἐν παρα-

to Jewish and to Greek sentiment to let women who respected themselves take such a public part, and though the Apostle could say that in Christ there was 'neither male nor female,' this did not mean that whatever a man could do a woman could do, nor did he encourage contempt for the usages and conventions of society. It was one of the earliest social results of Christianity to raise men's respect for womanhood, and to give woman a new place in good works. This beneficial change would have been impossible if it had been combined with an eccentricity of demeanour that every Greek lady would have thought immodest. The importance of the principle will be still more apparent if we remember that the Gentile world for a long time suspected the Church as a 'secret society,' and was not easily persuaded that it had no immoral rites. This made the conduct of its women before the world a consideration of great moment.

12. αὐθεντεῖν, a verb that occurs here first in literature, and only here in the N.T. The noun αὐθέντης meant one who does anything with his own hand, and so in late Greek, a masterful person or autocrat. Hence the meaning of the verb here —to exercise authority, R.V. *have dominion*. Our word *authentic* comes from it, 'that which is vouched for by the man himself.' [The frequent Classical association of αὐθέντης with murder is not essential to the word.]

13-14. The first part of the argument is the same as that of 1 Cor. xi. 9, viz., woman was formed after man, and for the sake of man, therefore she is meant to be subordinate to him. The second part is that woman incurred greater guilt than man in the Fall, and doubtless St. Paul has in mind that subjection to man was part of the punishment then pronounced for her: 'In sorrow thou shalt bring forth children; and thy desire shall be to thy husband, and he shall rule over thee' (Gen. iii. 16). In judging of St. Paul's argument, we may set aside all critical interpretations of the early chapters of Genesis—they were not present to him, and the words just quoted were taken by him simply as the actual words of God.

14. *I.e.* man's complaisance to his wife was less guilty than woman's listening to the tempter.

ἐν παραβάσει γέγονεν, R.V. 'hath fallen into transgression,' the perfect tense being used to indicate the continuance of the consequences to the present time. παράβασις is literally a stepping aside out of the path marked out, and therefore corresponds very closely to *transgression*, the stepping over a line.

15. R.V. 'But she shall be saved through the child-bearing.' This is ambiguous: (1) If διά be taken in the sense 'by means of,' the mean-

βάσει γέγονε· 15. σωθήσεται δὲ διὰ τῆς τεκνογονίας, ἐὰν μείνωσιν ἐν πίστει καὶ ἀγάπῃ καὶ ἁγιασμῷ μετὰ σωφροσύνης.ᵃ

ᵃ σωφροσύνης· πιστὸς ὁ λόγος.

ing of the sentence must be that woman by working out her curse ('In sorrow thou shalt bear children') will find healing. 'In God's face is light, but in His shadow healing too.' It is impossible to think that St. Paul meant ' by her being the mother of Christ,' or that he would have referred to the fact of the Incarnation in such a vague phrase. (2) But διά can mean 'through' of time, and σωθήσεται διά would then be 'shall be brought safe through.' There can be little doubt that this would have been the sense in which any ordinary Greek would have understood the phrase here, and this of course accords also with the looser use of διά in the N.T., to indicate the circumstances of an action (e.g. 2 Cor. ii. 4, ἔγραψα ὑμῖν διὰ πολλῶν δακρύων). This is substantially the interpretation of Alford, taking σωθήσεται in the higher sense of spiritual salvation, laying stress (very appositely) on 1 Cor. iii. 15, σωθήσεται οὕτω δὲ ὡς διὰ πυρός.

ἀγάπη. See n. on i. 5.

ἁγιασμῷ. The word ἅγιος seems first of all to have meant 'set apart for the service of God,' 'consecrated,' in the sense in which e.g. Israel was a consecrated people. But as that which is given to God must be perfect, the word came to mean the absence of blemish or guilt, which should characterise the worshippers of God—and so 'holy.' (See a full note in Sanday and Headlam's *Romans*, i. 7.) ἁγιασμός was properly the process of making ἅγιος; here it stands for the result, viz. 'holiness.'

σωφροσύνη. See n. on v. 9.

CHAPTER III

1. Πιστὸς ὁ λόγος, Εἴ τις ἐπισκοπῆς ὀρέγεται, καλοῦ

1. πιστὸς ὁ λόγος. See n. on i. 15. But here it is a question whether the saying referred to is contained in the preceding or in the following words. It certainly refers to following words in i. 15, and seems to in 2 Tim. ii. 11 ; but here, and in iv. 9, and Titus iii. 8, the reference is more doubtful.

It is to be noted that in the context of all five passages there is an allusion to salvation or eternal life, and this certainly suggests that a 'saying' (or more than one) is referred to which contains the promise of this, perhaps the saying that is actually quoted in i. 15. It is well to set the passages together. i. 15, 'Faithful is the saying and worthy of all acceptation that *Christ Jesus came into the world to save sinners*.' iii. 1, '*She shall be saved* through the childbearing if they continue in faith and love and sanctification with sobriety. Faithful is the saying. If a man seeketh the office of a bishop he desireth a good work.' iv. 9, 'Godliness is profitable for all things, *having promise of the life which now is and of that which is to come*. Faithful is the saying and worthy of all acceptation. For to this end we labour and strive because we have our hope set on the living God *who is the Saviour of all men*, specially of them that believe.' 2 Tim. ii. 11, '*That they also may obtain the sal-* vation which is in Christ Jesus with eternal glory. Faithful is the saying. For if we died with him we shall also live with him.' Titus iii. 8, 'That being justified by his grace we might be made *heirs according to the hope of eternal life*. Faithful is the saying. And concerning these things I will that thou affirm confidently, to the end that they which have believed God may be careful to maintain good works.'

In the present passage a reference to the preceding σωθήσεται seems more natural than a reference to a saying about the office of ἐπισκοπή. The abruptness of ending the former subject with 'Faithful is the saying' seems to us much greater than it really is because of our long familiarity with the ring of the A.V. The R.V. margin attaches the words to the preceding verse.

1-13. The qualifications of Bishops (1-7) and of Deacons (8-13).

1. ἐπισκοπῆς. This is the only passage in which this abstract noun is used of a definite office in the Church, but the name ἐπίσκοπος is used of a definite officer four times in the N.T. With regard to the use of the name in St. Paul's own lifetime, the student should make himself clear on the following points : (1) The words ἐπίσκοποι and πρεσβύτεροι stood for the same officials in the Church, as is shown by their use of the same men in Acts xx. vv. 17 and 28, and by the fact that neither in salutations nor elsewhere do we find such a combination as 'bishops and elders.' (2) The first mention of Christian πρεσβύτεροι is at Jerusalem in Acts xi. 30, and these are referred to twice again in the Acts. The passages where ἐπίσκοποι are spoken of in the N.T. all relate to churches in Greek or Gentile centres. It is safe to conclude that ἐπίσκοπος (=overseer) was adopted as a more natural word in Greek churches. It must be noted that such a Greek church frequently gathered round a nucleus of converts from the synagogue, and these Jewish converts would have been very loth to adopt for the officers of the Christian congregation a title which would have seemed to imply a rivalry in authority with the πρεσβύτεροι of the synagogue. This would be avoided by the use of the vague term ἐπίσκοποι, overseers.

As to the office indicated by the name ἐπίσκοπος or πρεσβύτερος, it should be noted (3) that the term πρεσβύτεροι was the recognised Greek for the Jewish 'elders.' The institution of these in every Jewish community dates from very ancient times, and it is probable that their civil authority in dealing justice came before the days of synagogues, and therefore before they had any clearly defined religious administration. But in the N.T. times the synagogue was the place from which they exercised their authority, and they had complete control of its services, funds, and arrangements. (4) It is as the equivalent of these Jewish officials that the Christian community needed πρεσβύτεροι or ἐπίσκοποι of its own when it was separated from the synagogue, and this fact is a guide to us in understanding the position of the 'bishops' or 'elders' of the church. They would thus be essentially *local* officials, with authority over the services, funds, and arrangements of a particular congregation. In one important respect they would necessarily differ from the Jewish elders, viz. that whereas these were everywhere recognised by the Romans as having a certain civil authority over members of the synagogue community (*e.g.* to inflict fines and scourge), no such authority could be assumed by the officials of the Christian congregation, who in this respect would be limited to what we should call ecclesiastical discipline.

As to the method of appointment, it is to be noted (5) that there is not any evidence at all in the N.T. that bishops or elders of the Church were elected or designated by the congregation (as there is the case of 'the seven,' *i.e.* deacons, Acts vi.). This may of course have preceded the appointment by apostolic authority, which itself is clearly indicated in such passages as Titus i. 5, Acts xiv. 23. Outside the N.T. the evidence is clear that the congregation had a voice in choosing men for the office. Cf. St. Clement's First Epistle, 44, where he speaks of those who were 'appointed by the apostles or afterwards chosen by other eminent men with the consent of the whole church,' and he rebukes the Corinthians for having presumed to expel some such. In the *Didache*, 15, we have 'Appoint for yourselves bishops and deacons worthy of the Lord.'

In the first place, then, the local authority over each church was a body of men called indifferently ἐπίσκοποι or πρεσβύτεροι. In the present note the further development of the organisation can only be briefly treated. The question is really threefold: (a) by what stages the two titles became differentiated in meaning; (b) by what stages and when episcopal organisation became established; (c) when bishops can be said to have been recognised as a separate 'order' with a 'consecration' different from the ordination of priests—for it must be noted that (b) and (c) are not necessarily the same question, nor is the answer to the one involved in the answer to the other. Unfortunately the direct evidence of the first three centuries is very inadequate, and the statements of fourth century writers are obviously inferences based upon little more knowledge of original institutions than we possess ourselves. The following facts are to be noted with regard to the above questions. (a) There is no evidence in St. Clement of Rome that he used the words with different signification, rather is it clear from his reference to 'bishops and deacons' in ch. 42 that he had no thought of a *threefold* division of the ministry. The same is true of the *Didache* (ch. 15). When we come, however, to the letters of St. Ignatius, we find a direct distinction drawn, *e.g.* in the letter to the Magnesians, ch. 2, 'Damas, your most excellent bishop, and your very worthy πρεσβύτεροι, Bassus and Apollonius.' (b) With regard to episcopal organisation (in the sense of one man's receiving authority over a number of πρεσβύτεροι or a number of churches) it is clear that this may be said to have begun with the commissions given to Timothy, Titus, and probably others. There is no other evidence of such exercise of authority over a whole *district* until we come to Ignatius, who speaks of himself as 'Bishop of Syria'; but from passages like that quoted above from the letter to the Magnesians [cf. the letter to the Ephesians, 2, 'being subject to your bishop and the presbytery'], it is safe to infer that by that time it was customary in some important churches for one man to be president and exercise some authority over the πρεσβύτεροι. But Ignatius does not mention a bishop at Rome, nor Polycarp a bishop at Philippi, nor Pliny a bishop in Bithynia. These facts, though perhaps capable of other incidental explanation, lend support to the theory that the establishment of bishops came gradually as a better organisation of the πρεσβύτεροι became necessary, and perhaps the system first became general in Asia Minor. (c) From the times of which we are speaking no evidence is forthcoming of the setting apart of bishops by any special act of consecration beyond their ordination as priests. Hence, it is said, they were at that time 'presidents of the presbytery,' differing from the priests in dignity and authority, not in 'order.' We can only allow to this the weight due to an argument from the silence of a period which has left us really little written authority for its institutions. St. Jerome, writing in the fourth century, says, 'Let bishops know that rather by custom

ἔργου ἐπιθυμεῖ. 2. δεῖ οὖν τὸν ἐπίσκοπον ἀνεπίληπτον εἶναι, μιᾶς γυναικὸς ἄνδρα, νηφάλιον, σώφρονα, κόσμιον,

than by the Lord's arrangement are they greater than priests'; and he states that the bishops of Alexandria down to the third century were elected by and received their authority from the priests. But in this it seems likely that he was misled by Arian statements. (See *Cambridge Mediaeval History*, vol. I. p. 160.) In the *Canons of Hippolytus* (third century) the bishop, after election by the people, is consecrated by 'one of the bishops and presbyters.' Nothing enables us to determine with certainty the practice of the earlier centuries.

In any inferences we may draw with regard to the practice during St. Paul's own life, it is most important to bear in mind that any arrangements which he made he thought of as almost temporary, to last for the short period before the Lord came again. This being so, we should hardly be justified in trying to find in his writings a definite 'constitution' which was to govern the Church of all future ages, but we are justified in seeing in the arrangements he made the germ which developed into the episcopal system. Where an apostolic delegate was present, as Titus in Crete (see Titus i. 5), he would probably exercise without question what we should call episcopal authority. But it is also probable that in other parts of the Church the arrangements varied according to local needs and possibilities, and that a complete organisation on the model of such commissions as those held by Titus and Timothy only came to prevail gradually.

1. **καλοῦ ἔργου ἐπιθυμεῖ**. The form of St. Paul's statement suggests, though vaguely perhaps, that the office was one which many were inclined to avoid. There was certainly a danger that men would undervalue the local and administrative office by comparison with the more obviously charismatic work of the 'prophets and teachers.' Hence the warning in *Didache* 15, 'not to despise the bishops and deacons.'

2. **ἀνεπίληπτος**, a Classical word, 'not open to attack,' 'irreproachable,' but only found in this epistle in the N.T.

μιᾶς γυναικὸς ἄνδρα. There are several things which St. Paul may here have in mind as a disqualification for the priesthood. (1) Polygamy was still not illegal among the Jews, and indeed cannot be said to have been illegal among them before A.D. 1000. If the law of the Levirate was ever observed it implied the possibility of polygamy, and Justin Martyr reproaches the Jews with it. But it was contrary to the best rabbinical teaching, and had probably fallen into general disuse. [See article 'Marriage' in Hastings' one vol. *Dict. of the Bible.*] If a Jew with two wives became a Christian it is possible that St. Paul would not have enjoined the putting away of one of them, but at the same time would have considered him unfit for office in the Church

φιλόξενον, διδακτικόν· 3. μὴ πάροινον, μὴ πλήκτην, ἀλλ᾽

because his life set an inferior example. (2) Among the Gentiles, as among the Jews, there was facility for divorce, and it was possible for a man to become a Christian who had put away one wife legally and married another legally. Here again it is only possible to infer what St. Paul would have done, but probably, while leaving the man as he was, he would have regarded the fact as making him unfit for the office of ἐπίσκοπος. The instinct which forbids men's preferring to the service of God anything which has a blemish (even an unavoidable blemish) was primitive, universal, and natural, and it has found drastic expression in the canon law of the Church. (3) There is thirdly the case of a man whose first wife had died, and who had married again. But St. Paul actually advises a second marriage to some women in v. 14, and allows it in 1 Cor. vii. 39, so that he cannot have thought it an unworthy course.

It is probable that St. Paul's reference here is to (1) and (2). Early authority refers his words to (1). Perhaps the reference to (3) would hardly have found support but for the phrase ἑνὸς ἀνδρὸς γυνή in v. 9, where see note.

νηφάλιος. The first use of this adjective was for things (*e.g.* drinks, libations) that contained no wine. Its use of men, 'sober,' 'not given to wine,' is later Greek.

σώφρων. See note on ii. 9.

κόσμιος, R.V. 'orderly.' It means doing 'quod decet,' avoiding 'quod dedecet,' and this from the point of view of station as well as of character generally. Some things not unseemly in an ordinary man would be unseemly in a priest, and the man chosen must be one who has this sense of respect for his office and work.

φιλόξενος. The need for hospitality in the early Church, even in large cities, must have been great. In inns and lodging-houses they must have come into hourly contact with that which called for their avoidance or protest. Apart from heathenish rites associated with the meals in a public room, there was frequent danger of contumelious treatment; so that the Jews had long carried to the West the Oriental ideas of hospitality in entertaining one another. Christians, whether Jew or Gentile, now had to do the same. (Cf. v. 10, Rom. xii. 13.)

διδακτικός. See n. on 2 Tim. ii. 24.

3. μὴ πάροινον, μὴ πλήκτην, R.V. 'no brawler (*margin* not quarrelsome over wine), no striker.' The offences here referred to are so scandalous in our eyes that attempts have been made to soften them down, *e.g.* to make the 'striking' only the castigation of rebuke. This is to make the words mean what no Greek reading them would understand by them. That St. Paul should think it necessary to give this injunction shows how difficult some of the converts found it to break with the standard of pagan life to which they had been accustomed. Public opinion did not brand excess in drinking as it does now, and it was not possible to make all converts see all things in a new light at once. It is evident

ἐπιεικῆ, ἄμαχον, ἀφιλάργυρον· 4. τοῦ ἰδίου οἴκου καλῶς προϊστάμενον, τέκνα ἔχοντα ἐν ὑποταγῇ μετὰ πάσης σεμνότητος· 5. (εἰ δέ τις τοῦ ἰδίου οἴκου προστῆναι οὐκ

from 1 Cor. that some members of the Church at Corinth were inclined to defend even a case of gross immorality. When we find that such an estimate of these things was possible, it may suggest to us that our own estimate of the comparative heinousness of offences is not perfect, and there are things that we in our turn attach too slight a stigma to. A man is sometimes punished more severely for one act of dissipation (because it is obvious and tangible) than for a lifetime of malice and evil-speaking.

ἐπιεικής. This word, derived from εἰκός, meant first that which is fitting, and so that which is reasonable and equitable. Its ethical meaning to Classical writers is shown by the passage in Aristotle's *Rhetoric* i. 13: 'It is ἐπιείκεια to pardon human failings, to look to the lawgiver and not to the law, to the spirit and not to the letter, to the intention and not to the action, to the whole and not to the part, to the character of the actor in the long run and not in the present moment, to remember good rather than evil, and good that one has received rather than good that one has done.' The adjective, therefore, naturally came to mean *considerate*, *gentle*, and this is its meaning in the N.T.

ἀφιλάργυρος. Cf. note on 2 Tim. iii. 2. It means that he keeps the motive of personal gain in its proper subordinate position, even though he has to earn his living. He does not measure the service he is prepared to render by the greatness of the expected fee. Some of the best examples of ἀφιλάργυροι one comes across among doctors who lavish on poor men the skill acquired by a lifetime's work.

4. μετὰ πάσης σεμνότητος. Cf. note on ii. 2 for σεμνότης. It is questioned whether it is meant here for the quality shown by the father or the quality produced in the children. Alford says the latter. But why should it not include both?— i.e. the attitude of mutual respect, due partly to the consciousness of sharing great spiritual aims, and partly (even where that is absent) to the fact that neither father nor son ever forgets his own self-respect or what is due to the other. Each is 'libertatis alienae et dignitatis suae memor.' The manner of some is such that they can never be either affectionate or stern without some sacrifice of respect. This is the opposite of σεμνότης.

The noun σεμνότης occurs three times in the Pastoral Epistles, the adjective σεμνός occurs three times in them and once in Phil. iv. 8. Neither occurs elsewhere in the N.T. It looks as if the need for the quality had been brought home to St. Paul in his later experience, as if there were a danger of the serious standard of Christian life being contaminated by compromise with Gentile habits.

5. τοῦ ἰδίου οἴκου, so comparatively small a charge, so completely under his own authority. ἐκκλησίας Θεοῦ,

CH. III. 5-8.] FIRST EPISTLE TO TIMOTHY 31

οἶδε, πῶς ἐκκλησίας Θεοῦ ἐπιμελήσεται;) 6. μὴ νεόφυτον, ἵνα μὴ τυφωθεὶς εἰς κρῖμα ἐμπέσῃ τοῦ διαβόλου. 7. δεῖ δὲ καὶ μαρτυρίαν καλὴν ἔχειν ἀπὸ τῶν ἔξωθεν, ἵνα μὴ εἰς ὀνειδισμὸν ἐμπέσῃ καὶ παγίδα τοῦ διαβόλου. 8. δια-

so great a charge, over which authority must be won and kept by proof of personal fitness.

6. **νεόφυτον**, a word that meant 'newly planted,' hence of a 'new convert,' but not occurring elsewhere in the N.T. The precept has been sometimes disregarded in times of stress, *e.g.* St. Ambrose was chosen bishop of Milan before he was baptized.

τυφωθείς. τυφόω meant by derivation 'to wrap in smoke,' and, though never used literally, expressed by very rigorous metaphor the clouding and darkening of the mind by pride. Pride prevents one's thinking or judging clearly. R.V. 'puffed up,' but this is not very happy, because the metaphor is different. Better 'blinded with pride.'

κρῖμα τοῦ διαβόλου. The natural interpretation of this is that favoured by most early commentators, viz. condemnation such as the devil fell into through pride. For the word διάβολος, see note on i. 20.

7. **ἀπὸ τῶν ἔξωθεν** – from those who are not Christians. A ruler in the Church must be one whose life naturally commends his profession even to those who do not think with him, so that they will say of him: 'God cannot be far from him in doctrine to whom He is so gracious in life' (George Herbert).

εἰς ὀνειδισμόν. Both the sense and the order are rather against taking this with τοῦ διαβόλου. Such a man first of all falls into the 'reproach' of men, and gives them occasion for speaking contemptuously of himself and his office, and consequently of the Church. Then he becomes painfully conscious of this, and feels that by some means or other he must re-establish his influence—hence he may be led to unworthy compromise, gives away point after point on which he should have stood. This is falling into the 'snare of the devil.' There is, of course, no greater temptation to compromise than the consciousness of failure in one's present line.

8. The word **διάκονος** (probably from the root of διώκω, *follow*), with its cognates διακονία and διακονέω, could indicate any form of *service*, and these words are used freely for the ministry of the apostles and our Lord. The first use of διάκονος for a specific office in the Church is Phil i. 1. For the Seven appointed in Acts vi. for the Church at Jerusalem, are not called διάκονοι in any writing earlier than Irenaeus (*c.* 180 A.D.), and we can only say that there was some analogy between the work assigned to them and the work of later deacons. It is evident, however, that in the present passage St. Paul is referring to a definite office with definite functions. His words support the usual tradition, which makes visiting and the ministration of alms the first duty of the deacon. The warnings in μὴ διλόγους, μὴ διαβόλους suit the former, that in μὴ αἰσχρο-

κόνους ὡσαύτως σεμνούς, μὴ διλόγους, μὴ οἴνῳ πολλῷ προσέχοντας, μὴ αἰσχροκερδεῖς, 9. ἔχοντας τὸ μυστή-

κερδεῖς suits the latter. The omission of διδακτικός, φιλόξενος, and all reference to *ruling* the church suggests the subordination of the office of deacon to that of the ἐπίσκοπος. We find the deacon's functions well established in the *Canons of Hippolytus* (about 200 A.D.). Besides serving the bishops and priests in all things, he is specially to visit the sick and report on cases of poverty and suffering. At that time he was ordained by the bishop, who laid hands on him with a set form of prayer. St. Paul does not refer to any *ordination* of deacons in the Pastoral Epistles. The permission given to deacons in the Church of England to preach, 'if they be licensed thereto by the Bishop,' is a comparatively modern innovation. It is also to be noted that the modern conception of the office as only the first step to the priesthood, and leading to that almost as a matter of course, was not inherent in the primitive conception: a man might have special gifts for the work of a deacon without the gifts for ruling and teaching the Church, which specially appertain to the priesthood. St. Paul's words mark this clearly.

σεμνούς. See above ii. 2 and iii. 4.

διλόγους, a word used only here, though διλογέω and διλογία are used in Xenophon for *repeat* and *repetition*. R.V. here 'double-tongued.' Nothing was more natural than that Christianity should invent some new words to express the qualities of truthfulness and falseness. Among the ancients the sanction for truth in ordinary life was simply utilitarian—the breaking of an oath would bring punishment, and the habit of deceit would probably not pay. In Christian ethics truth is on a different footing: any falseness of speech is a sin against the community, as destroying that confidence between man and man on which the ideal Christian state of ἀγάπη must in part depend. Note also what George Herbert says: 'The Parson is very strict in keeping his word, though it be to his own hinderance, as knowing that if he be not so he will quickly be discovered and disregarded; neither would they believe him in the pulpit whom they cannot trust in his conversation.'

μὴ οἴνῳ πολλῷ προσέχοντας. Their duty of visiting would expose them to much well-meant hospitality.

αἰσχροκερδεῖς. The idea is rather different from that of ἀφιλάργυρον in v. 3, where see n. Here the idea is the sordid grasping after petty gains. Possibly there is allusion to a special temptation of a poor man having the charge of church funds. Theophrastus describing the αἰσχροκερδής says: 'When he makes a distribution he will say that the distributor is entitled to a double share, and thereupon will help himself.' But the whole of this character (xxvi.) in Theophrastus should be read. George Herbert is thinking of the same character when he writes, 'If a man hath wherewithal to buy a spade and yet he chuseth rather to use his neighbour's and wear out

CH. III. 9-11.] FIRST EPISTLE TO TIMOTHY 33

ριον τῆς πίστεως ἐν καθαρᾷ συνειδήσει. 10. καὶ οὗτοι δὲ δοκιμαζέσθωσαν πρῶτον, εἶτα διακονείτωσαν ἀνέγκλητοι ὄντες. 11. γυναῖκας ὡσαύτως σεμνάς, μὴ διαβό-

that, he is covetous. Nevertheless, few bring covetousness thus low or consider it so narrowly, which yet ought to be done, since there is a justice in the least things, and for the least there shall be a judgment.'

9. The Greek 'mysteries' were certain religious celebrations or rites (notably those of Demeter at Eleusis), to which only the initiated were admitted. But the word was used (in Plato and elsewhere) in a perfectly general sense, and when St. Paul speaks of the Christian mysteries there is no reason to suppose anywhere that he is expressing an analogy. The phrase 'the mystery of the faith' means those truths which could only be known to man by direct revelation, truths which could not be reached by any process of reasoning from natural observation. The deacon is to hold fast to these. It was not his business to teach (as explained above), but in his visiting he would have many an opportunity of saying the right thing at the right moment both to believers and unbelievers. In such case it would be his special temptation (more especially as he was not an authorised teacher) to indulge in argument and that 'wisdom of the world' which St. Paul disclaims for himself in 1 Cor., instead of stating boldly the unpalatable 'mystery' of 'Jesus Christ and him crucified.' (See 1 Cor. ii. 1, 2.) The present words are a reminder that this latter is his duty rather than the other. St. Paul adds ἐν καθαρᾷ συνειδήσει.

See n. on i. 5. But though the phrase may imply that there must be nothing in his conduct to contradict his faith, it is naturally taken here of the way in which the faith is held and maintained. The faith is held 'with a pure conscience' when there is absolute correspondence between what we think and what we say, when there is no acting a part for the sake of being orthodox.

10. δοκιμαζέσθωσαν, 'let them be tested'—the word having been first used of testing metals, etc. No particular method is specified by St. Paul, but the kind of δοκιμασία that would occur to a Greek reader would be the scrutiny that a man elected to an office at Athens would have to undergo to prove that he was a full citizen, etc. No doubt some opportunity was given to the congregation to challenge the fitness of a candidate before Timothy appointed him to the office.

11. γυναῖκας. Standing as it does in the middle of instructions about deacons, this word must stand for either (1) women holding a position analogous to that of deacons; or (2) the wives of deacons. The form of the Greek γυναῖκας ὡσαύτως (without τάς or αὐτῶν) seems to make (2) impossible. Therefore, even if it stands by itself, this passage points to the institution of what we should call deaconesses. There is no other certain allusion to them in the N.T.; for they must not be confused with the 'widows' of ch. v. 9, and it is not likely that St. Paul is referring

C

λους, νηφαλίους, πιστὰς ἐν πᾶσι. 12. διάκονοι ἔστωσαν μιᾶς γυναικὸς ἄνδρες, τέκνων καλῶς προϊστάμενοι καὶ τῶν ἰδίων οἴκων. 13. οἱ γὰρ καλῶς διακονήσαντες βαθμὸν ἑαυτοῖς καλὸν περιποιοῦνται, καὶ πολλὴν παρρησίαν ἐν πίστει τῇ ἐν Χριστῷ Ἰησοῦ.

14. Ταῦτά σοι γράφω ἐλπίζων ἐλθεῖν πρός σε ἐν τάχει·

to a specific office when he calls Phoebe a διάκονος of the Church in Cenchreae in Rom. xvi. 1. But we may add to the present passage the fact that Pliny in his letter to Trajan mentions those who were called *ministrae* in the Church in Bithynia; and though this is the only other evidence in the first two centuries, the fact that social usages made it quite impossible for deacons, as a rule, to visit the women leaves no doubt that very early there must have been women appointed for this duty. See Sanday and Headlam's note on Rom. xvi. 1: 'An office in the Church of this character, we may argue on *a priori* grounds, there must have been; but an order in the more ecclesiastical sense of the term need not have existed.'

μὴ διαβόλους, in the ordinary Greek sense of διαβάλλω, 'not slanderous.'

πιστὰς ἐν πᾶσι, 'trustworthy in all things,' in their word as in their distribution of alms.

12. See notes on verses 2 and 4.

13. The rare word βαθμός is difficult. It seems to have been used for *threshold* in the LXX (1 Sam. v. 5, also Sirach vi. 36) and for the *degrees* of a sundial, which were possibly marked by a flight of *steps* (2 Kings xx.). But apart from this there seems no instance of its use in the literal sense of *step*. The R.V. has *gain to themselves a good standing*, and this clearly gives the sense. But the question is asked whether it means a good standing in the eyes of God (at the day of judgment) or in the eyes of the Church; and in support of the former interpretation the parallel of vi. 19 is quoted ('laying up in store for themselves a good foundation against the time to come, that they may lay hold on the life which is life indeed'). But is the question necessary? St. Paul must have been well aware of it when his language was ambiguous and he seems to have left it so—in other words he includes both. The man who has done well in the duties of ministering to others increases in favour both with God and with man. And, as St. Paul adds, he increases in boldness towards both also—the boldness with which he presents his faith before men and the boldness with which faith enables him to approach the throne of grace. (Heb. iv. 16 προσερχώμεθα οὖν μετὰ παρρησίας τῷ θρόνῳ τῆς χάριτος.)

14-16. 'I write thus in order that, if I cannot come myself, you may know what you ought to do in the church, that body which is chosen by God to maintain the mystery of the faith.'

14. See Introd., p. x.

15. ἐὰν δὲ βραδύνω, ἵνα εἰδῇς πῶς δεῖ ἐν οἴκῳ Θεοῦ ἀναστρέφεσθαι, ἥτις ἐστὶν ἐκκλησία Θεοῦ ζῶντος, στῦλος

15. **πῶς δεῖ**, *how thou oughtest* is more natural here than *how men ought*.

ἐν οἴκῳ Θεοῦ naturally carries back to the thought of v. 5. It is not the metaphor of a building as in Eph. ii. 20-22, but the Church is God's household, the οἰκεῖοι τοῦ Θεοῦ of that passage. Cf. Heb. x. 21, ἱερέα μέγαν ἐπὶ τὸν οἶκον τοῦ Θεοῦ.

The word ἐκκλησία was the common Greek word for the assembly of citizens in a free city called together to transact the business of the city. (So used in Acts xix. 39.) In the LXX it was adopted for a Hebrew word meaning 'assembly,' in the sense of the whole people of God gathered together or spoken of collectively (*e.g.* Deut. xxxi. 30. Of this we have an instance in Acts vii. 38: 'This is he that was in the ἐκκλησία in the wilderness'). That this use of it was continued in N.T. times is shown by our Lord's use of it as represented in the Greek of St. Matthew xvi. 18, 'Upon this rock I will build my ἐκκλησία,' which might be paraphrased as 'the new and true Israel of God.' The ordinary word for a local congregation was συναγωγή; but that ἐκκλησία could also be used for this is shown by the other passage where the word appears in the Gospels, viz. St. Matthew xvii. 17, 'If he refuse to hear them, tell it unto the ἐκκλησία.' The word συναγωγή is used for a Christian congregation in St. James ii. 2, but there was an obvious reason why the recognised name for the Jewish congregation should not be used also for the Christian congregation in a place where both existed. Therefore in the earliest writings of St. Paul we find the local use of ἐκκλησία already well established, *e.g.* 1 Thess. i. 1, 'Unto the church of the Thessalonians'; 2 Thess. i. 4, 'We ourselves glory in you in the churches of God.' Its use for 'the Church considered collectively is shown in such passages as 1 Cor. xii. 28, but especially in the Epistle to the Ephesians (i. 22, etc.), where the unity of the Church is most strongly brought out. This is its use in the present passage, where the unity of the whole is further emphasised by the figure of the 'household of God.' In the other two passages where the word is used in this epistle (iii. 5, v. 16), it is capable of the local sense.

στῦλος καὶ ἑδραίωμα, *pillar and foundation*. R.V. for ἑδραίωμα (which occurs only here) has *ground*, margin *stay*. In any case the metaphor is that of the Church as the support of the truth. This does not compel us to take ἐν οἴκῳ above as the *house* rather than the *household*, the change of metaphor being easily paralleled. The words στῦλος καὶ ἑδραίωμα have been taken of Timothy as the unexpressed subject of ἀναστρέφεσθαι; this would be grammatically possible, but is not so natural a sense.

16. The thought of the Church as the support of the truth leads the Apostle to an exclamation as to the greatness of the mystery in that truth.

καὶ ἑδραίωμα τῆς ἀληθείας. 16. καὶ ὁμολογουμένως μέγα ἐστὶ τὸ τῆς εὐσεβείας μυστήριον· "ὃς ἐφανερώθη ἐν σαρκί, ἐδικαιώθη ἐν πνεύματι, ὤφθη ἀγγέλοις, ἐκηρύχθη ἐν ἔθνεσιν, ἐπιστεύθη ἐν κόσμῳ, ἀνελήφθη ἐν δόξῃ.

" ὅ·

ὁμολογουμένως, *confessedly*, by the admission of all who have approached it.

τὸ τῆς εὐσεβείας μυστήριον, *the mystery of the religious life*. For the words see n. on iii. 9, vi. 11.

ὃς ἐφανερώθη, κ.τ.λ. The following words have been variously described as part of an early creed or part of an early hymn. The former idea may be set aside. The only evidence we have in the N.T. of a special creed-form is in connection with Baptism, and it seems to have taken the simple form of a statement that 'Jesus is the Lord.' (Cf. Rom. x. 9 and 1 Cor. xii. 3.) The present passage is manifestly unsuitable for the purpose. On the other hand it may have had some liturgical use. Such passages as Eph. v. 19 ('psalms and hymns and spiritual songs'), and the early origin of such canticles as the *Magnificat* and *Benedictus* in St. Luke i., show conclusively that the Church from the beginning used at least the Hebrew Psalms and special Christian hymns, based in form upon them. The freedom of this form would quickly give rise to variations under Christian inspiration, and besides the present passage we may reasonably conclude that Eph. v. 14 contains part of another hymn—ἔγειραι ὁ καθεύδων καὶ ἀνάστα ἐκ τῶν νεκρῶν καὶ ἐπιφαύσει σοι ὁ Χριστός. See article 'Hymn' in Hastings' *D. of the B.* and p. 276 in Bigg's *Origins of Christianity*.

If we recognise the passage as a quotation (especially if from a hymn) we shall be saved from seeking to find in it a special order, chronological or other, and from finding a meaning in antitheses which may be more in the rhythm of the verse than in the statement. The subject is clearly the manifestation of Christ, —Christ was manifested in the flesh by His Incarnation, He was proved to be righteous (in all that He claimed and did and taught) by the present power of the Spirit (in Himself and His servants), was seen of angels, was preached among the nations, was believed on in the world, was received up in glory.

The correct reading is ὅς, not ὅ or Θεός. Regarding the passage as a quotation it is not necessary to regard μυστήριον as grammatically the antecedent of ὅς, though it is certainly true to say that Christ in believers is Himself the 'mystery'; but it is a more natural form of speech to take the mystery as being the facts of Christ's manifestation as stated in the quoted words.

ὤφθη ἀγγέλοις. It is natural to take these words as meaning that Christ Incarnate was a revelation to angels as well as to men. Cf. 1 Pet. i. 12, 'which things angels desire to look into.'

ἐν ἔθνεσιν, not necessarily of Gentiles only, as A.V.

CHAPTER IV

1. Τὸ δὲ Πνεῦμα ῥητῶς λέγει, ὅτι ἐν ὑστέροις καιροῖς ἀποστήσονταί τινες τῆς πίστεως, προσέχοντες πνεύμασι

1-5. Warning that the danger from false beliefs will increase.

The passage should be compared with 2 Tim. iii. 1-5, but there is a marked difference in that here St. Paul emphasises false beliefs, there moral perversion.

1. ῥητῶς, *expressly*. ῥητός means *expressed in words*, and so *definite*. Cf. παρεῖναι εἰς ῥητὴν ἡμέραν (to be present on the day named), ῥητὸν ἀργύριον (a definitely named sum of money). Here the reference is to the inspired utterances of prophets in the Church. See note on i. 18. For the nature of these prophecies relating to a great apostasy to precede the second coming of our Lord, cf. 2 Thess. ii.

ἐν ὑστέροις καιροῖς, *in later times*, not 'the latter times' as A.V.

πνεύμασι πλάνοις, *deluding spirits*. The reference is presumably to men speaking in the Church as if by inspiration of God, but really under the influence of evil spirits. See 1 Cor. xii. 10 for the need of a 'discerning of spirits' (διακρίσεις πνευμάτων), and compare 2 Thess. ii. 2. The test suggested by St. Paul in 1 Cor. xii. 3 obviously applied to some utterances that had happened at Corinth, but was not applicable to all utterances; it shows, however, that he wished the authorities of the Church to judge the prophets by the nature of what they said. This serious necessity was one reason for ranking highest in the Church the ministry that required *rule* and *judgment*. Wherever 'inspiration' has been allowed to be supreme over all rule (a very natural inclination in times of religious excitement), the door has been opened to 'deluding spirits.' The difficulty continued, and we read in *Didache* xi. 'Not every one that speaketh in the spirit is a prophet, but only if he have the ways of the Lord . . . Whoever in the spirit says, Give me money, or something else, ye shall not hear him; but if for others in need he bid you give, let no one judge him.' So when the gift of prophetic utterance seems to have disappeared, and Montanus in Phrygia (about A.D. 156) claimed that in himself and others the spirit of prophecy was revived, there were many ready to accept it as true utterance of the Spirit, but the Church generally rejected it, judging it partly by its frenzied manner, partly by the nature of what the new prophets said.

St. Paul's description shows that in the main he is referring to conscious impostors. The desire for notoriety produces strange results, and in this case there may have been the possibility of maintenance

πλάνοις καὶ διδασκαλίαις δαιμονίων, 2. ἐν ὑποκρίσει ψευδολόγων, κεκαυτηριασμένων τὴν ἰδίαν συνείδησιν, 3. κωλυόντων γαμεῖν, ἀπέχεσθαι βρωμάτων, ἃ ὁ Θεὸς

by the Church. Cf. *Didache* xiii., 'Every true prophet who will settle among you is worthy of his support.' By the following words, διδασκαλίαις δαιμονίων, *teachings of evil spirits*, St. Paul shows that he regarded such persons as taken advantage of by the devil, who made them utter what he wished. For St. Paul's belief as to the power of evil spirits, see note on i. 20. But apart from conscious imposture, every strong manifestation of religious emotion is apt to produce imitation among the weak-minded, who have an idea that by sharing in the emotion they must share in the religion also.

2. ἐν ὑποκρίσει ψευδολόγων—with ἀποστήσονται—men will be led to decline from the faith *through* the false pretences of liars. For ἐν expressing cause, cf. St. Matt. vi. 7, ἐν τῇ πολυλογίᾳ αὐτῶν εἰσακουσθήσονται (they will be heard on account of their much speaking).

κεκαυτηριασμένων τὴν ἰδίαν συνείδησιν. The only meaning for καυτηριάζω quoted by L. and S. (apart from this passage) is *to cauterise*, and as cauterising is remedial the metaphor is inapplicable here. There are two possible meanings: (1) having their conscience burnt to insensibility of the truth, they not only deceive others, but have come to the point when they can no longer discern between truth and falsehood if they want to; (2) having their conscience branded as with a mark of infamy. If the latter were the meaning, we have again an alternative: (*a*) branded, like a runaway slave, they are apostates and they know it; (*b*) branded like a temple slave, they teach the teaching of devils and are branded willingly and consciously with their mark. But as there is no evidence that καυτηριάζω was ever used in a technical sense for branding, the phrase here used would not have been so understood by any Greek reader without some addition. It is best, therefore, to take it with the meaning (1).

3. κωλυόντων γαμεῖν, ἀπέχεσθαι βρωμάτων. In these words we have some definite intimation of the nature of the false teaching, or one form of the false teaching, prevalent at Ephesus. But three views have been held as to the special reference here, viz.: (1) that the words refer to the beginnings of what we call Gnosticism; (2) that they refer to Jewish teaching of the Essene kind; (3) that we must look for the explanation in the combination of these two influences—in a kind of Gnostic Judaism.

As Gnosticism had little hold till the early part of the second century, while the power of Judaism to influence Christianity was at its highest in St. Paul's time and had greatly lessened by the second century, it is natural that those who accept the Pauline origin of these epistles prefer (2), while those who doubt the Pauline origin from other points of evidence are in this matter inclined to (1). 'Intellectus

humanus in iis quae semel placuerunt alia etiam omnia trahit ad suffragationem et consensum cum illis' (*Novum Organum*, i. 46). The words used by St. Paul are certainly capable of application to either.

(1) Gnosticism is the name applied, not to any one definite philosophy or heresy, but to a type of doctrine which appeared in many forms and exercised much influence during the second and third centuries. It must not be regarded as an offshoot of Christianity, but as a form of philosophy which, accepting many of the facts of Christianity, tried to include them in its system, and at any rate found it necessary to explain them on the basis of its own philosophical tenets. Nor can it be regarded as a type of Greek philosophy, though in various tenets it reproduces older Greek speculations. It must rather be looked upon as a combination of oriental theosophy with Greek philosophy and some speculative Christianity, but in its main tenets the oriental character is most prominent. The first beginnings of Gnosticism can hardly be traced, but such teachings had certainly begun in St. Paul's days, and in the first century such men as Simon Magus, Dositheus, Cerinthus are classed as Gnostics.

The Syrian sect of Ophites is said to have been the first to adopt the name of Gnostics, but the word γνῶσις had probably been used earlier to express the special 'illumination' which Gnostics laid such stress on. It was by the capacity for, and the acquiring of, this esoteric illumination that they thought man could be saved; and they divided men into three classes —the spiritual, who were possessed of such illumination; the psychic or animal, who might be led on to it; and the hylic or material, who were incapable of it. Religion therefore is progress in this illumination, not dependent on any faith, and is confined to the limited number of those capable of it.

The problem which the Gnostics set themselves to solve was therefore cosmological rather than religious, and here the oriental character of their tenets is apparent. Starting from the fact that there is evil in the world, they tried to find a way of making this consistent with the existence of a God who is altogether good. From the supreme being, they imagined, had emanated a number of aeons or angelic powers, and from these in succession other series of inferior aeons, by the lowest of whom the material world had been created.

Involved in this is the conclusion that matter is altogether evil. Wherever a dualism of this kind, opposing mind and matter, has prevailed, the consequential moral doctrine has always had dangerous results. On the one hand, the idea of freeing the spirit from its bondage in a material body led some of the Gnostics to asceticism, by which they taught that the spirit could make progress in its emancipation. On the other hand, contempt for what was material led others to teach that what happened in the body was of no concern, and so to permit an antinomianism which gave licence for conduct of any description.

It is obvious that such systems

had difficulty in incorporating anything of catholic Christianity. Their views of matter forbade any doctrine of the resurrection of the body and they could only teach an immortality of the soul. But the majority of Gnostics accepted in their own sense the whole of the Gospel narrative, explaining in various ways the personality of our Lord. The commonest teaching was that He was an aeon, an emanation from the Father, who came to us in an apparent body, but it was really only a phantasm which suffered and was crucified. According to others He was a combination of two aeons, one an emanation from the Creator aeon and born of the Virgin Mary, the other a higher aeon who descended on the first at the Baptism. His work was to restore their proper perfection to those of mankind who were capable of it, by undoing the work of creation and setting the spirit free from matter.

There was an extensive literature of Gnosticism, but almost all of it has perished except the *Pistis Sophia*, which survived in a Coptic version. We depend for our information mainly on the Catholic writers against Gnosticism. Much of their mysticism is therefore incomprehensible. It is clear that they had much secret ritual whereby their γνῶσις was expressed and conveyed. They claimed also elaborate knowledge of the angels or aeons and of magic. In order to justify their attitude to the Gospel narrative as ordinarily received, they claimed that this was only for the unspiritual or uninitiated, and that they had themselves received from the apostles a tradition to be handed on orally, by which they received their esoteric knowledge. They wove many romances about the persons of the apostles, and some of these, adapted in a catholic form, gave rise to widely received legends.

(2) The type of Jewish doctrine to which, according to the second view, St. Paul is supposed to be referring is that which passes under the name of Essenism. The Essenes were the only body of Jews who could really be spoken of as a 'sect' because they stood aside from the national worship. They seem never to have been very numerous.

Essenism probably originated in the troubled period following the Maccabaean revolt (about 168 B.C.), and was a protest for the law and strict ceremonial purity. To secure their end the Essenes had to withdraw from all ordinary life, and they formed themselves into monastic communities, living in villages near the Dead Sea, having all their goods in common, observing the Mosaic law, and especially the Sabbath, with fanatical scrupulousness, and living a life of great simplicity. So far we might have regarded them as a community determined at all costs to carry out the Pharisee ideal. It is impossible to say at what date they adopted the tenets and practices which not only marked them off from the Pharisees, but from all Judaism, and which present a striking parallel to the Gnostic doctrines already described.

Their asceticism in the time when we get information about them (mostly from Philo and Josephus) included abstention from marriage, from wine and all meat, from participation in the sacrifices of the temple. Their simple diet was carefully guarded against uncleanness by

being prepared by their special priests, and they seem to have regarded every meal as a sacrifice. They (unlike the Pharisees) denied the resurrection of the body. All these things point to a belief in the essential evil of matter, but that this was a dogma with them is not as clear as it is in the case of the Gnostics. They had secret books, and with regard to these and with regard to 'the names of the angels,' every Essene was sworn to secrecy. They practised magical arts, and we are expressly told that they allowed philosophy 'as to the being of God and the origin of the universe.' One of the most striking facts related of them is that they prayed towards the sun at dawn, apparently regarding the sun as the visible symbol of God.

It is clear from the above account that the avoidance of marriage and asceticism in matters of food resulted from the teaching both of Gnostics and of Essenes. The origin of Gnostic teachings is wrapt in obscurity, but unless we reject the practically unanimous statement of our authorities that Simon Magus was a Gnostic, we must assume that Gnosticism made some headway during St. Paul's lifetime. There is no sufficient evidence that Essenes, strictly so called, travelled far from Palestine, and the tenets of their faith must have made it difficult for them to live in pagan cities; but the admiration expressed for them by our Jewish authorities makes it at least possible that teaching on the lines of their ideal would occur in every great centre of Jewish life. Lightfoot (in his excursus on the Colossian heresy) regards the heresy of this part of Asia Minor as a result of the combined influences of Gnostic speculation and Judaism of the Essene type. But the evidence is slight, and all we can say is that Ephesus was a place where any religion and any philosophy, whether of East or of West, would be likely to find some welcome.

The words used by St. Paul here seem to the present writer to favour the Gnostic explanation. It seems more likely that he would have used the phrase διδασκαλίαι δαιμονίων of something distinctly pagan than of Essenism. His use of ἐπεγνωκόσι, taken with the ἀντιθέσεις τῆς ψευδωνύμου γνώσεως of vi. 20, suggests that he is using pointedly the word in which Gnostics summed up their claims. While, if we may assume that he has the same subject still in mind in verse 10, the phrase σωτὴρ πάντων ἀνθρώπων is directed against the Gnostic doctrine of exclusiveness explained above.

ἀπέχεσθαι βρωμάτων. Before ἀπέχεσθαι must be understood commanding from κωλυόντων, just as it has to be understood from οὐκ ἐπιτρέπω in ii. 12.

St. Paul's teaching, both on celibacy and on eating or not eating particular kinds of food, can be gathered more fully from 1 Cor. vii.-viii. It is hardly necessary to say that he is not belittling fasting for its proper use. (See also n. on v. 23.) But whereas the false teachers taught either that, on account of the essential evil of matter, there was a virtue in eating as little as possible, or that there was a distinction between 'pure' and 'impure' in matters of food, St. Paul denies both of these. There

ἔκτισεν εἰς μετάληψιν μετὰ εὐχαριστίας τοῖς πιστοῖς καὶ ἐπεγνωκόσι τὴν ἀλήθειαν. 4. ὅτι πᾶν κτίσμα Θεοῦ καλόν, καὶ οὐδὲν ἀπόβλητον, μετὰ εὐχαριστίας λαμβανόμενον· 5. ἁγιάζεται γὰρ διὰ λόγου Θεοῦ καὶ ἐντεύξεως, 6. Ταῦτα ὑποτιθέμενος τοῖς ἀδελφοῖς καλὸς ἔσῃ διάκονος Χριστοῦ Ἰησοῦ, ἐντρεφόμενος τοῖς λόγοις τῆς πίστεως καὶ τῆς καλῆς διδασκαλίας ᾗ παρηκολούθηκας· 7. τοὺς δὲ

is no gain in abstinence for the sake of abstinence only from any food natural to man. All that God has made is good—St. Paul is here quoting the refrain of Genesis i., 'God saw that it was good' (εἶδεν ὁ Θεὸς ὅτι καλόν).

But, he goes on, there is a difference between those who receive it as the gift of God and those who do not. To the former it has a kind of consecration that it cannot have to others. We may illustrate this point by what George Herbert says of a certain kind of labour: 'Then they labour *profanely* when they set themselves to work like brute beasts, never raising their thoughts to God, nor sanctifying their labour with daily prayer.' The same may be said of eating.

4-5. **μετὰ εὐχαριστίας ... διὰ λόγου Θεοῦ καὶ ἐντεύξεως.** The thanksgiving, the 'word of God' and the prayer are here all naturally referred to the 'grace' said before and after meat. The phrase 'word of God' probably refers to a passage or passages from the O.T. forming part of this grace. The custom was probably a very early one—see Deut. viii. 10. Cf. *Sibylline Oracles*, Bk. iv. 24: 'Happy among men shall they be upon earth who love to bless the great God before taking food and drink.'

6-16. '**Teach these things. Apply them also to your own life and practice, and so be a strenuous example to others, proving to them the power of your ordination gift.**'

6. **ὑποτιθέμενος**, R.V. *put in mind of*. ὑποτίθεμαι means to *suggest* in any way, therefore *remind, advise, warn*, according to the context.

διάκονος, in the quite general sense. See n. on i. 12.

ἐντρεφόμενος. Do not translate as R.V. *nourished*. The word ἐντρέφω meant *to bring up* children, including, of course, their nourishment. But in its metaphorical sense the word means *train* rather than *feed*. See the examples in L. and S., ἐντρέφεσθαι γυμνασίοις, μουσικῇ, ὅπλοις, νόμοις, in which the metaphor of feeding is out of place. Here, therefore, 'keeping thyself trained.'

τῆς καλῆς διδασκαλίας ᾗ παρηκολούθηκας. The 'teaching which thou hast followed' here, as in 2 Tim. iii. 10, is the teaching of St. Paul especially. If παρηκολούθησας be read (W.H. margin) it refers the teaching rather more definitely to

CH. IV. 7-8.] FIRST EPISTLE TO TIMOTHY 43

βεβήλους καὶ γραώδεις μύθους παραιτοῦ. γύμναζε δὲ
σεαυτὸν πρὸς εὐσέβειαν· 8. ἡ γὰρ σωματικὴ γυμνασία
πρὸς ὀλίγον ἐστὶν ὠφέλιμος· ἡ δὲ εὐσέβεια πρὸς πάντα

a past time ('which thou didst follow') instead of representing, as the perfect does, its continuance to the present. παρακολουθέω means 'to follow at the side of,' and so 'to attend closely to,' 'to trace throughout its course.' Cf. its use in St. Luke i. 3, 'having traced the course of all things accurately.'

It is worth while to note the phrases in which St. Paul in these epistles applies the epithet καλός to the Christian life, conduct, etc.: τὴν καλὴν στρατείαν, i. 18; τὸν καλὸν ἀγῶνα τῆς πίστεως and τὴν καλὴν ὁμολογίαν, vi. 12; τὴν καλὴν παραθήκην, 2 Tim. i. 14, etc. The word has, of course, a very wide meaning, but its frequent recurrence in such phrases suggests the intense feeling with which St. Paul realised the surpassing excellence of the way of life in Christ Jesus as compared with all else that the world might call καλόν. The philosopher called virtue τὸ καλόν, the artist called beauty τὸ καλόν. The soldier used it of his honour, the merchant of uprightness. But all the excellences of them all are combined in the Christian life and faith.

7. **βεβήλους μύθους**. See n. on i. 4.

γραώδεις, *old-womanish*—the traditional imputation against old women being idle gossip and credulity.

παραιτοῦ, *ask to be excused, have nothing to do with*. Cf. St. Luke xiv. 18, 'They all with one consent began to make excuse' (παραιτεῖσθαι); Acts xxv. 11, 'I refuse not to die' (οὐ παραιτοῦμαι τὸ ἀποθανεῖν).

γύμναζε, *train, keep in training*, i.e. do everything that may make you more fit for. As εὐσέβεια covers the whole 'religious life,' the training thought of includes all that conduces to it, *e.g.* regularity in prayer, voluntary self-denial; but the preceding words suggest that St. Paul has specially in mind study and reading, and such things as fit us to face intellectual difficulties of the faith. The reminder is important in view of the fact that while modern thought has added to the problems of the clergy, modern demands of another kind tend to steal from them more and more the time of study, with the natural result in sterile sermons and timid teaching. One good rule is always, where possible, to read one new book when in the annual round you come to what you have done before, *e.g.* one new book bearing on the special teaching of Confirmation, when you are teaching candidates for this. The teacher who draws only from past study is soon 'dipping buckets into empty wells,' and his preaching is apt to become what Herbert calls 'crumbling a text into small parts.'

8. The use of the word γύμναζε suggests this comparison to St. Paul. 'If the training of the body is cheerfully endured for the limited benefit that it confers, how much more readily should we endure training πρὸς εὐσέβειαν.'

πρὸς ὀλίγον, not 'little' as A.V., but 'for a little' as R.V., *i.e.* it is

ὠφέλιμός ἐστιν, ἐπαγγελίαν ἔχουσα ζωῆς τῆς νῦν καὶ τῆς μελλούσης. 9. πιστὸς ὁ λόγος καὶ πάσης ἀποδοχῆς ἄξιος. 10. εἰς τοῦτο γὰρ κοπιῶμεν καὶ ἀγωνιζόμεθα, ὅτι ἠλπίκαμεν ἐπὶ Θεῷ ζῶντι, ὅς ἐστι σωτὴρ πάντων ἀνθρώπων, μάλιστα πιστῶν. 11. παράγγελλε ταῦτα καὶ

useful but only for the body. πρὸς πάντα prevents our translating 'for a little time,' which otherwise would have been natural, as in St. James iv. 14 ('a vapour that appeareth *for a little time*').

ἐπαγγελίαν ἔχουσα ζωῆς, κ.τ.λ. Comparing 2 Tim. i. 1, it is impossible to take the genitive otherwise than as expressing the thing promised, 'having promise of life, that which now is and that which is to come.' τῆς νῦν is of course not opposed to τῆς μελλούσης in the sense of 'natural' life as opposed to spiritual life; it is rather as if St. Paul said that such a man 'has a more real life than others, in the life he is living now as well as in the life to come.'

9. See n. on i. 15, iii. 1. The γάρ of the following sentence here, as well as the natural sense, make it more likely here that the λόγος is to be found in the sentence ἠλπίκαμεν ... πιστῶν.

10. **εἰς τοῦτο**, 'to this end,' is most naturally taken as referring back to the thought of ζωῆς τῆς νῦν καὶ τῆς μελλούσης.

κοπιῶμεν. This verb and the noun κόπος imply labour to weariness. In the life of a clergyman, as in the life of a business man, external standards will make a certain amount of industry and a certain amount of attention to duty necessary; but in the case of the former there is a greater danger, because he more often apportions his own labour, and there is no one to bring him to account if he is content with a minimum. But beyond all that can be bargained for, that is 'in the bond,' lies all the margin of voluntary strenuous effort that makes the difference between a merely competent man and an effective man.

ἀγωνιζόμεθα, *strive, contend*, is a better reading than T.R. (and W.H. margin) ὀνειδιζόμεθα, *suffer reproach*.

ἠλπίκαμεν ἐπὶ Θεῷ ζῶντι, *we have our hope set on the living God.* If εἰς τοῦτο refers back to ζωῆς the addition of ζῶντι here is the more natural; striving for life ourselves we think of God as 'Him who lives,' just as *e.g.* in a prayer for protection we should naturally use the attribute '*Almighty* God,' and in a prayer for pardon '*Merciful* God.'

σωτὴρ πάντων ἀνθρώπων. This is one of the passages that have been quoted to prove that (after whatever further trying and purification) all men will be saved. But this phrase must be taken in the sense that is very clear in other passages quoted (*e.g.* Rom. xi. 32, Eph. i. 10, etc.) as expressing the fact that it is God's *will* to include all. There is no authority in the N.T. for a doctrine of 'universal salvation,' but much that can be quoted decisively against it; and those who argue for it depend on their own theories as to what God

CH. IV. 11-14.] FIRST EPISTLE TO TIMOTHY 45

δίδασκε. 12. μηδείς σου τῆς νεότητος καταφρονείτω, ἀλλὰ τύπος γίνου τῶν πιστῶν ἐν λόγῳ, ἐν ἀναστροφῇ, ἐν ἀγάπῃ, ἐν πίστει, ἐν ἁγνείᾳ. 13. ἕως ἔρχομαι, πρόσεχε τῇ ἀναγνώσει, τῇ παρακλήσει, τῇ διδασκαλίᾳ. 14. μὴ

must do, or on considerations of the psychology of man. The expression added, viz. μάλιστα πιστῶν, will not seem so difficult if we remember not only that God is potentially the saviour of all men, but that He is actually endeavouring to save all, that all men living are, so far as their wills permit it, the objects of His saving grace.

12. **μηδείς σου τῆς νεότητος καταφρονείτω.** According to a probable chronology it was now seventeen years since St. Paul's first missionary journey, and about fifteen years since he took Timothy with him. See Introd., p. xiv. We may therefore presume that Timothy was now between thirty and forty. The warning 'Let no one despise thy youth' is possibly a suggestion to a timid man to be rather more masterful, because men will often take you at your own estimate of yourself, and it is not well, if you have the right to command, to let your modesty be taken for doubt or timidity; but having regard to the τὰς νεωτερικὰς ἐπιθυμίας φεῦγε of 2 Tim. ii. 22, we are more justified in taking it to mean 'Do nothing which will justify men in despising you as young for your office.' Men cannot despise youth if it adds to its own freshness the judgment and self-restraint of age.

Compare *A Priest to the Temple*, ch. xxviii.: The Country Parson, 'according to the Apostle's rule, endeavours that none shall despise him; especially in his own parish he suffers it not to his utmost power; for that, where contempt is, there is no room for instruction. This he procures, *First*, by his holy and unblameable life; which carries a reverence with it, even above contempt. *Secondly*, by a courteous carriage and winning behaviour: he that will be respected must respect. ... *Thirdly*, by a bold and impartial reproof, even of the best in the parish, when occasion requires: for this may produce hatred in those that are reproved, but never contempt either in them or others.'

τύπος originally meant the mark of a blow and so the impression of a seal, hence the general form or outline of anything, so a model or (as here) pattern.

ἐν λόγῳ, ἐν ἀναστροφῇ, *in word, in conduct,* in the widest sense. The A.V. *conversation* for ἀναστροφή was of course meant, according to the proper Latin force of the word, for *conduct, manner of life.*

ἐν ἁγνείᾳ. See n. on v. 22. Here probably in the widest sense of the word.

13. **ἕως ἔρχομαι,** *till I come.* The indicative in this construction, though not Classical, is quite regular in later Greek.

τῇ ἀναγνώσει. It is generally taken for granted that this means the *public* reading of the Scriptures in the Church. As the ordinary service

ἀμέλει τοῦ ἐν σοὶ χαρίσματος, ὃ ἐδόθη σοι διὰ προφητείας

of the Church doubtless at first followed the model of the synagogue, and in this the reading of Scripture had an important part, this interpretation is more probable here, more especially as it is connected with τῇ παρακλήσει, τῇ διδασκαλίᾳ. Where the noun ἀνάγνωσις occurs elsewhere in the N.T. it refers to public reading, though ἀναγιγνώσκω is used of any reading. The consideration mentioned in the note on γύμναζε, v. 7, is the only one that might suggest a reference to Timothy's private study.

It is to be noted that among the ancients it was very customary to read *aloud* even when reading to oneself. The Ethiopian was reading aloud in Acts viii. 30. St. Augustine (*Conf.*, vi. 3) expresses surprise at finding St. Ambrose reading silently. To this practice we may partly attribute their great feeling for rhythm and sound in language. To read aloud by oneself what one is going to read in public would probably increase the effectiveness of our own utterance.

τῇ παρακλήσει, in the ordinary Classical sense of *exhortation*.

14. This verse must be considered in connection with 2 Tim. i. 6, ἀναμιμνήσκω σε ἀναζωπυρεῖν τὸ χάρισμα τοῦ Θεοῦ, ὅ ἐστιν ἐν σοὶ διὰ τῆς ἐπιθέσεως τῶν χειρῶν μου. For though it has been held that they may refer to different occasions, the balance of probability is against this.

The passages have been interpreted in three ways, viz.: (1) as referring to nothing so definite as what we should call ordination, but rather to a general 'commending to the grace of God'; (2) as referring to Timothy's ordination as a *Bishop*, with apostolic authority over presbyters; (3) as referring to his earlier ordination, for which see Introd., p. xiv.

The considerations adduced above in the n. on iii. 1, 2 enable us to leave (2) without further comment.

With regard to (1) it has been argued that the laying on of hands was a very ancient accompaniment of blessing or intercessory prayer for an individual (as in Gen. xlviii. 14), that our Lord used it both in blessing the children (St. Matt. xix. 15) and in healing (St. Mark viii. 23, etc.), that the apostles continued to use it in this way (*e.g.* Acts xxviii. 8). But (*a*) the precision of the words used in the present passage (διὰ προφητείας, μετὰ ἐπιθέσεως, κ.τ.λ.) is strongly against any indefiniteness in the reference; (*b*) the Aorist ἐδόθη most naturally points to some one occasion in the past; (*c*) the laying on of hands was *specially* used in the early Church in the imparting of some special charismatic gift of the Holy Ghost (Acts viii. 17, xix. 6, etc.); (*d*) the word χάρισμα, though used in Rom. v. and vi. of the 'free gift' of God in eternal life, is generally used elsewhere of *special* endowments of the Christian man, whether miraculous or non-miraculous.

It is hardly possible, therefore, to refer these passages to any other occasion than that on which Timothy was appointed to his office, and therefore we must accept the third interpretation given above. To use the word 'ordination' might seem to be assuming too much as to the

form and intention of this appointment. But the word is not necessary. That what the word signifies to us was involved in the appointment of πρεσβύτεροι or ἐπίσκοποι will seem practically certain if we consider the following facts: (a) Though we do not know what was the method of appointment of the *local* πρεσβύτεροι of a Jewish community, we have sufficient evidence to show that there was an ordination of the πρεσβύτεροι of the Sanhedrin at Jerusalem. (See *Jewish Encyclopaedia*, article 'Ordination.') The idea of such a ceremony was therefore familiar to the apostles, and would naturally pass into the Christian Church. (b) Acts vi. 6 (προσευξάμενοι ἐπέθηκαν αὐτοῖς τὰς χεῖρας) implies an ordination of 'the Seven,' whom we speak of as the first deacons. It is not likely, therefore, that the ceremony was omitted for the 'elders.' (c) The present passages conform to the practice followed by the later Church in μετὰ ἐπιθέσεως τῶν χειρῶν τοῦ πρεσβυτερίου and διὰ τῆς ἐπιθέσεως τῶν χειρῶν μου.

Taking both passages as referring to this we see that parts in it were taken (1) by the Apostle; (2) by the πρεσβύτεροι collectively; (3) by the prophets. It is natural to see in (1) and (2) the later usage whereby (and this is the case from the time when the usage is clearly evidenced) the episcopal act is regarded as that which is essential to ordination, the act of the πρεσβυτέριον as a natural but not necessary accompaniment. If we could reckon that the Classical force of prepositions was maintained (which we cannot do), the prepositions διά and μετά would point to the same principle. But other considerations give us pause in coming to any such conclusion. (a) The fact that in the present passage St. Paul omits to mention the laying on of his own hands is striking. Is it conceivable that in modern times any one could refer to an ordination simply by such words as 'the gift that was given thee when the priests laid their hands upon thee,' without any reference to the bishop? This at any rate shows a change in point of view. (b) We must always keep in mind that the apostles thought they were making arrangements that were only to last for a short time— until the Lord came—and that therefore they probably did not contemplate any complete or invariable system, either of appointment or of administration. It was left to later generations to establish regular custom on the lines of apostolic teaching. It is possible that there were divergencies in practice (see n. on p. 27) down to the third century, and all that we can say further is that wherever apostolic authority was present (either in the person of an apostle or in the person of his delegate, as in Titus i. 5), it probably took precedence over all local authority, and that when this was absent the act of the president of the πρεσβύτεροι was probably thought essential to the appointment of others.

This is the only place where πρεσβυτέριον is used thus of the body of Christian πρεσβύτεροι. Elsewhere in the N.T. it is used for the Jewish elders or Sanhedrin. Presumably the reference here is to the elders of Lystra, and the occasion that recorded in Acts xvi. 1-3. We

μετὰ ἐπιθέσεως τῶν χειρῶν τοῦ πρεσβυτερίου. 15. ταῦτα μελέτα, ἐν τούτοις ἴσθι, ἵνα σου ἡ προκοπὴ φανερὰ ᾖ πᾶσιν. 16. ἔπεχε σεαυτῷ καὶ τῇ διδασκαλίᾳ. ἐπίμενε αὐτοῖς· τοῦτο γὰρ ποιῶν καὶ σεαυτὸν σώσεις καὶ τοὺς ἀκούοντάς σου.

do not know what number was usual in a church, probably it varied as in the local Jewish bodies of elders.

The part taken by the prophets may have been one of two things, viz. either the designation of Timothy beforehand or an inspired utterance at the time of his ordination—probably the former, cf. Acts xiii. 1-2.

From what has been said of the word χάρισμα, it will be seen that St. Paul regards Timothy's appointment as meaning, not only the bestowal of office and authority, but an inward gift of 'grace and power faithfully to fulfil the same.' This sacramental side of ordination needs emphasising. If a man is called by God to be a priest and remains faithful, his ordination is an assurance to him of a divinely imparted capacity to fulfil his office worthily. But the μὴ ἀμέλει of this verse and the ἀναζωπυρεῖν of 2 Tim. i. 6 show that our co-operation is needed to keep the gift at its full value. Many things tend to lessen it: the sense of monotony, the loss of heart where our work appears ineffective, the tendency to expect too easy a life ('nimis avide consolationem quaerere,' as Thomas à Kempis puts it). But we must not mistake our own *feelings* for a verdict against ourselves. Health and many other things may lessen our consciousness of spiritual power, but even then we need not distrust our ordination gift. 'Quotidie novis visitationibus (*of Divine grace*) interior homo secundum imaginem Dei reformatur' (*De Imitatione*, iv. 54).

15. ταῦτα, τούτοις and the αὐτοῖς of v. 16 are naturally taken as referring generally to the precepts of the preceding verses.

ἐν τούτοις ἴσθι, *be wholly occupied with them.* The verb is here equal to the Latin *versari.*

16. ἔπεχε, take heed to. His life and his teaching are both parts of his ministry.

ἐπίμενε, of *continuing* in an occupation or state. Cf. Rom. vi. 1, ἐπιμένωμεν τῇ ἁμαρτίᾳ.

CHAPTER V

1. Πρεσβυτέρῳ μὴ ἐπιπλήξῃς, ἀλλὰ παρακάλει ὡς πατέρα, νεωτέρους ὡς ἀδελφούς, 2. πρεσβυτέρας ὡς μητέρας, νεωτέρας ὡς ἀδελφὰς ἐν πάσῃ ἁγνείᾳ. 3. χήρας

1-16. Rules of conduct towards special classes in the Church—older and younger men, older and younger women, widows.

1. **πρεσβυτέρῳ**, *an elder man* in the natural sense of age, as in St. Luke xv. 25, etc. The context requires this obviously. Where Timothy has occasion for censuring an older man, it must not take the form of stern rebuke (ἐπιπλήσσειν), but exhortation with all respect for age.

ὡς ἀδελφούς, and therefore in some sense as equals and comrades, even if he himself be 'primus inter pares.'

2. **ὡς ἀδελφάς, ἐν πάσῃ ἁγνείᾳ.** The second phrase amplifies the first. Just as the younger men are ἀδελφοί so the younger women are ἀδελφαί, but in their case there must be most careful guarding against any suspicion of familiarity. The difficulty of striking the right balance is accentuated in our own days, when young women think it right to talk of every subject, and therefore naturally show little reticence in their conversation with the clergy. However justifiable this may be in theory, it is in practice advisable for the younger clergy to refer them often to their seniors in office.

3. In the following passage St. Paul is giving directions for the treatment of widows. He is obviously mainly concerned with preventing their becoming unjustifiably a burden to the Church. This difficulty arose very early in the Church at Jerusalem (see Acts vi. 1), and was bound to occur wherever (as was probably the case in most places) the majority of the Christians were of the poorer classes. The maintenance of widows thus became an act of piety, and later on we read that this principle was much abused. The present passage shows that there was already danger of it, and St. Paul directs in the first place that those who have children or grandchildren shall not be allowed to become a burden to the Church. We must remember that the difficulty would be enhanced by the fact that (whatever Greek or Jewish custom prescribed in such cases) the relatives who might have maintained them would often not be Christians, and would be inclined to disown responsibility.

But beyond the directions for

D

τίμα τὰς ὄντως χήρας. 4. εἰ δέ τις χήρα τέκνα ἢ ἔκγονα ἔχει, μανθανέτωσαν πρῶτον τὸν ἴδιον οἶκον εὐσεβεῖν, καὶ ἀμοιβὰς ἀποδιδόναι τοῖς προγόνοις· τοῦτο γάρ ἐστιν ἀπόδεκτον ἐνώπιον τοῦ Θεοῦ. 5. ἡ δὲ ὄντως χήρα καὶ μεμονωμένη ἤλπικεν ἐπὶ Θεόν, καὶ προσμένει ταῖς δεήσεσι καὶ ταῖς προσευχαῖς νυκτὸς καὶ ἡμέρας. 6. ἡ δὲ σπατα-

widows generally, St. Paul seems to refer to a special 'roll' of widows in v. 9, widows with special claims and qualifications, presumably expected in return for their recognition by the Church to devote themselves to special service. These must not be confused with deaconesses (see n. on iii. 11), though of course some of these latter may have been on the roll of widows. For the later development of this recognised class of widows, see Bigg's *Origins of Christianity*, p. 268.

3. τίμα, *i.e.* especially by greater readiness in recognising them as fit objects of the Church's bounty. But also in a more general sense, because their loneliness would make them feel more acutely their dependent position, and honour done them by the whole brotherhood of the Church would make up for this.

4. ἔκγονα, *offspring*; here naturally grandchildren. The A.V. *nephews* was presumably meant in the sense of grandchildren, a sense which the word (from Latin *nepos*) frequently bore in English. Cf. in Jeremy Taylor, 'Nephews are very often liker to their grandfathers than to their fathers.'

μανθανέτωσαν. The subject is naturally τέκνα ἢ ἔκγονα. It has been said that τὸν ἴδιον οἶκον is an unsuitable phrase if this be the sense, but the headship of the house naturally devolved on the son (though young), and it was quite natural to speak of it as 'his own household.'

πρῶτον, *first* because to honour one's father and mother is the most elementary act of εὐσέβεια, and if a man does not do that no other devotion or generosity will be equally acceptable in God's sight. 'People are apt to glorify all sorts of bravery, except the bravery they might show on behalf of their nearest neighbours.'

5-6. These verses give parenthetically the reason for discriminating between widows, a reason further enlarged upon in 11-13. The contrast is one that is not *necessarily* one of age, but is apt to depend largely on age; the one woman has her thoughts centred on God, having lost with her husband the interest in further worldly occupation, advancement, or pleasure, while the other has thoughts still mainly centred on these.

5. δεήσεσι . . . προσευχαῖς. See n. on 2 Tim. i. 3.

6. σπαταλῶσα, living in self-indulgence.

λῶσα ζῶσα τέθνηκε. 7. καὶ ταῦτα παράγγελλε, ἵνα ἀνεπίληπτοι ὦσιν. 8. εἰ δέ τις τῶν ἰδίων καὶ μάλιστα οἰκείων οὐ προνοεῖ, τὴν πίστιν ἤρνηται καὶ ἔστιν ἀπίστου χείρων. 9. χήρα καταλεγέσθω μὴ ἔλαττον ἐτῶν ἑξήκοντα γεγονυῖα, ἑνὸς ἀνδρὸς γυνή, 10. ἐν ἔργοις καλοῖς μαρτυρουμένη, εἰ ἐτεκνοτρόφησεν, εἰ ἐξενοδόχησεν, εἰ

ζῶσα τέθνηκε. The contrast in this and all similar passages is doubtless based on what seems to have been a common saying of our Lord, recorded in St. Mark viii. 35, 36, and elsewhere ('Whosoever would save his life shall lose it,' etc.), though the Greek word for *life* in those passages is ψυχή. But Alford well draws attention to Sophocles' *Antigone*, 1165, as illustrating a pagan application of the idea of 'death in life':—

τὰς γὰρ ἡδονὰς
ὅταν προδῶσιν ἄνδρες, οὐ τίθημ'
ἐγὼ
ζῆν τοῦτον, ἀλλ' ἔμψυχον ἡγοῦμαι
νεκρόν.

('For when a man hath forfeited his pleasures, I count him not as living; I hold him but a breathing corpse.')

7. The A.V. 'give in charge' is Old English for 'give by way of command.' The noun is the same as in the expression 'a bishop's charge.'

8. Omitting the τῶν of T.R. before οἰκείων it is most natural to take it as 'those who are his own and most closely related to him.' In this verse St. Paul's thought goes back to what he said in v. 4.

τὴν πίστιν ἤρνηται. ἀρνεῖσθαι is the opposite of ὁμολογεῖν (to profess) —he has disowned the faith by not acting on it in its simplest application. The meaning is, of course, much the same as is conveyed by St. James—ἡ πίστις χωρὶς ἔργων νεκρά ἐστιν.

9. **καταλεγέσθω**, 'let her be entered on the roll.' See n. on v. 3. When next we have definite information about the roll of widows (about 200 A.D.) the qualifying age is fifty. At that time definite services were expected of the 'widows on the roll.' It cannot be said that vv. 9-10 point yet to this very clearly— the qualities required (viz. a blameless private life and general good service to the Church) are merely such as would recommend them for the bounty of the Church. The one phrase that seems to point to it is ἑνὸς ἀνδρὸς γυνή, which can only mean that she must have been married only once, a qualification which in view of v. 14 could hardly be required as a condition of maintenance by the Church in old age.

10. **τεκνοτροφέω** and **ξενοδοχέω** only here in N.T.

εἰ ἐτεκνοτρόφησεν has been taken of bringing up orphan children as an act of charity. This is unnatural without a clear indication from the context. Rather it is mentioned by the Apostle as one among other recommendations to consideration that a woman has had children and brought them up instead of avoiding the duties of motherhood. With

ἁγίων πόδας ἔνιψεν, εἰ θλιβομένοις ἐπήρκεσεν, εἰ παντὶ ἔργῳ ἀγαθῷ ἐπηκολούθησε. 11. νεωτέρας δὲ χήρας παραιτοῦ· ὅταν γὰρ καταστρηνιάσωσι τοῦ Χριστοῦ, γαμεῖν θέλουσιν, 12. ἔχουσαι κρῖμα ὅτι τὴν πρώτην

regard to this it may be remembered that the law did not forbid the exposure of newly-born infants, a practice which was only limited by custom till 315 A.D., when the growth of Christian influence brought legislation to bear on it.

εἰ ἐξενοδόχησεν. Another recommendation to be reckoned in favour of a woman who has ever been in a position to show hospitality, with regard to which see n. on iii. 2

εἰ ἁγίων πόδας ἔνιψεν—in a general sense of performing the lowliest services. With us a practical equivalent would be 'if she has nursed the sick.' To a Christian the phrase would necessarily recall our Lord's words recorded in St. John xiii. 12-14. It is obvious that when the present passage was written the phrase had become more or less proverbial for kindness and humility combined. The metaphor is, of course, derived from the necessity in Palestine of washing the feet on entering a house from the street—the feet having been only shod with sandals.

θλιβομένοις, *those in distress.* The literal meaning of θλίβω was *press.*

11. **παραιτοῦ,** *i.e.* do not put them on the roll. In vv. 11-12 we have perhaps a clearer indication that the widows in question are appointed to a definite position in Church work —otherwise St. Paul could hardly have used such an expression as τὴν πρώτην πίστιν ἠθέτησαν. The duties of those on the roll seem to have been incompatible with married life and its duties. If a younger woman were appointed to it at all she would by implication, if not by vow, promise to remain unmarried. If she afterwards married she might be said, therefore, τὴν πρώτην πίστιν ἀθετῆσαι. St. Paul's direction is not to appoint such women at all. He recognises that their impulse to marry again is not wrong in itself (v. 14), but *they have made it wrong* by undertaking after the death of their first husband to give the rest of their lives to Christ's work. This is why he speaks of their conduct as καταστρηνιᾶν τοῦ Χριστοῦ, *growing wanton against Christ, i.e.* rebelliously preferring their own inclinations to His service.

This passage may serve on the one hand as a warning against emotionalism, *i.e.* against letting a great sorrow or a great experience of any kind hurry one without counting the cost into something that is not really one's vocation. 'Master, I will follow Thee whithersoever Thou goest' is perhaps not so good as 'Master, I will go whithersoever Thou biddest me go,' and even the enthusiasm of self-surrender does not dispense a man from the necessity of judging his own faculties and vocation. The bidding of the Master may be in some cases to go back to the ordinary life. A schoolmaster once joined a

CH. V. 12-13.] FIRST EPISTLE TO TIMOTHY 53

πίστιν ἠθέτησαν. 13. ἅμα δὲ καὶ ἀργαὶ μανθάνουσι, περιερχόμεναι τὰς οἰκίας, οὐ μόνον δὲ ἀργαί, ἀλλὰ καὶ φλύαροι καὶ περίεργοι, λαλοῦσαι τὰ μὴ δέοντα. 14. βού-

religious order to escape the drudgery of teaching. The first work his superiors assigned to him was ten years' teaching in their own school.

On the other hand, the passage serves to remind us that the Church should not be too ready to accept any and every service offered to it. It in its turn is not dispensed by the enthusiasm of a votary from the necessity of judging. The women whom St. Paul had in mind would doubtless be sincere in their intention, but he saw greater danger in the possibility of their subsequent defection than benefit in the temporary use of their enthusiasm. The saying is perhaps a hard one in our days when Church workers are not often too numerous; but the danger is even greater now because of the prevalent idea that he who does Church work in any capacity is conferring a benefit on the Church rather than receiving a benefit from the Church.

13. ἀργαὶ μανθάνουσι. R.V. *learn to be idle*. But there is no other instance of the omission of εἶναι after μανθάνω in this way, since the reading cannot be substantiated in the instance quoted by L. and S. (Plato, *Euthyd.* 276). The alternative, 'They learn in idleness, going about from house to house' (of the members of the Church), does not give a clear enough meaning to μανθάνουσι, although the picture of these younger women, bereft of their natural instructors, their husbands, and keenly interested in the teaching of the Church, going from one church-officer to another, ostensibly to be taught, is not an impossible picture nor inconsistent with other phrases in these Epistles. Cf. 2 Tim. iii. 7, where certain women are described as 'ever learning and never able to come to knowledge of the truth.' Cf. also what is said of men in 2 Tim. iv. 3, 'They will heap to themselves teachers according to their own desires.'

φλύαροι, given to silly talk (from a root meaning *babble*). λαλοῦσαι τὰ μὴ δέοντα goes a little further— their talk is not only silly but mischievous, the reference being presumably to social gossip.

With περίεργοι, cf. 2 Thess. iii. 11, μηδὲν ἐργαζομένους ἀλλὰ περιεργαζομένους.

14. The advice that these younger widows should marry again, become mothers and rule homes of their own, is not really inconsistent with the approval that seems to be given in v. 9 to the ideal of being married only once. A comparison of St. Paul's various statements shows that he thought that in the stress in which they were living, Christians did well not to marry at all, but if their nature unfitted them for a celibate life, it was permissible for them to marry and (for the same reason) to marry again. But this concession to nature is quite consistent with his thinking that such persons were not the most fit for church office. In the first century it is probable that the position of a young widow, unless she could

λομαι οὖν νεωτέρας γαμεῖν, τεκνογονεῖν, οἰκοδεσποτεῖν, μηδεμίαν ἀφορμὴν διδόναι τῷ ἀντικειμένῳ λοιδορίας χάριν· 15. ἤδη γάρ τινες ἐξετράπησαν ὀπίσω τοῦ Σατανᾶ. 16. εἴ τις πιστὴ ἔχει χήρας, ἐπαρκείτω αὐταῖς, καὶ μὴ βαρείσθω ἡ ἐκκλησία· ἵνα ταῖς ὄντως χήραις ἐπαρκέσῃ.

17. Οἱ καλῶς προεστῶτες πρεσβύτεροι διπλῆς τιμῆς

definitely return to her father's house, was much more difficult than it would be now, and the advice given had to be in accordance with the circumstances.

τῷ ἀντικειμένῳ, *i.e.* the outside critic, on the watch for any evidence of lax conduct in the Church. λοιδορίας χάριν with ἀφορμήν, 'opportunity for reproach.'

15. ὀπίσω τοῦ Σατανᾶ, see n. on i. 20. St. Paul here means that some Christian widows, in their unprotected condition, have done what brought reproach on the Church.

16. Cf. vv. 3-4. The widow was (unless she married again) to be cared for and protected by any woman relation she had (omitting T.R. πιστὸς ἤ).

βαρέω = the more regular Classical βαρύνω.

17-25. This passage consists mainly of certain precepts with regard to the principles on which Timothy was to exercise his authority in his judgment of men who bore office in the Church, and in his choice of such men.

Even with the bishop's authority clearly defined and undisputed, we know what mischief can arise through any appearance of partiality (towards individuals or groups in the Church).

If Timothy's authority was indefinite (see n. on p. 27), its enforcement might depend temporarily on the fact that he represented the distant Apostle, but would depend ultimately on its own commendation of itself by evident rightness in judgment and administration. We need not be surprised at the strong words in v. 21.

17-18. These two verses taken together certainly imply (*a*) what we should call a paid ministry; (*b*) a ministry in which efficiency was to be recognised by enhanced position and probably enhanced salary. The first of these points is important as indicating (1) a rather more complete organisation in the Church than we might have been inclined to imagine at this stage; (2) a very definite distinction between the position of the Christian πρεσβύτεροι and that of the Jewish πρεσβύτεροι. The latter were never paid, and their office brought them no such duty as that implied in the words κοπιῶντες ἐν λόγῳ καὶ διδασκαλίᾳ. With regard to (*b*), we need only remark that it implies the application of a business principle to the tenure of a sacred office—a thing very difficult to bring about, because the result of a priest's work is not 'fixed and embodied in material objects,' and therefore can only be judged by the personal

ἀξιούσθωσαν, μάλιστα οἱ κοπιῶντες ἐν λόγῳ καὶ διδασκαλίᾳ. 18. λέγει γὰρ ἡ γραφή, Βοῦν ἀλοῶντα οὐ φιμώσεις· καί, Ἄξιος ὁ ἐργάτης τοῦ μισθοῦ αὐτοῦ. 19. κατὰ πρεσβυτέρου κατηγορίαν μὴ παραδέχου ἐκτὸς εἰ μὴ ἐπὶ δύο ἢ τριῶν μαρτύρων. 20. τοὺς ἁμαρτάνοντας ἐνώπιον πάντων ἔλεγχε, ἵνα καὶ οἱ λοιποὶ φόβον ἔχωσι.

judgment of his superior. But obviously St. Paul regards it as a principle to be aimed at, and it is one of the abnegations implied in our seeking the office of the priesthood that we undertake to submit to this judgment loyally, though we do not agree with it.

μάλιστα οἱ κοπιῶντες, κ.τ.λ. It is natural to take λόγῳ of preaching, διδασκαλίᾳ of such instruction as that of catechumens. The phrase is generally taken to imply that some πρεσβύτεροι had these duties and some had not. This may be so, but as κοπιῶντες generally implies *hard* toil, 'toil to weariness,' the stress may lie on this word, and the meaning be 'those who give themselves laboriously to preaching and teaching.'

18. βοῦν ἀλοῶντα οὐ φιμώσεις. Deut. xxv. 4. A precept of humanity to cattle. Corn was threshed on a hard piece of ground by driving round and round on it a team of oxen drawing a weighted sledge. In the intervals of their labour they were not to be prevented from picking up straw. St. Paul takes this as implying the general principle that a man has a right to charge his maintenance to that on which he labours, and to this the ministry of the Church is no exception.

ἄξιος ὁ ἐργάτης, κ.τ.λ. This corresponds to no definite passage of Scripture, but is obviously quoted as a current saying, as by our Lord in St. Luke x. 7.

19. This is sometimes taken as a reminder to Timothy that the Law required two witnesses for conviction. But the position of κατὰ πρεσβυτέρου and the more natural meaning of ἐπί ('in the presence of') indicate the precept to mean that Timothy is not to allow an accusation against a πρεσβύτερος to be brought to him privately. The occasional advantage to authority of receiving information from an informer too timid to face publicity is more than counterbalanced by the atmosphere of mistrust produced by such methods. Authority that is known to use them is feared but not trusted. It is particularly fatal where one official is allowed to accuse another privately to their common chief.

20. τοὺς ἁμαρτάνοντας, *i.e.* πρεσβυτέρους, but πάντων and οἱ λοιποί mean the whole Church. Faults that are known to all should be rebuked before all. With this verse and v. 22 below, compare what Herbert says in *The Priest to the Temple*, ch. xiv. : 'One way or other he ever reproves them that he may keep himself pure and not be entangled in others' sins.' (Cf. v. 22), 'Neither in this doth he forbear,

21. διαμαρτύρομαι ἐνώπιον τοῦ Θεοῦ καὶ Χριστοῦ Ἰησοῦ καὶ τῶν ἐκλεκτῶν ἀγγέλων, ἵνα ταῦτα φυλάξῃς χωρὶς προκρίματος μηδὲν ποιῶν κατὰ πρόσκλισιν. 22. χεῖρας ταχέως μηδενὶ ἐπιτίθει, μηδὲ κοινώνει ἁμαρτίαις ἀλλοτρίαις· σεαυτὸν ἁγνὸν τήρει. 23. μηκέτι ὑδροπότει, ἀλλ' οἴνῳ

though there be company by: for as when the offence is particular and against me, I am to follow our Saviour's rule and to take my brother aside and reprove him, so, when the offence is publick and against God, I am then to follow the Apostle's rule, 1 Tim. v. 20, and to *rebuke openly* that which is done openly.'

21. The word μαρτύρομαι (and its compounds) originally meant 'I call to witness,' and naturally took an acc. of the person; then they came to mean 'adjure,' 'protest,' and the construction was adapted to these meanings. For the great emphasis given by the triple adjuration here, see n. on v. 17 above.

τῶν ἐκλεκτῶν ἀγγέλων is usually taken as meaning 'the holy angels,' the epithet being one of reverence towards the whole angelic order. But, as we have no reason to suppose that St. Paul questioned the current Jewish recognition of different classes among the angels (cf. Col. i. 16 and Eph. i. 21), it cannot be positively asserted that the phrase here does not mean what we mean by 'archangels.' Cf. such a passage as Tobit xii. 15, 'I am Raphael, one of the seven angels, which stand and enter before the glory of the Lord.' For the various orders of angels according to Jewish ideas, see *Testaments of the Twelve Patriarchs*, Levi 3.

ταῦτα, i.e. my injunctions with regard to the treatment of elders.

προκρίμα and πρόσκλισις are both ἅπαξ λεγόμενα in the N.T. The former means 'judging before inquiry,' the latter 'inclination' and therefore 'partiality.'

22. The context shows that the laying on of hands refers here to the ordaining of πρεσβύτεροι. For this see n. on iv. 14.

μηδὲ κοινώνει ἁμαρτίαις ἀλλοτρίαις, do not let yourself be a partner in the sins of others, as you are if they get their opportunity by your hasty choice of them. The reference is firstly to the choice of fit and proper persons for holy orders. In leaving this choice to the almost unfettered discretion of the bishop in each diocese, the Church has relied upon his sense of the responsibility implied in St. Paul's words—he is in the eyes of God a sharer in the faults of an unworthy priest whom he has ordained without due inquiry. But, of course, the principle applies also much more widely, *e.g.* to the parish priest himself in his choice of helpers. In the responsibility for consequences the saying is true, *qui facit per alium facit per se*. For which reason those who move in great affairs would generally rather have rules binding them than the freedom of an 'unfettered choice.'

σεαυτὸν ἁγνὸν τήρει. The word ἁγνός is here in its most general sense, 'free from guilt'—neither by conduct of his own nor by the con-

CH. V. 23-24.] FIRST EPISTLE TO TIMOTHY 57

ὀλίγῳ χρῶ διὰ τὸν στόμαχον καὶ τὰς πυκνάς σου ἀσ-
θενείας. 24. τινῶν ἀνθρώπων αἱ ἁμαρτίαι πρόδηλοί εἰσι,

duct of others for whom he is morally responsible is he to give cause of reproach against himself.

23. The insertion of this advice here can only, as Alford says, have one explanation, viz. : the bodily weaknesses referred to must have made Timothy specially liable to one or other of the faults mentioned in v. 17-22, to hasty or unsympathetic or undiscriminating judgment of men ; and for this reason he is urged to use wine as a means of strengthening himself physically. The words used make it most likely that the weakness was weak digestion. A fuller recognition of physical causes as affecting judgment and conduct would improve most men in themselves, and would also lead to more charitable criticism of others' motives. St. Paul warns Timothy that any extreme of asceticism is not for him. What is bad for a man physically is bad for his work, which must be the ultimate criterion in all acts of self-denial.

Compare the words of Herbert's *Priest to the Temple*, ch. x., especially the words, 'For meat was made for man, not man for meat. To all this may be added, not for emboldening the unruly, but for the comfort of the weak, that not only sickness breaks these obligations of fasting, but sickliness also. For it is as unnatural to do anything that leads me to a sickness to which I am inclined as not to get out of that sickness, when I am in it, by any diet.'

24-25. We must take these verses also in close connection with the preceding passage. Timothy is reminded that while character, bad or good, may often be obvious and more often seem obvious, it is not always so. The hypocrisy of the bad and the modesty of the good may both give wrong impressions, and he who has to choose between men for office must in his judgment see through both hypocrisy and modesty.

The κρίσις means ordinary human judgment in choosing between men ; it has no reference to the judgment of God. The word πρόδηλος more often means 'manifest beforehand,' and this is the natural sense here, viz. 'manifest before you even come to investigate them.' But the word can also mean 'openly manifest,' as in Heb. vii. 14, 'It is evident that our Lord sprang out of Juda.' ἐπακολουθοῦσιν, *follow after*, in the sense of becoming manifest later on, when their work brings them out.

One's judgment of character is apt to be misled, not only by the hypocrisy that conceals sins, but by the obviousness of some sins, and the subtle nature of other sins which may nevertheless be just as serious a hindrance in a man who is to be selected for office. See Herbert's *Priest to the Temple*, ch. xxvi. : 'The Countrey Parson at spare times from action, standing on a Hill, and considering his Flock, discovers *two sorts of vices and two sorts of vicious persons*. There are some vices, whose natures are always clear and evident, as Adultery, Murder, Hatred, Lying, etc. There are other vices whose

προάγουσαι εἰς κρίσιν, τισὶ δὲ καὶ ἐπακολουθοῦσιν. 25. ὡσαύτως καὶ τὰ ἔργα τὰ καλὰ πρόδηλα, καὶ τὰ ἄλλως ἔχοντα κρυβῆναι οὐ δύναται.

natures, at least in the beginning, are dark and obscure; as Covetousness and Gluttonie. So likewise there are some persons who abstain not even from known sins; there are others who when they know a sin evidently they commit it not. It is true, indeed, they are long in knowing it, being partial to themselves and witty to others, who shall reprove them of it. A man may be both Covetous and Intemperate and yet hear sermons against both, and himself condemn both in good earnest; and the reason hereof is because the natures of these vices being not evidently discussed, or known commonly, the beginnings of them are not easily observable: and the beginnings of them are not observed, because of the sudden passing from that which was just now lawful to that which is presently unlawful, even in one continued action . . .'

CHAPTER VI

1. Ὅσοι εἰσὶν ὑπὸ ζυγὸν δοῦλοι τοὺς ἰδίους δεσπότας

1-2. Instructions to slaves.

For St. Paul's treatment of the question of slavery compare 1 Cor. vii. 21-24, and the way in which he dealt with the actual case of Onesimus in the Epistle to Philemon. He must have realised that the spirit of brotherhood in Christianity would eventually destroy the slave system, and he trusted to the leaven of this spirit to bring the change gradually. Meanwhile he took each opportunity of teaching that in the eyes of God there is 'neither bond nor free,' and therefore there could be no such distinction in the Church; of inculcating also such humanity on the one side and such willing obedience on the other as combined would rob slavery of its worst features. But he made no formal attack upon slavery as the basis of the social system. If we add to domestic slaves the gangs which tilled the fields and worked the mines, there were probably as many slaves as free men in the Roman Empire; and without any system to take its place, a sudden change in the slave system, even if it could have been brought about by a miraculous revulsion of human conscience, would have dislocated all agriculture and commerce. In estimating the meaning of St. Paul's silence, we must, as always, bear in mind his expectation of the second coming of our Lord. Any advice that he gives is but for the time, and we need not speculate as to what teaching he would have given on such subjects as slavery on any other supposition. But we need hardly doubt that he would have maintained the principle of attacking the social system *by changing the spirit in men*, and would have trusted to this for a gradual revolution. For centuries the Church maintained this attitude, and those who, like Celsus, attacked Christianity never found occasion for accusing it (as they certainly would have done if they could) of provoking a servile war. Eventually the leaven of Christianity, together with economic changes (especially in the tenure and tilling of land), caused the worst features of slavery to disappear in Western Europe.

It is interesting to note that Mahomet followed a similar line when faced with the same problem among his Arabs. He set free his own slaves and inculcated the humane treatment of slaves, but did not attempt to abolish outright the system of slavery.

1. ὑπὸ ζυγὸν δοῦλοι, to be taken together, 'slaves under the yoke.'

ἰδίους. This word, which first meant *private* as opposed to *public*,

πάσης τιμῆς ἀξίους ἡγείσθωσαν, ἵνα μὴ τὸ ὄνομα τοῦ
Θεοῦ καὶ ἡ διδασκαλία βλασφημῆται. 2. οἱ δὲ πιστοὺς
ἔχοντες δεσπότας μὴ καταφρονείτωσαν, ὅτι ἀδελφοί εἰσιν·
ἀλλὰ μᾶλλον δουλευέτωσαν, ὅτι πιστοί εἰσι καὶ ἀγαπητοὶ
οἱ τῆς εὐεργεσίας ἀντιλαμβανόμενοι. ταῦτα δίδασκε καὶ
παρακάλει.

is in N.T. Greek a frequent equivalent for the possessive ἑαυτοῦ, but sometimes also expresses the possessive without any such emphasis as is implied by the English *own*. Here 'their masters' is better than 'their own masters.' Cf. St. Matt. xxii. 5, 'They went their ways, one to his farm,' τὸν ἴδιον ἀγρόν.

βλασφημῆται. For the word see n. on i. 13. The reproach would be that in the name of religion they upset the foundation of society and taught the doctrine of 'equality of classes,' in a sense not dreamed of by St. Paul when he said that in Christ there was 'neither bond nor free.' Monstrous as it seems to us, the relation between master and slave seemed to most men of the time as natural as the division of labour between 'employers and employed' seems to us; and teaching which encouraged slaves to be insubordinate seemed to them a breach of natural principle as well as actual law.

2. The preceding verse refers mainly to Christian slaves of pagan masters. If the masters also are converted, the slaves are not to show disrespect on the excuse that they are brethren and 'equal' in the Church (take ὅτι ... εἰσιν with καταφρονείτωσαν, not with μὴ καταφρονείτωσαν): on the contrary, they are to render them all the better service because those who thus enjoy the benefit of their service are believers and beloved. The meaning of the last few words is somewhat doubtful. The A.V. 'because they are faithful and beloved, partakers of the benefit' is quite contrary to the grammar—οἱ ... ἀντιλαμβανόμενοι must be the subject of εἰσιν. There is no difficulty in understanding it as it is taken above, unless we think it necessary to press the more common force of ἀντιλαμβάνομαι, viz. to *help* or *have a mutual share in*. But it seems hardly necessary to do so with examples before us where it means simply *attain* or *secure*, e.g. Thuc. iii. 22, πρὶν ... τοῦ ἀσφαλοῦς ἀντιλάβοιντο; vii. 77, ἦν ἀντιλαβώμεθά του φιλίου χωρίον.

3-10. It is natural to take v. 3 as the beginning of a new paragraph, not in connection with the ταῦτα of the preceding sentence. It is in fact the beginning of the final section of the letter.

St. Paul naturally reverts to the subject which he has so much in mind, viz. the false teaching becoming so rife. Cf. i. 3. Here (v. 3-10) he lays bare the motives underlying this false teaching—

CH. VI. 3-4.] FIRST EPISTLE TO TIMOTHY 61

3. Εἴ τις ἑτεροδιδασκαλεῖ, καὶ μὴ προσέρχεται ὑγιαί-
νουσι λόγοις, τοῖς τοῦ Κυρίου ἡμῶν Ἰησοῦ Χριστοῦ, καὶ
τῇ κατ' εὐσέβειαν διδασκαλίᾳ, 4. τετύφωται, μηδὲν
ἐπιστάμενος, ἀλλὰ νοσῶν περὶ ζητήσεις καὶ λογομαχίας,
ἐξ ὧν γίνεται φθόνος, ἔρις, βλασφημίαι, ὑπόνοιαι πονηραί,

it is partly pride of mind, partly desire to make profit of religion.

3. ἑτεροδιδασκαλεῖ teaches a different doctrine, *i.e.* different from the ὑγιαίνοντες λόγοι. For this use of ὑγιαίνω, see i. 10. Here the Apostle definitely claims that the 'healthful words' are the words of Christ Himself. In fact he is not condemning men for differing from himself in interpretations or deductions, but for rejecting the admitted words of Christ and 'teaching that is according to godliness.' In the following words he contrasts this with teaching that has other motives, viz. personal glorification or gain.

προσέρχεται. No Classical use of the word seems to give an exact parallel to its use here, but the literal meaning could naturally lead to the sense 'to associate oneself with,' and so 'to consent to.'

4. The attitude described is one of intellectual pride—an attitude which consists far more in the desire to raise questions than in the desire to find their answer. 'Curiositie in prying into high speculative and unprofitable questions is a great stumbling-block to the holiness of scholars.' For τετύφωται, see iii. 6.

λογομαχίας, disputes about words where there is no reality dependent on the dispute. In one sense many martyrs have died 'for words' because they thought that realities of the faith depended on them. On the distinction between ὁμοούσιον and ὁμοιούσιον depended the maintenance of the Catholic faith as to the divine nature of our Lord. But the Apostle is not here emphasising so much the nature of a contention as the *motive* of it—the people referred to were mostly concerned with establishing their intellectual superiority. The remark of Whateley is apposite: 'It is one thing to wish to have truth on one's side, quite another to wish to be on the side of truth.' The latter may require a good deal of humility, and to 'change one's mind' is often a proof of real greatness of character. 'Regnum scientiae, ut regnum caeli, non nisi sub persona infantis intratur' (Bacon).

The word νοσῶν is translated 'doting' in the R.V. It suggests a kind of mental disease.

βλασφημίαι, speaking evil of others. See n. on 2 Tim. iii. 2.

ὑπόνοιαι πονηραί, malicious suspecting of others, the imputing of wrong motives. The speaking evil of parties (religious or political) and the misrepresentation of their motives are two of the most subtle breaches of the Ninth Commandment. They always seem to be

5. διαπαρατριβαὶ διεφθαρμένων ἀνθρώπων τὸν νοῦν καὶ ἀπεστερημένων τῆς ἀληθείας, νομιζόντων πορισμὸν εἶναι τὴν εὐσέβειαν. 6. ἔστι δὲ πορισμὸς μέγας ἡ εὐσέβεια

justifiable on 'public' grounds, and they are difficult to combat because they do not come home to individual persons, who could refute them in their own cases. 'Si aliquid boni habueris crede de aliis meliora.'

5. **διαπαρατριβαί** is the better reading—violent disputings, wrangling. The A.V. 'perverse disputings' was a translation of the inferior reading παραδιατριβαί, where the emphasis lay rather on the παρά.

διεφθαρμένων . . . τὸν νοῦν, who have lost the power of thinking straight. The idea is best explained by the words τετύφωται and νοσῶν. Giving the rein to intellectual speculation a man may become unable to see any line of thought but that which he has followed—it becomes a disease with him, and his mind is befogged. He no longer sees things in their right relations or proportions. But, though this apart from the context would be a sufficient meaning for διεφθαρμένος τὸν νοῦν, the context here shows that the Apostle means men with whom the corruption has gone further—they have come to see the worldly profit that can be made out of the exploitation of their point of view, perhaps become popular and fashionable, and (by unconscious steps perhaps) they have come to think of the value of it in keeping them in funds. To them the service of God has become a πορισμός, a means of getting money.

For **νοῦς** see n. on 2 Tim. iii. 8.

ἀπεστερημένων τῆς ἀληθείας. A man who 'argues for arguing's sake' gets a reputation for cleverness, but is apt to pay dearly for it in several ways. He may become identified with a cause that he never meant to champion. He may begin to take a pride in 'holding the balance' and 'seeing all sides of a question,' until 'mistiness is the mother of wisdom' with him, and 'he never enunciates a truth without guarding himself against being supposed to exclude the contradictory.' But worst of all is when he is 'robbed of the truth' by being*half convinced himself. The constant repetition of one point of view may have this result, especially if the point of view is popular and profitable.

6. The turn of words that he has used suggests to St. Paul another thought, viz. that in a true sense the service of God *is* a πορισμός, and this leads him to speak (vv. 7-10) of the danger always involved in the desire for wealth.

αὐτάρκεια means independence of outward circumstances, 'self-sufficiency' in a good sense, and therefore the contentment that results from such independence. St. Paul gives his idea of it in Phil. iv. 11-12, 'I have learned in whatsoever state I am, therein to be content (αὐταρκής). . . . In all things have I learned the secret both to be filled and to be hungry.' There are two ways of increasing such 'independence,' viz.: (1) reducing one's needs; (2) having in one's own power the means to satisfy one's desires as they occur. Most of us, when urged by

μετὰ αὐταρκείας· 7. οὐδὲν γὰρ εἰσηνέγκαμεν εἰς τὸν κόσμον, ὅτι οὐδὲ ἐξενεγκεῖν τι δυνάμεθα· 8. ἔχοντες δὲ διατροφὰς καὶ σκεπάσματα τούτοις ἀρκεσθησόμεθα. 9. οἱ δὲ βουλόμενοι πλουτεῖν ἐμπίπτουσιν εἰς πειρασμὸν καὶ παγίδα καὶ ἐπιθυμίας πολλὰς ἀνοήτους καὶ βλαβεράς,

desire, try the second way first, and it is the excessive indulgence of this inclination that St. Paul is condemning here. The Stoic glorified the first method, and this is one point of contact between his thought and the Apostle's. Every time that a man adds to the number of things *which he cannot do without* he lessens his αὐταρκεία. ('Erue me de necessitatibus meis.' — Thomas à Kempis.) There is more independence in the man whose habits are naturally simple than in the man of expensive habits, even if he generally has the power to satisfy them.

7. The attempts to render the sense easier by inserting δῆλον or ἀληθές before ὅτι have no good MSS. support. The text without these words is translated in the R.V., 'For we brought nothing into the world, for neither can we carry anything out'; apparently meaning, 'We bring nothing into the world to remind us throughout our life that we shall carry nothing out.' But it is hardly possible to believe that St. Paul said this or expressed himself thus. It would be somewhat better if, taking ὅτι as the neuter of ὅστις, we could translate it *wherefore*. We have no exact parallel for such a usage, but ὅ is used in this sense, e.g. in several passages of Euripides, *Hecuba* 13, ὅ καί με γῆς ὑπεξέπεμ-ψεν—and as ὅς and ὅστις are not

regularly distinguished in N.T. Greek, it might be possible to infer from ὅ a similar use of ὅτι.

8. σκεπάσματα, covering, i.e. clothing and a roof over our heads.
ἀρκεσθησόμεθα, we shall be sufficiently provided.

9. οἱ δὲ βουλόμενοι πλουτεῖν. The A.V., 'they that will be rich,' suggests an emphasis on βουλόμενοι which is not in the Greek. The emphasis is rather on the πλουτεῖν, as opposed to the simple life of v. 8.

εἰς πειρασμόν, into a position in which it is much harder to do right, a position against which they are daily praying in the Lord's Prayer, μὴ εἰσενέγκῃς ἡμᾶς εἰς πειρασμόν.

παγίδα. The kind of life they lead is a net in which their weapons of spiritual defence get more and more tangled and incapable of use, so that deliverance is difficult.

ἐπιθυμίας . . . βλαβεράς, many foolish and harmful desires. Very few can use wealth altogether sensibly— when once wealth is an object in itself we want to outshine others. It is not enough to be 'well off'—we must show it. ἀνοήτους, unjustifiable to reason, βλαβεράς, not only serving no good end but doing positive harm.

αἵτινες βυθίζουσιν, such as sink men. The metaphor is from the sinking of a ship.

αἵτινες βυθίζουσι τοὺς ἀνθρώπους εἰς ὄλεθρον καὶ ἀπώλειαν. 10. ῥίζα γὰρ πάντων τῶν κακῶν ἐστιν ἡ φιλαργυρία· ἧς τινὲς ὀρεγόμενοι ἀπεπλανήθησαν ἀπὸ τῆς πίστεως, καὶ ἑαυτοὺς περιέπειραν ὀδύναις πολλαῖς. 11. Σὺ δέ, ὦ ἄνθρωπε Θεοῦ, ταῦτα φεῦγε· δίωκε δὲ δικαιοσύνην, εὐσέβειαν, πίστιν, ἀγάπην, ὑπομονήν, πραϋ-

10. ῥίζα, more naturally translated *a root* (R.V.) than *the root*. The saying was probably a common one among the Jews and appears in various forms in Greek. Cf. *Sibylline Oracles*, iii. 235, φιλοχρησμοσύνη τίς γ᾽ ἦ κακὰ μυρία τίκτει θνητοῖς ἀνθρώποις.

With this verse compare the emphasis on φιλαργυρία in 2 Tim. iii. 2. If you take each of the Ten Commandments in turn, it is easy to find instances of their being broken by men once obsessed with the idea of getting rich quickly. More completely than any other vice it brings men to treat others (*e.g.* dependents and employés) as mere pawns in their own game, instead of 'counting nothing so much his own as that he may be unjust to it.' Its deadly effect on professing *Christians* is implied in ἀπεπλανήθησαν ἀπὸ τῆς πίστεως. Its special danger is of course that we all have to earn money, and it is not easy to say *at what particular point* the desire to secure independence and make proper provision passes into covetousness. In judging ourselves in this matter (as in other 'temptations of the world'), we must keep steadily in view our 'vocation and ministry' ('sint temporalia in usu, aeterna in desiderio')—what may be natural in one life may be harmful in another.

The surest safeguard against covetousness is to have as few things as possible that 'one can't do without.' For obvious reasons covetousness is the special vice of those who in their youth have had to 'fight their way up.' They have known poverty and they want to get as far from it as possible.

ἧς, *i.e.* τῆς φιλαργυρίας, but of course the expression is loose, it is the *money* that they desire.

ὀδύναις. Perhaps St. Paul is thinking especially of the remorse of an old man as he remembers all the comradeship and affection that he has missed by the way through his anxiety for riches.

11-16. A final charge to Timothy as to his life and conduct.

11. ἄνθρωπε Θεοῦ, only here and 2 Tim. iii. 17 in the N.T., but the common appellation of prophets in the O.T. It reminds Timothy that he has a commission from God, as they had, and must live up to his call.

δικαιοσύνην, εὐσέβειαν. When these words are conjoined they mean respectively right conduct towards men, and right relation towards God. The former of course is *righteousness* in the fullest sense, not *justice* in the narrow sense.

ἀγάπην. See n. on i. 5.

ὑπομονήν. The willing endurance

πάθειαν. 12. ἀγωνίζου τὸν καλὸν ἀγῶνα τῆς πίστεως, ἐπιλαβοῦ τῆς αἰωνίου ζωῆς, εἰς ἣν ἐκλήθης, καὶ ὡμολόγησας τὴν καλὴν ὁμολογίαν ἐνώπιον πολλῶν μαρτύρων.. 13. παραγγέλλω σοι ἐνώπιον τοῦ Θεοῦ τοῦ ζωογονοῦντος τὰ πάντα καὶ Χριστοῦ Ἰησοῦ τοῦ μαρτυρήσαντος ἐπὶ Ποντίου Πιλάτου τὴν καλὴν ὁμολογίαν, 14. τηρῆσαί σε

of hard and trying things, whether labour or suffering.

πραϋπάθειαν is the correct reading for πραότητα, meaning the same. It is a late form, here only in the N.T. See n. on 2 Tim. ii. 25.

12. 'Fight the good fight of the faith' (R.V.). Probably the familiar rendering cannot be bettered, but one may regret that the word *good* has to stand for so many shades of meaning. καλός here implies that it is a contest in which one is contending for *right and honour*. Cf. n. on iv. 6.

τῆς αἰωνίου ζωῆς. See n. on i. 16.

τὴν καλὴν ὁμολογίαν. The preceding words, referring to a call common to all Christians, make it likely that 'the good confession' is the profession of faith made at baptism. The reference here to the contest of the Christian life will naturally call to the mind of an English Churchman the words of our own rite: 'We receive this person into the congregation of Christ's flock; and do sign him with the sign of the cross, in token that hereafter he shall not be ashamed to confess the faith of Christ crucified and manfully to fight under his banner, against sin, the world, and the devil; and to continue Christ's faithful soldier and servant unto his life's end.' The priest who has received Jews in baptism, and has known what it means to them in breach with all their kinsfolk, will perhaps understand more than others why St. Paul calls it τὴν καλὴν ὁμολογίαν. But the use of the same phrase in v. 13 of our Lord's witness before Pilate makes it impossible to refer it to any set form of words in baptism—rather it is the whole of the challenge to the world involved in every baptism.

13. **ζωογονοῦντος** [ζωοποιοῦντος, T.R.], giveth life or preserveth life. Is it possible that St. Paul has in mind the words of our Lord recorded in St. Luke xvii. 33, ὃς δ' ἂν ἀπολέσῃ [τὴν ψυχὴν αὐτοῦ] ζωογονήσει αὐτήν? At any rate he is exhorting Timothy ἀπολέσαι τὴν ψυχήν, and he reminds him that God alone is the author and preserver of life.

ἐπί, in the presence of.

14. **ἐντολή** is naturally used of a particular commandment or injunction, and there seems to be no clear instance of its being used in the singular for laws collectively. Nevertheless it seems to be used here generally for the will or commandments of God as revealed by our Lord. There was an obvious reason why ὁ νόμος, the natural collective, should not be used in this sense by Christians.

τὴν ἐντολὴν ἄσπιλον, ἀνεπίληπτον, μέχρι τῆς ἐπιφανείας τοῦ Κυρίου ἡμῶν Ἰησοῦ Χριστοῦ· 15. ἣν καιροῖς ἰδίοις δείξει ὁ μακάριος καὶ μόνος δυνάστης, ὁ βασιλεὺς τῶν βασιλευόντων καὶ κύριος τῶν κυριευόντων, 16. ὁ μόνος ἔχων ἀθανασίαν, φῶς οἰκῶν ἀπρόσιτον, ὃν εἶδεν οὐδεὶς ἀνθρώπων οὐδὲ ἰδεῖν δύναται, ᾧ τιμὴ καὶ κράτος αἰώνιον. ἀμήν.

τηρῆσαι ... ἄσπιλον, ἀνεπίληπτον. The phrase suggests that the law of Christ is a precious treasure, entrusted to the Christian, which he is to guard so that he can present it before God at the day of judgment, unstained by his own sin and beyond the reach of criticism. The words μέχρι τῆς ἐπιφανείας suggest that this is the thought—otherwise we might take the adjectives as meaning beyond reproach *in the eyes of men*, in the sense in which St. Paul speaks of 'adorning the doctrine,' and in which we sometimes speak of a man's *commending* his faith by his conduct.

μέχρι τῆς ἐπιφανείας. The phrase undoubtedly implies that the Apostle still hoped for the return of Christ in their own time, but his doubt about this is immediately indicated by the word ἰδίοις (God's own appointed time) and (as Bengel observed) by the very use of a plural καιροῖς.

15. **ὁ μακάριος καὶ μόνος δυνάστης, κ.τ.λ.** The phraseology of this sentence suggests convincingly that St. Paul is using an ascription of praise which had some liturgical use. It does not follow that it was a part of a Christian hymn. It is just as likely that he is quoting from synagogue usage words that would be familiar to Jews. See n. on i. 17.

The word μακάριος (in its more exalted sense) was applied even by a Greek to his gods as implying a happiness beyond being touched by the ills that affect mankind, and could be applied to men in so far as they shared in this. It is in this sense of their being now beyond the touch of evil that we speak of 'the blessed dead.'

βασιλεύς. See n. on i. 17.

16. **ὁ μόνος ἔχων ἀθανασίαν.** God alone has immortality in His own being and power. There are those to whom He grants immortality, just as also we read in 1 Cor. xv. 53, 'this mortal must put on immortality.' This is the only other passage in the N.T. where ἀθανασία is used, and ἀθάνατος nowhere occurs. ἄφθαρτος and ἀφθαρσία are the usual words.

ᾧ τιμὴ καὶ κράτος αἰώνιον. ἀμήν. See nn. on i. 16, 17.

17-19. **To his other exhortation of Timothy the Apostle adds a special admonition as to his duty in connection with the subject of v. 10, to which he here reverts.**

CH. VI. 17-19.] FIRST EPISTLE TO TIMOTHY 67

17. Τοῖς πλουσίοις ἐν τῷ νῦν αἰῶνι παράγγελλε μὴ ὑψηλοφρονεῖν, μηδὲ ἠλπικέναι ἐπὶ πλούτου ἀδηλότητι, ἀλλ᾽ ἐπὶ Θεῷ τῷ παρέχοντι ἡμῖν πάντα πλουσίως εἰς ἀπόλαυσιν· 18. ἀγαθοεργεῖν, πλουτεῖν ἐν ἔργοις καλοῖς, εὐμεταδότους εἶναι, κοινωνικούς, 19. ἀποθησαυρίζοντας

πλουσίοις ἐν τῷ νῦν αἰῶνι, rich in the present life (world). This is a good illustration of the transition of αἰών from its temporal to its ethical meaning. It is impossible here to separate the two. It is 'the rich in this life' as opposed to those who lay up treasure for the life to come (v. 19), and it is also the 'rich in the riches of the world.' For αἰών see i. 16, 17.

ὑψηλοφρονεῖν. Pride in their special advantage is meant. Cf. Rom. xi. 20, where the same word is used of the possible pride of Gentiles in the special privilege their faith has brought them. The verb is not classical, but the adj. ὑψηλόφρων is.

μηδὲ ἠλπικέναι ἐπὶ πλούτου ἀδηλότητι, not to rest hopes on uncertain riches. This is the natural translation, but we also can speak of 'depending on an uncertainty.' The following words, of course, bring out by way of contrast the idea of *certain* riches as in St. Matthew vi. 19-20.

πάντα πλουσίως εἰς ἀπόλαυσιν. The reminder in πάντα is 'All these things shall be added unto you' (St. Matt. vi. 33). - God does not forget the natural needs of His children, and their desiring things to enjoy is no sin. The sin comes when they are preferred to 'the Kingdom of God,' and are sought without regard to our 'vocation and ministry.' The word ἀπόλαυσιν further emphasises this—temporal gifts are primarily for *use*, not to give pride of possession, nor to raise our standard of needless luxury, nor to secure us against a vague fear of 'coming down in the world.' 'Seeke not proud riches but such as thou maist get justly, use soberly, distribute cheerfully, and leave contentedly' (Bacon, *Essays*, 34).

18. ἀγαθοεργεῖν, κ.τ.λ. Bacon also says, in the Essay just quoted, 'Deferre not charities till death: for certainly, if a man weigh it rightly, he that doth so is rather liberall of another man's than of his owne.' He might have added that such a man is passing on his *opportunities* to another instead of using them.

ἀγαθοεργεῖν, εὐμεταδότους, κοινωνικούς, ἀποθησαυρίζοντας are all words peculiar to this passage in the N.T., and L. and S. quote no earlier instance of the first two. The word κοινωνικός, which in Classical Greek meant *social* or *between man and man*, here certainly means *ready to share*. Cf. the use of κοινωνέω in Gal. vi. 6.

19. The phrase 'laying up as a treasure for themselves a good foundation for the future' is peculiar; but θεμέλιον means 'something on which to build,' and implies that these good works are a foundation for future progress in Christian life. It is not necessary to refer εἰς τὸ μέλλον to

ἑαυτοῖς θεμέλιον καλὸν εἰς τὸ μέλλον, ἵνα ἐπιλάβωνται τῆς ὄντως ζωῆς.

20. Ὦ Τιμόθεε, τὴν παραθήκην φύλαξον, ἐκτρεπόμενος τὰς βεβήλους κενοφωνίας καὶ ἀντιθέσεις τῆς ψευδωνύμου γνώσεως, 21. ἥν τινες ἐπαγγελλόμενοι περὶ τὴν πίστιν ἠστόχησαν.

Ἡ χάρις μεθ' ὑμῶν.

the life to come exclusively, but it includes doubtless the thought of St. Luke xvi. 9, 'Make to yourselves friends by means of the mammon of unrighteousness; that when it shall fail they may receive you into the eternal tabernacles.'

20. A final exhortation, returning to his first point, that Timothy should be faithful to the ministry of the word entrusted to him. The affectionate use of the personal name expresses perhaps more forcibly than anything else could have done the depth of the Apostle's feeling that all his former work at Ephesus depended for its continuity on the faithfulness of the disciple.

τὴν παραθήκην [τὴν παρακαταθήκην, T.R.], 'the deposit,' 'the thing entrusted to thee.' The following words ἐκτρεπόμενος κ.τ.λ. make only one interpretation of this word possible (though several have been proposed)—it is the 'deposit' of sound doctrine which he must keep inviolate against all assaults of Judaism and pseudo-philosophy. The comment of St. Vincent of Lerins on this word (quoted by Alford) is full of warning to the critical intellect: 'Quid est "depositum"? id est quod tibi creditum est, non quod a te inventum: quod accepisti, non quod excogitasti: rem non ingenii sed doctrinae, non usurpationis privatae sed publicae traditionis: rem ad te perductam, non a te prolatam, in qua non auctor debes esse sed custos.'

βεβήλους. See n. on i. 9.

κενοφωνίας, vain talking, futile wordiness.

ἀντιθέσεις coupled with κενοφωνίας must be taken, not as 'oppositions to sound doctrine,' but in some dialectical or logical sense. Probably 'subtle distinctions' is the nearest English equivalent, but the exact reference must depend on the nature of the heresies which St. Paul has specially in view. See n. on iv. 3. Without assuming too much with regard to the growth of 'Gnostic' heresies, it is nevertheless fairly evident from τῆς ψευδωνύμου γνώσεως that he refers to some who claimed esoteric knowledge and exalted too much their 'philosophical' treatment of Christianity, whether from a Jewish or from a Greek standpoint.

21. ἠστόχησαν. See n. on i. 6.

ἡ χάρις μεθ' ὑμῶν. See n. on i. 2.

Η ΠΡΟΣ ΤΙΜΟΘΕΟΝ

ΕΠΙΣΤΟΛΗ ΔΕΥΤΕΡΑ

CHAPTER I

1. Παῦλος ἀπόστολος Χριστοῦ Ἰησοῦ διὰ θελήματος Θεοῦ κατ' ἐπαγγελίαν ζωῆς τῆς ἐν Χριστῷ Ἰησοῦ 2. Τιμοθέῳ ἀγαπητῷ τέκνῳ· χάρις, ἔλεος, εἰρήνη ἀπὸ Θεοῦ πατρὸς καὶ Χριστοῦ Ἰησοῦ τοῦ Κυρίου ἡμῶν.

1-2. **The Greeting.** See notes on name and designation and form of greeting in 1 Tim. i. 1-2.

διὰ θελήματος Θεοῦ. God's will is the *cause* of his apostleship.

κατ' ἐπαγγελίαν. The connection indicated by κατά may be very varied. Here it seems most natural to take it as implying purpose, as in such phrases as κατὰ θέαν ἥκειν, and it might be paraphrased by 'to further' or 'to proclaim the promise.'

ζωῆς τῆς ἐν Χριστῷ Ἰησοῦ. The ἐν in such phrases may be regarded both as local (the life is in Christ, and we have it only by union with Him) and as causal (our life depends on Christ, and is only given to us through Him).

For ζωή see n. on 1 Tim. i. 16.

3-14. **The Apostle expresses his thankfulness for Timothy's faith (3-5), and exhorts him to make full use of the gifts he has received as** a minister of Christ (6-14), especially by boldness in facing the opinion of the world and the hardships of his task (7-8), and by maintaining without compromise the doctrine committed to him (13-14).

The outline of this paragraph is best seen if verses 9-12 be regarded as a digression. See notes.

3-5. This involved sentence is capable of two constructions: (*a*) The ground for χάριν ἔχω may be expressed in the words ὡς ἀδιάλειπτον ἔχω, κ.τ.λ.; or (*b*) it may be expressed by the words ὑπόμνησιν λαβών, in which case ὡς ἀδιάλειπτον ... πληρωθῶ must be taken as a parenthesis, ὡς being translated *as* or *since*. In favour of (*a*) is the natural order of the words and the fact that a Greek reader could hardly avoid taking ὡς ἀδιάλειπτον

3. Χάριν ἔχω τῷ Θεῷ, ᾧ λατρεύω ἀπὸ προγόνων ἐν καθαρᾷ συνειδήσει, ὡς ἀδιάλειπτον ἔχω τὴν περὶ σοῦ μνείαν ἐν ταῖς δεήσεσί μου, νυκτὸς καὶ ἡμέρας 4. ἐπι-

in the sense of 'how unceasing' (cf. Rom. i. 9), at any rate until he got to ὑπόμνησιν λαβών and found that he had mistaken the intended sense. For (b) it may be said that in similar expressions of thanksgiving (Rom., Col., 1 Thess., 2 Thess.) the direct ground of thanksgiving is the *faith* of those addressed, as here expressed in v. 5, and that the frequency of his remembrance of Timothy in prayer, while intelligible as a ground for thanksgiving, is not so natural a one. Nevertheless (a) becomes more natural if we might paraphrase it by 'how unceasingly I have occasion to remember thee in my prayers when I remember the bond that unites us, and when I have been reminded of thy unfeigned faith.' The balance of argument seems to favour (a). So R.V. and the punctuation of W. H. suggests the same.

3. **χάριν ἔχω**. Except in these two Epistles St. Paul's word is εὐχαριστῶ.

λατρεύω originally meant *to serve for hire*. Its use for religious service of the gods is found in Classical Greek, and this use is the only one in the LXX.

ἀπὸ προγόνων. Cf. Phil. iii. 6, κατὰ δικαιοσύνην τὴν ἐν νόμῳ γενόμενος ἄμεμπτος. St. Paul implies here that he came of a strictly religious family, and that for himself as for his race Christianity was the natural development of Judaism, not a discarding of it. May we not with all reverence assume that God's choice of him for the wonderful vision by which his conversion came about was not 'arbitrary,' but was God's answer to previous 'faith and clear conscience,' however unenlightened the way in which these had for a time been shown? It is right to think of every special call from God as an illustration of the principle 'To him that hath shall be given.'

St. Paul's personal attitude to the religion of his father, the religion from which he had advanced, may be a lesson to many who in the course of life think they have 'found a better way' in religion than the one in which they were brought up, and who are too apt to speak slightingly, even scornfully, of the latter. Rather they should keep in mind how much good there must have been in it since it made them capable of receiving further light from God.

ἐν καθαρᾷ συνειδήσει. See 1 Tim. iii. 9. καθαρός is 'clear from stain.'

ὡς ἀδιάλειπτον, R.V. 'how unceasing is my remembrance of thee,' *i.e.* 'because of the unceasing remembrance I have of thee.' μνεία means both 'remembrance' and 'mention,' but with ἔχω it naturally means the former.

δεήσεσι, 'petitions,' 'supplications'—the word involves perhaps a little more of the idea of 'earnest entreaty' than προσευχή does. See n. on 1 Tim. ii. 1.

νυκτὸς καὶ ἡμέρας, R.V. and W. H. take with ἐπιποθῶν. The phrase occurs three times in the Epistles to the Thessalonians, each time pre-

CH. I. 4-6.] SECOND EPISTLE TO TIMOTHY 71

ποθῶν σε ἰδεῖν, μεμνημένος σου τῶν δακρύων, ἵνα χαρᾶς
a πληρωθῶ· 5. ὑπόμνησιν λαβὼν τῆς ἐν σοὶ ἀνυποκρίτου
πίστεως, ἥτις ἐνῴκησε πρῶτον ἐν τῇ μάμμῃ σου Λωΐδι
καὶ τῇ μητρί σου Εὐνείκῃ, πέπεισμαι δὲ ὅτι καὶ ἐν σοί.
6. δι' ἣν αἰτίαν ἀναμιμνήσκω σε ἀναζωπυρεῖν τὸ χάρισμα

a πληρωθῶ

ceding a participle and necessarily taken with it. If we regard the little habits of expression which all writers acquire, this makes it more likely that it should be taken here with ἐπιποθῶν than with μνείαν ἔχω.

4. τῶν δακρύων, i.e. at their parting. .The verse shows strong reciprocal affection.

ἵνα χαρᾶς πληρωθῶ goes closely with σε ἰδεῖν.

5. For the connection of ὑπόμνησιν λαβών see n. on v. 3. But with the arrangements there adopted these words may either be taken with ἵνα χαρᾶς πληρωθῶ, 'that I may be filled with joy by being reminded' (so R.V. margin, and the punctuation in W. H.), or may be taken as in R.V. text, 'that I may be filled with joy; having been reminded...' In the latter case ὑπόμνησιν λαβών would naturally go back to χάριν ἔχω, and would refer to some message or report that had recently reached St. Paul. But probably the former is better.

ὑπόμνησιν is *reminder*, not *remembrance*.

ἀνυπόκριτος, 'unfeigned,' i.e. on which there is no acting a part or forcing of what does not come naturally. The word is apparently peculiar to religious language— LXX and N.T.—but once also in M. Antoninus.

For Lois and Eunice see Introd., p. xiii.

ἐνῴκησε. The word ἐνοικεῖν could be used in Classical Greek metaphorically for 'to be occupied with.' St. Paul's use of it, 'took up its abode in,' implies steady and persistent faith. Cf. v. 14.

πέπεισμαι δὲ ὅτι καὶ ἐν σοί, 'Yes, and I am persuaded also in thee.' The form of this phrase makes it impossible not to see that, however slight it may have been, there was some shadow of fear in St. Paul's mind for Timothy's steadfastness in his difficult circumstances. See Introd., p. xix.

6. δι' ἣν αἰτίαν. Because the faith is there Timothy is urged to make his service correspond.

ἀναζωπυρεῖν. The word literally meant 'rekindle,' but was commonly used in metaphor, and 'stir up' is probably the best rendering. St. Chrysostom compares 1 Thess. v. 19, τὸ πνεῦμα μὴ σβέννυτε.

τὸ χάρισμα ... χειρῶν μου. For this as a reference to Timothy's ordination, see n. on 1 Tim. iv. 14. It is abundantly clear from these passages that St. Paul regarded ordination as not only an appointment to office, but the sacramental gift of capacity for that office—a capacity which depended for its maintenance on our faithfulness. The verse before us

τοῦ Θεοῦ, ὅ ἐστιν ἐν σοὶ διὰ τῆς ἐπιθέσεως τῶν χειρῶν μου. 7. οὐ γὰρ ἔδωκεν ἡμῖν ὁ Θεὸς πνεῦμα δειλίας, ἀλλὰ δυνάμεως καὶ ἀγάπης καὶ σωφρονισμοῦ. 8. μὴ οὖν

speaks home to every ordained man. St. Chrysostom mentions as chief dangers to our keeping our gifts steadily burning ἀκηδία and ῥᾳθυμία —terms which are to some extent mutually convertible, but cover between them all slackness due to loss of heart or love of ease, and perhaps we may include the dulness due to monotonous labour. Each priest has his own danger, but the special gift at ordination is, as St. Paul says, a spirit of power and of love and of discipline which is capable of facing all dangers if we realise the gift, trust it, and use the proper means for keeping it alive.

7. 'For God gave us' (at ordination) 'not a spirit of cowardice but a spirit of power and of love and of discipline.' All three words, δύναμις, ἀγάπη, σωφρονισμός, are here meant to characterise the attitude of God's minister in his dealings with others. δύναμις here means strength of character in dealing with others, due primarily to the consciousness of authority from God, but depending for its effectiveness on its first being shown in our dealings with ourselves. It is not mere authority—it is the stiffness in the background which men recognise instinctively and which attracts their confidence, so that they come to it again and again for advice and help when they would not come either to learning or to eloquence. ἀγάπη (for which see n. on 1 Tim. i. 5), here represents the restraining influence in the exercise of authority and our dealing with those who oppose. It corrects hardness and makes us enter, so far as we can, into the motives of those with whom nevertheless we feel bound to interfere. σωφρονισμός is not 'a sound mind,' as A.V., but 'discipline,' as R.V. It is the opposite of the temper which is ready to compromise for the sake of peace and quietness.

These three are the virtues of authority. Their opposite is expressed by one word δειλία, for ἀγάπη is as much opposed to cowardice as are the other two. E.g. δειλία often excuses and so takes sides with a man's weaker self—ἀγάπη rebukes it and sides with his higher self.

8. The οὖν refers to the thought of δειλίας and δυνάμεως. The greatest proof of strength of character is not to be ashamed of a cause that meets with general contempt. It is extremely difficult to the imagination of modern Christians, to whom the cross has become the symbol of everything noble, to realise that in Ephesus and Rome it was thought of simply as the means of execution, and to realise the shrinking of a sensitive man from preaching that the salvation of the world depended on one who, himself a member of a despised race, has been done to death as a criminal on the cross. That this is the special reference in τὸ μαρτύριον τοῦ Κυρίου seems certain. The genitive τοῦ Κυρίου is objective ('the witness about Christ'), not subjective ('the witness borne by Christ')—indeed it is difficult to

ἐπαισχυνθῇς τὸ μαρτύριον τοῦ Κυρίου ἡμῶν, μηδὲ ἐμὲ
τὸν δέσμιον αὐτοῦ· ἀλλὰ συγκακοπάθησον τῷ εὐαγγελίῳ
κατὰ δύναμιν Θεοῦ 9. τοῦ σώσαντος ἡμᾶς καὶ καλέ-

think how even in the worst heathen surroundings, tolerant as they were of all philosophies, the 'witness borne by Christ,' even the witness borne by His submission to a humiliating death, could have been matter of shame. The Greek world well understood the meaning of sacrificing one's life for a cause, and it was the 'witness borne by Christ' which overbore the shame of 'the witness about Christ' which His disciples found at first so hard a task.

τὸν δέσμιον αὐτοῦ. St. Paul had used the same phrase in his first imprisonment—Eph. iii. 1, ὁ δέσμιος τοῦ Χριστοῦ Ἰησοῦ. It goes far beyond all Stoical submission ('Minds innocent and quiet take that for a hermitage')—it accepts the chains as part of Christ's purpose, imposed by Him to work a special result.

συγκακοπάθησον τῷ εὐαγγελίῳ, R.V., 'suffer hardship with the Gospel.' But the same verb is used absolutely in ii. 3; and in ii. 9 we have the expression τὸ εὐαγγέλιόν μου, ἐν ᾧ κακοπαθῶ, which seems to suggest the form that the thought would naturally take in St. Paul's mind. Therefore perhaps the better rendering would be 'Take thy share of hardship for the Gospel.'

κατὰ δύναμιν Θεοῦ, referring to the δυνάμεως of v. 7. One manifestation of the πνεῦμα δυνάμεως is to be the readiness to endure hardship. But as this is the power of God Himself imparted to us, the thought carries St. Paul on to speak of that power as manifested in the whole process

of their call and salvation in vv. 9-12.

9-12. We may regard these verses as a parenthesis (see n. on v. 3), but of course they bear on the main thought as suggesting triumphant reasons both for endurance and for realising to the full the gift we have received. The connection of thought may be thus summarised: 'Endure hardship, making full use of the power of God which He has already manifested in delivering and calling us—a deliverance and call which was His purpose from eternity, but has been made actual now that Jesus Christ has revealed life in the Gospel—the Gospel which I have been appointed to preach; for which reason I myself suffer without shame, knowing that our Lord is faithful and will fulfil all that for which I have trusted Him.'

9. σώσαντος. The Christian use of the word σώζω (and its cognates) doubtless had its origin in the Jewish use. To a Jew it implied the being saved from 'the wrath' and being made a participator in the Messianic kingdom. In Christian theology, therefore, it is used of the whole process whereby a man is saved from the power of sin with all the consequences of this. It can, therefore, sometimes be used as if 'salvation' were a thing accomplished in the past, referring to the beginning of the Christian life, a man's union with Christ in baptism and his 'justification,' as carrying with it naturally all that is to follow.

σαντος κλήσει ἁγίᾳ, οὐ κατὰ τὰ ἔργα ἡμῶν, ἀλλὰ κατ' ἰδίαν πρόθεσιν καὶ χάριν τὴν δοθεῖσαν ἡμῖν ἐν Χριστῷ Ἰησοῦ πρὸ χρόνων αἰωνίων 10. φανερωθεῖσαν δὲ νῦν διὰ τῆς ἐπιφανείας τοῦ σωτῆρος ἡμῶν Χριστοῦ Ἰησοῦ, καταργήσαντος μὲν τὸν θάνατον φωτίσαντος δὲ ζωὴν καὶ ἀφθαρσίαν διὰ τοῦ εὐαγγελίου, 11. εἰς ὃ ἐτέθην ἐγὼ

So in the present passage. Or it can be regarded as a process now going on in the Christian, referring to his gradual sanctification. For this compare such a passage as 1 Cor. i. 18 (τοῖς σωζομένοις ἡμῖν) and Phil. ii. 12 ('Work out your own salvation with fear and trembling'). Or it can be referred to as a thing to be finally accomplished in the future in the sanctification of the Christian and his ultimate acceptance in God's judgment. For this compare such passages as Rom. v. 9, 10 (σωθησόμεθα δι' αὐτοῦ ἀπὸ τῆς ὀργῆς, etc.).

καλέσαντος κλήσει ἁγίᾳ. For the full meaning of καλεῖν, cf. 1 Thess. ii. 12, τοῦ καλοῦντος ὑμᾶς εἰς τὴν ἑαυτοῦ βασιλείαν καὶ δόξαν. All to whom the Gospel comes are 'called'—the word in itself emphasises the divine source of the opportunity which makes the life in Christ possible for a man, and the following words οὐ κατὰ τὰ ἔργα ἡμῶν emphasise it still more. κλήσει ἁγίᾳ means in effect 'with a calling to a state of holiness.' Cf. St. Paul's use of κλητοῖς ἁγίοις in Rom. i. 7.

For the word ἅγιος, see n. on 1 Tim. ii. 15.

πρόθεσιν. Cf. Rom. ix. 11, ἡ κατ' ἐκλογὴν πρόθεσις τοῦ Θεοῦ. The purpose of God in the salvation of man is here spoken of as formed (and the grace therefore conferred), πρὸ χρόνων αἰωνίων, 'from all eternity' ('before age-long periods of time'—see n. on 1 Tim. i. 16).

10. φανερωθεῖσαν, 'manifested,' brought into evident application, in the Incarnation of our Lord.

ἐπιφάνεια, elsewhere used of what we refer to as the 'Second Coming' of our Lord, here refers naturally to the revelation of His First Coming. In the Apostle's thoughts the two were not quite so separable as they are in ours.

καταργεῖν, 'to make of none effect,' 'to render powerless.' (Cf. Rom. vi. 6, ἵνα καταργηθῇ τὸ σῶμα τῆς ἁμαρτίας, 'that the body which is subject to sin may be deprived of its power in us.') Of course this may be equivalent to *abolish* according to the context in which the word is used, but this is not so natural a rendering here. τὸν θάνατον should be taken in the literal sense—St. Paul regards death as the penalty of sin (Rom. v. 12), and Christ has made it 'of no effect'—it is at most a trifling incident in the developing life of the Christian.

φωτίζειν, 'to shed light on'—to bring into light that which before was hidden. Cf. 1 Cor. iv. 5, ὅς καὶ φωτίσει τὰ κρυπτὰ τοῦ σκότους. The double phrase ζωὴν καὶ ἀφθαρσίαν

κήρυξ καὶ ἀπόστολος καὶ διδάσκαλος. 12. δι' ἣν αἰτίαν καὶ ταῦτα πάσχω· ἀλλ' οὐκ ἐπαισχύνομαι, οἶδα γὰρ ᾧ πεπίστευκα, καὶ πέπεισμαι ὅτι δυνατός ἐστι τὴν παραθήκην μου φυλάξαι εἰς ἐκείνην τὴν ἡμέραν. 13. ὑποτύπωσιν ἔχε ὑγιαινόντων λόγων, ὧν παρ' ἐμοῦ ἤκουσας, ἐν πίστει καὶ ἀγάπῃ τῇ ἐν Χριστῷ Ἰησοῦ. 14. τὴν καλὴν παραθήκην φύλαξον διὰ Πνεύματος Ἁγίου τοῦ ἐνοικοῦντος ἐν ἡμῖν.

covers life present and life to come, the continuous life which the Christian has in union with Christ.

11. **διδάσκαλος.** Cf. 1 Tim. ii. 7, where the phrase is διδάσκαλος ἐθνῶν. In the present passage ἐθνῶν is not read in the best MSS., and is omitted by W. H. and the Revisers.

12. **παραθήκην.** For the word cf. 1 Tim. vi. 20, but the thing signified there is something entrusted to Timothy, here it is obviously something entrusted by St. Paul to Christ. By this he means *himself*, his soul and life, and we can compare 1 Pet. iv. 19, 'Let them that suffer according to the will of God commit (παρατιθέσθωσαν) their souls ... unto a faithful Creator.' Every one who chooses, as St. Paul did, a life of suffering in place of what the world can give is conscious of having entrusted his all to Christ, to Whom he looks as Saviour and vindicator.

13. For the connection see outlines given under v. 3. He now resumes what he was saying in verses 6-8, and reminds Timothy that one of the first duties of the ordained man is to guard the truth committed to him as carefully as a banker guards a deposit.

ὑποτύπωσιν. This word properly means a *sketch* or *outline*, giving the main points of a subject. 'Keep ever in mind an outline of sound words.' The main points of St. Paul's teaching must be ever in his thoughts and must be pressed home at every opportunity.

ὑγιαινόντων. See n. on 1 Tim. i. 10.

ἐν πίστει καὶ ἀγάπῃ — naturally with ἔχε.

14. **τὴν καλὴν παραθήκην.** Cf. 1 Tim. vi. 20, which makes clear what is meant here. For the use of καλός see n. on 1 Tim. iv. 6. The double use of the word παραθήκη here and in v. 12 is not without a special point — as we have trusted something to God which we expect Him to keep safe, so He has trusted something to us which we must keep safe. Our faithfulness must correspond to God's.

διὰ Πνεύματος Ἁγίου. All men realise that their spiritual and moral faculties require the help of the Holy Spirit, but we have a reminder here that the reason also as used in the judgment of truth is equally dependent on divine light. We are apt to think of reason as an infallible critic, or at least think ourselves blameless

15. Οἶδας τοῦτο, ὅτι ἀπεστράφησάν με πάντες οἱ ἐν τῇ Ἀσίᾳ· ὧν ἐστι Φύγελος καὶ Ἑρμογένης. 16. δῴη ἔλεος ὁ Κύριος τῷ Ὀνησιφόρου οἴκῳ· ὅτι πολλάκις με ἀνέψυξε, καὶ τὴν ἅλυσίν μου οὐκ ἐπῃσχύνθη, 17. ἀλλὰ γενόμενος ἐν Ῥώμῃ σπουδαίως ἐζήτησέ με καὶ εὗρε 18. (δῴη αὐτῷ

if we follow it, but the fact is that no man's thinking faculty is uninfluenced by inherited and acquired *habits* of thought and by moral prejudices. *E.g.* the argument 'I cannot think of God as acting otherwise' is dangerous—what is the faculty by which we are thus determining how God is bound to act?

[12-14. The interpretation of these verses adopted above is not without difficulty. It accounts for the use of παραθήκη in two different senses in 12 and 14, and it keeps the proper meaning of ὑποτύπωσις. Neither is there any objection to the force given to ἔχε (cf. 1 Tim. i. 19, iii. 9). It does not meet the remaining difficulty, viz. that in the order of words ὑποτύπωσιν is made emphatic and ἔχε unemphatic. A rendering has been suggested which may be thus paraphrased—'Take (this) as a summary of the healthful teaching thou hast received from me, viz. In faith and love GUARD THE DEPOSIT.' Or 'In faith and love' may still be taken with ἤκουσας, but in any case the words 'Guard the deposit' *are* the ὑποτύπωσις, and the thought is suggested, as in the above interpretation, by the use of the phrase in v. 12. From its use in 1 Tim. vi. 20 it is plain that the words 'Guard the deposit' had been often on St. Paul's lips, and that Timothy well understood them.]

15-18. The desertion of many and the loyalty of one are mentioned as an incentive to Timothy to be loyal to his master. The facts are left to speak—the conclusion is not urged except by the emphatic and contrasted Σύ with which ii. 1. begins.

15. ἀπεστράφησαν. The occasion may have been the 'first defence' of iv. 16, but with equal probability it may have been the time of St. Paul's arrest. The phrase οἱ ἐν τῇ Ἀσίᾳ will then refer to some of St. Paul's travelling companions, who deserted him at the sight of danger and returned to Asia, probably there putting the best colour on their conduct. It is as if St. Paul said, 'You probably know—and if not, I wish you to know—that those of my companions who returned to Asia, and whom you may meet, deserted me because of the danger.' Nothing is known of Phygelus and Hermogenes.

16. Nothing further is known of Onesiphorus except that his family were living at Ephesus (iv. 19). St. Paul's words (especially the form of prayer in v. 18) make it likely that Onesiphorus was now dead.

ἅλυσιν—probably literal, St. Paul being chained to a soldier-guard.

18. εὑρεῖν—the repetition of the word from εὗρε is of course inten-

ὁ Κύριος εὑρεῖν ἔλεος παρὰ Κυρίου ἐν ἐκείνῃ τῇ ἡμέρᾳ)· καὶ ὅσα ἐν Ἐφέσῳ διηκόνησε, βέλτιον σὺ γινώσκεις.

tional. Bengel's note is excellent, 'Invenit me in tanta multitudine: inveniat misericordiam in illa panegyrei.'

διηκόνησε. The student will note that in the word διακονέω the δια- was mistaken for the preposition and the augment was adapted to this. The word is probably from the same stem as διώκω—the *a* being long.

CHAPTER II

1. Σὺ οὖν, τέκνον μου, ἐνδυναμοῦ ἐν τῇ χάριτι τῇ ἐν Χριστῷ Ἰησοῦ. 2. καὶ ἃ ἤκουσας παρ' ἐμοῦ διὰ πολλῶν μαρτύρων, ταῦτα παράθου πιστοῖς ἀνθρώποις, οἵτινες ἱκανοὶ ἔσονται καὶ ἑτέρους διδάξαι. 3. συγκακοπάθησον ὡς

1-13. Verses 1 and 2 give two injunctions: (a) show in thyself the strength of grace; (b) secure the continuity of true teaching in the church under thy care. The first of these is amplified in vv. 3-13, the second is returned to in v. 14.

1. Σύ—emphatic. 'Seeing then that many show themselves weak in face of danger, do thou for thy part...'

ἐνδυναμοῦ, R.V. *be strengthened*. But there is no reason why it should not be taken as middle, 'show thyself strong.' Cf. Eph. vi. 10, R.V., 'Be strong in the Lord' (ἐνδυναμοῦσθε).

The strength of character referred to (cf. δύναμις in i. 7) is explained in the following verses—the strength to face suffering, hard living, toil, especially as required in the ministerial life. Timothy especially was in a position that demanded a forceful character in his dealings with others. To do his duty in any place of authority a man needs not only ability and judgment, but that indefinable strength which we call 'character' without an adjective—a stiffness for which it is easy to mistake eccentricity or mere self-assertion.

2. διὰ πολλῶν μαρτύρων. For the use of διά see n. on 1 Tim. ii. 15. For the occasion cf. 1 Tim. vi. 12—it is natural to think that this refers to the same occasion, though we cannot be quite sure. If on the other hand it refers to his ordination, we may suppose that St. Paul gave Timothy a charge when he was appointed to his ministry. The reference to *witnesses* certainly seems to make it necessary to assume some formal and special occasion, and excludes any interpretation that would refer the words to the general course of St. Paul's teaching on sundry occasions.

3-6. Three precepts for the ministerial life, derived from the examples of men who in ordinary professions give themselves wholeheartedly to their work if they mean to succeed. When St. Paul thus makes men in ordinary civil occupations an example to men whose calling is preeminently sacred and God-appointed, we are reminded of our Lord's parable of the unjust steward, with its concluding words, 'For the children of this world are in their generation wiser than the children of light.'

CH. II. 3-4.] SECOND EPISTLE TO TIMOTHY 79

καλὸς στρατιώτης Χριστοῦ Ἰησοῦ. 4. οὐδεὶς στρατευό-
μενος ἐμπλέκεται ταῖς τοῦ βίου πραγματείαις, ἵνα τῷ

The first example is from the soldier—his readiness to endure hardship and the readiness with which he breaks away from all ties that are inconsistent with the life of a soldier.

The second example is from the athlete—his submission to all the rules of the training school and of the course.

The third is from the farmer—the hard toil by which he earns his right, before all others, to share in the fruits of the earth.

Endurance of hardship—detachment—submission to discipline—toil to weariness—these are doubtless necessary in their degree for success in any calling, but they are pre-eminently needed for the minister who is to be the example as well as the teacher of others.

3. The correct reading is συγκακοπάθησον, found only here and i. 8, 'Take thy share of hardship.' The soldier's profession may bring honour —so may the clergyman's. The soldier's may give absorbing interest —so may the clergyman's. But the first condition of both is the readiness to face what human nature shrinks from. We may quote what Ruskin says in *Unto This Last* of the soldier when comparing his with other ordinary occupations: 'The consent of mankind has always, in spite of the philosophers, given precedence to the soldier. And this is right. For the soldier's trade, verily and essentially, is not slaying, but being slain. This, without well knowing its own meaning, the world honours it for. . . . Our estimate of him is based on this ultimate fact— of which we are well assured—that put him in a fortress breach, with all the pleasures of the world behind him, and only death and his duty in front of him, he will keep his face to the front ; and he knows that his choice may be put to him at any moment, and has beforehand taken his part—virtually takes such part continually—does, in reality, die daily.' This is why in the first place St. Paul says the minister of Christ must be a 'good soldier.'

4. ταῖς . . . πραγματείαις—the business or ties that would be natural in ordinary civil life, *e.g.* trade or law-suits. A Roman soldier could not even marry lawfully while he was on service. In the case of the clergyman it is of course the *spirit* of detachment that matters. St. Paul, who on occasion kept himself by a trade, would not have said that under no circumstances ought a clergyman to have another occupation, nor that a man with another occupation ought not to be a clergyman. Nevertheless in a more settled order the principle has been observed that a priest must not have another definite occupation. This is probably best, but in view of future contingencies it may be well to remember that this is not a necessary nor an apostolic law. It would be better for a priest to be making boots on six days of the week than to spend his time trying to add to his stipend by a study of Stock Exchange prices—yet the

στρατολογήσαντι ἀρέσῃ. 5. ἐὰν δὲ καὶ ἀθλῇ τις, οὐ
στεφανοῦται ἐὰν μὴ νομίμως ἀθλήσῃ. 6. τὸν κοπιῶντα

former is considered an impossibility, the latter is not only a possibility but a snare to many. The fact is that the danger of αἱ τοῦ βίου πραγματεῖαι is less in the loss of time (though that of course is important) than in the *anxiety*, which is much more fatal to the detachment of spirit required for priestly work. A priest must 'inter multas curas quasi sine cura transire, non more torpentis sed praerogativa quadam liberae mentis' (*De Imitatione*). These remarks are very apposite in discussions as to the value of a permanent diaconate open to men maintaining themselves by secular occupations.

τοῦ βιοῦ—see n. on 1 Tim. i. 16.

5. A second example from the athlete who submits himself to discipline both before and during the contest in order that he may win the wreath. There were of course a stadium and games at Ephesus, but the idea was familiar to the whole Greek world. The word νομίμως could mean 'according to the rules of the course,' but probably means also 'with the customary training'—a man could not hope to win in these contests unless he submitted to this. The competitors in the Olympic Games had to swear before the statue of Zeus that they had undergone training for ten months. To 'contend νομίμως' would therefore mean that this rule and oath had been fulfilled. For the word see n. on 1 Tim. i. 8.

The phrase, then, may be taken as referring in the first place to the training required for ministerial work—the training of the mind to readiness and fruitfulness, especially by hard study of the Scriptures and doctrine, the training of oneself in the habit of devotion so that it may remain real amid the constant repetitions required in one's office, and—above all—the training of the will to go without things cheerfully. 'Tantum proficies quantum tibi ipsi vim intuleris.' And again, taking νομίμως as 'according to the rules of the course,' we may apply it both to this training continued (for it never ends, and it does not do 'to let go the reins as soon as the horse goes easy') and also to the habit of discipline as required in *e.g.* carrying out the use of the Church even where one thinks one could improve it. And it is well to remember that discipline does not mean obeying where one approves, but obeying often where one does not approve —because the advantage of unity is greater than the advantage of the improvement one could oneself effect.

6. A third example from the farmer. The emphatic word is τὸν κοπιῶντα—'it is the farmer who toils hard who has the first right to . . .' The word κόπος means *toil to weariness*, and a certain bishop kept a card over his mantelpiece with this one word inscribed ΚΟΠΟΣ. He meant that you must not stop because you were tired nor because you had done what was reasonable, but only because you had done all there was to do.

γεωργὸν δεῖ πρῶτον τῶν καρπῶν μεταλαμβάνειν. 7. νόει
ὃ λέγω· δώσει γάρ σοι ὁ Κύριος σύνεσιν ἐν πᾶσι.
8. μνημόνευε Ἰησοῦν Χριστὸν ἐγηγερμένον ἐκ νεκρῶν
ἐκ σπέρματος Δαβὶδ κατὰ τὸ εὐαγγέλιόν μου· 9. ἐν ᾧ

Doctors—to their honour be it said—often set us the finest example of this quality when they drag themselves out in obedience to a summons at night. 'A clergyman, even though his power of intellect be small, is respected on the presumed ground of his unselfishness and serviceableness.'

7. 'Consider what I say; for the Lord will give thee understanding in all things.' St. Paul means in effect, 'I suggest these thoughts—our Lord will help you to apply them further.'

σύνεσις is best translated 'understanding'—it means the critical faculty which enables one to understand a subject in all its bearings.

8-10. The main point of the whole passage 1-13 is the need of patience in suffering and hardship. Verses 8-10 may therefore be paraphrased, 'Remember that our Lord passed to His resurrection and glory through suffering. And in the same cause I also suffer that I may help to bring others to share His salvation and glory.' The thought of Christ's *suffering* is not expressed in so many words, but having regard to the whole passage one feels that it is necessarily implied in the contrast of ἐγηγερμένον, and in the reference to His manhood in ἐκ σπέρματος Δαβίδ. The risen and glorified Christ is called to mind as our great assurance that suffering is not purposeless or in vain.

The best illustration may be taken from the words of the office for the Visitation of the Sick: 'There should be no greater comfort to Christian persons than to be made like unto Christ, by suffering patiently adversities, troubles, and sicknesses. For he himself went not up to joy, but first he suffered pain; he entered not into his glory before he was crucified. So truly our way to eternal joy is to suffer here with Christ; and our door to enter into eternal life is gladly to die with Christ; that we may rise again from death and dwell with him in everlasting life.'

8. ἐγηγερμένον. The Perfect denotes the continuance of the state brought about, as if he said 'now living the risen life.' Besides the contrast implied (see note above) with His life of suffering on earth, the words remind us of Christ as a now living power, 'able to succour them that are tempted—because he himself hath suffered being tempted' (Heb. ii. 18).

ἐκ σπέρματος Δαβίδ is taken, according to the above interpretation, as simply emphasising the true manhood of Christ. It is otherwise taken as referring to the fulfilment of prophecy in Him.

κατὰ τὸ εὐαγγέλιόν μου is best taken with the whole phrase preceding. St. Paul's teaching was that in Christ true man was raised and exalted to the right hand of God.

F

κακοπαθῶ μέχρι δεσμῶν ὡς κακοῦργος, ἀλλ' ὁ λόγος τοῦ Θεοῦ οὐ δέδεται. 10. διὰ τοῦτο πάντα ὑπομένω διὰ τοὺς ἐκλεκτούς, ἵνα καὶ αὐτοὶ σωτηρίας τύχωσι τῆς ἐν Χριστῷ Ἰησοῦ μετὰ δόξης αἰωνίου. 11. πιστὸς ὁ *ᵃλόγος, Εἰ γὰρ συναπεθάνομεν, καὶ συζήσομεν· 12. εἰ ὑπομένομεν, καὶ

ᵃ λόγος· εἰ

9. **ὡς κακοῦργος.** St. Luke xxiii. 32, 'There were also two others, κακοῦργοι, led with him to be put to death.' Perhaps in thinking of his own suffering with Christ, St. Paul has those others in mind. See also Introd., p. xi.

ἀλλ' ὁ λόγος, κ.τ.λ. A triumphant parenthesis.

'God's word, for all their craft and force,
One moment will not linger,
But, spite of hell, shall have its course;
'Tis written by his finger.
And though they take our life,
Goods, honour, children, wife,
Yet is their profit small;
These things shall vanish all,
The city of God remaineth.'

10. **ὑπομένω** and **ὑπομονή** include all patience in enduring hardship and all perseverance in making for one's end in spite of obstacles.

ἐκλεκτοί. As in the Catechism, 'who sanctifieth me and all the elect people of God.' There is no opposition between 'called' and 'chosen' in this use of the word—it only emphasises the fact that we all depend primarily for our salvation from sin on the will and choice of God.

σωτηρίας. See n. on i. 9.

δόξης αἰωνίου. See n. on 1 Tim. i. 16.

11-13. A quotation summing up the correspondence between Christ's suffering and glory and our suffering and glory. It is probable that the quotation is from some canticle already in use among Christians. See n. on 1 Tim. iii. 16. The phrase πιστὸς ὁ λόγος here is usually taken as referring to the following words. But see n. on 1 Tim. iii. 1.

The use of singing among the earliest Christians as part of their worship is not only a natural inference from the model of synagogue worship, but is proved by such a passage as Col. iii. 16 ('psalms and hymns and spiritual songs'), confirmed by Pliny, who describes the Christians in Bithynia as assembling before daybreak and singing by turns a hymn to Christ as God (*Ep.* 97, A.D. 112). The earliest hymns would doubtless have been modelled on Jewish psalmody (like the *Magnificat, Benedictus, Nunc Dimittis*), and where the rhythm and balance of clauses is present in a quotation (as here) it is reasonable to suppose it to be part of such a hymn. We have had one such passage in 1 Tim. iii. 16. Cf. Eph. v. 14, and many passages in the Apocalypse. The development of metrical hymns, as we understand them, came at a later date.

συμβασιλεύσομεν· εἰ ἀρνησόμεθα, κἀκεῖνος ἀρνήσεται ἡμᾶς· 13. εἰ ἀπιστοῦμεν, ἐκεῖνος πιστὸς μένει· ἀρνήσασθαι γὰρ ἑαυτὸν οὐ δύναται.

14. Ταῦτα ὑπομίμνησκε, διαμαρτυρόμενος ἐνώπιον τοῦ

11. **συναπεθάνομεν.** The Aorist naturally refers to the time of baptism (cf. Rom. vi. 3-4), but refers to this as the beginning of our suffering with Christ, thus adding to the thought of the preceding verses.

12. **εἰ ἀρνησόμεθα.** Cf. St. Matt. x. 33.

14-26. **The whole of this passage is an expansion of the second precept, viz. that given in v. 2.** In vv. 20-22 the Apostle might seem to have turned aside from this thought, but he has not really done so; see notes on those verses.

To understand the emphasis laid by St. Paul on due provision for continuity of sound doctrine, we should keep in mind two considerations: (1) Even if there were already in existence books containing the Gospel message or the sayings of Christ, the possession of copies of such books would have been very uncommon, and therefore the Church had to rely on oral teaching both of catechumens and of others. The corruption of doctrine was therefore much easier than where there is a written standard to appeal to. This greater dependence on oral teaching may even be said to have continued down to the 15th century, when printing and new methods of making paper began to make the possession of books commoner. One of the causes which led to the growth of the College system at Oxford was the need of using books in common —in a certain sense the College may be said to have grown round its Library. (2) The centres where Christianity was most active and influential were great centres of Judaism and of Greek thought. In these places, therefore, there was on the one hand a temptation to graft Christian teaching too closely on Jewish teaching—not to break completely with the old order; and on the other hand a temptation to try to capture what was best in the Greek world by rationalising that which in Christian doctrine appeared to a Greek as incredible or grotesque. Both these things tended to compromise and assimilation, and it is compromise of this kind that St. Paul has in mind. So much in Plato was so near to the kingdom of God that we can well understand the attraction; the danger was that in such appreciation the Christian might try to lighten the ship by throwing over anything in Christianity which Plato would have thrown over, thus making philosophy the judge of revelation.

14. **διαμαρτυρόμενος.** See n. on 1 Tim. v. 21.

λογομαχεῖν. See n. on 1 Tim. vi. 4.

ἐπὶ καταστροφῇ. The ἐπὶ denotes *result*, really the same use as the Classical *on the condition of*, *at the cost of*. Cf. 1 Thess. iv. 7, 'God called us not ἐπὶ ἀκαθαρσίᾳ.' καταστροφή, overthrowing, the opposite of edification, building up (οἰκοδομή).

ᵃΚυρίου μὴ λογομαχεῖν ἐπ' οὐδὲν χρήσιμον ἐπὶ καταστροφῇ τῶν ἀκουόντων. 15 σπούδασον σεαυτὸν δόκιμον παραστῆσαι τῷ Θεῷ, ἐργάτην ἀνεπαίσχυντον, ὀρθοτομοῦντα τὸν λόγον τῆς ἀληθείας. 16. τὰς δὲ βεβήλους κενοφωνίας περιΐστασο· ἐπὶ πλεῖον γὰρ προκόψουσιν ἀσεβείας, 17. καὶ ὁ λόγος αὐτῶν ὡς γάγγραινα νομὴν

ᵃ Θεοῦ

---

15. δόκιμος, that has stood the test. A metaphor from metals.

ὀρθοτομοῦντα. The parallel is quoted from Prov. iii. 6, 'In all thy ways acknowledge him, and he shall direct thy paths'—ἵνα ὀρθοτομῇ τὰς ὁδούς σου—but there, on account of the ὁδούς, the metaphor of *cutting straight* may be retained. Here, with the object τὸν λόγον, the metaphor of τέμνω is probably lost. R.V. *handling aright*, Vulg. *recte tractantem*. The loss of metaphor is pointed to also by the use of ὀρθοτομία for 'orthodoxy' in later ecclesiastical writers.

16. βεβήλους. See n. on 1 Tim. i. 9. From meaning simply 'not hallowed' it came to have a worse meaning—'impure,' 'unfit to take part in holy things.' So the Latin *profanus*—as in Vir. *Aen*. vi. 258, 'Procul este, profani.'

κενοφωνίας, talking on subjects that have no relation to reality, or speculative questions which from their nature are incapable of answer: *e.g.* the Jewish question, how many angels could stand on the point of a needle. In such speculations— even theological—a man 'may be perfectly at home without ever submitting to the demands of religion.'

περιΐστασο properly meant *stand round, encircle*, and so came in later Greek to mean *go round in order to avoid, keep away from*.

προκόψουσι, metaphor from pioneers—work their way on.

ἀσεβείας, irreligion, especially wrong beliefs about God and things divine. Such speculations as St. Paul refers to tend to cast off the religious element altogether in favour of quasi-philosophical explanations.

17. γάγγραινα, a gangrene, a rapidly spreading disease.

νομὴν ἕξει. νομή literally meant *pasturage*, and the phrase therefore came to be used of anything spreading rapidly, like fire or disease. The statement here means primarily, like the preceding words, that such teaching gets worse and worse in the individual.

For Hymenaeus, see 1 Tim. i. 20. Philetus is unknown. The heresy was based probably not so much on the incredibility of the resurrection of the body as on the pagan notion that matter is essentially evil and that the spirit could only aim at complete and final liberation from it. See n. on 1 Tim. iv. 3. Hence the resurrection had to be explained as a spiritual resurrection from ignorance to the knowledge of God—

CH. II. 17-19.] SECOND EPISTLE TO TIMOTHY 85

ἔξει· ὧν ἐστιν Ὑμέναιος καὶ Φιλητός, 18. οἵτινες περὶ τὴν ἀλήθειαν ἠστόχησαν, λέγοντες ^aτὴν ἀνάστασιν ἤδη γεγονέναι, καὶ ἀνατρέπουσι τήν τινων πίστιν. 19. ὁ μέντοι στερεὸς θεμέλιος τοῦ Θεοῦ ἕστηκεν, ἔχων τὴν σφραγῖδα ταύτην, Ἔγνω Κύριος τοὺς ὄντας αὐτοῦ, καὶ

^a om. τήν

an idea probably familiar enough to a Greek from the conception of the mysteries. It is possible that such words of St. Paul as those in Rom. vi. 3-4 were wrested by these men to favour their argument. Notice the R.V. marg. 'a resurrection' (omitting τήν with W. H.)—this does not alter the interpretation, but doubtless the men in question taught that the resurrection was a spiritual change continually going on.

18. ἠστόχησαν. See n. on 1 Tim. i. 6, 'Missed the mark.'

19. 'Nevertheless the firm foundation of God standeth (immovable), having this seal-mark, "The Lord knoweth them that are His." . . .' The general meaning is clear, viz. that, opposed to the speculative doctrine just described, the truth of God stands invincible. But the exact application of some of the words is difficult.

Having regard to such a passage as 1 Tim. iii. 15, where the Church is spoken of as the 'pillar and ground' or 'stay' of the truth (στῦλος καὶ ἑδραίωμα), it is natural to suppose that St. Paul meant the Church here by 'the foundation of God,' though elsewhere it is represented as the building, with Christ Himself as the corner-stone and the apostles and prophets as foundation (Eph. ii. 20-22). In favour of this application is the fact that the seal-inscriptions given in the following words describe the character of *persons* as if they, so to speak, composed the foundation so described. At the same time the contrast meant in the whole passage is that between men's fleeting, quasi-philosophical speculations and the permanent truth of God; and therefore it is not impossible to apply the words 'foundation of God' to the truth as revealed by God in Christ. Are we obliged to suppose that St. Paul meant one of these to the exclusion of the other? If we used in English the equivalent expression, 'that which God hath laid as a foundation,' we could include under it both the truth and the Church.

ἔχων τὴν σφραγῖδα ταύτην, having this seal, *i.e.* seal-inscription. The reference is to the mark or inscription impressed by a seal. The commonest inscription on a seal was the name of the owner preceded by the word for 'belonging to,' but it was possible to have any figure or motto which could serve as a private emblem. The use of the seal was to mark ownership, especially on sealed-up packets or vessels, and also to mark authenticity (like a signature)

Ἀποστήτω ἀπὸ ἀδικίας πᾶς ὁ ὀνομάζων τὸ ὄνομα Κυρίου. 20. ἐν μεγάλῃ δὲ οἰκίᾳ οὐκ ἔστι μόνον σκεύη χρυσᾶ καὶ ἀργυρᾶ, ἀλλὰ καὶ ξύλινα καὶ ὀστράκινα, καὶ ἃ μὲν εἰς τιμήν, ἃ δὲ εἰς ἀτιμίαν. 21. ἐὰν οὖν τις ἐκκαθάρῃ ἑαυτὸν ἀπὸ τούτων, ἔσται σκεῦος εἰς τιμήν, ἡγιασμένον, εὔχρηστον τῷ δεσπότῃ, εἰς πᾶν ἔργον ἀγαθὸν ἡτοιμασμένον. 22. τὰς δὲ νεωτερικὰς ἐπιθυμίας φεῦγε, δίωκε δὲ δικαιο-

on any writing. Both ideas are included here—they are marked as God's possession, and they are authenticated as His messengers—but the former is pointed to by the words of the inscription τοὺς ὄντας αὐτοῦ. Cf. Rev. vii. 2-4.

For the idea of an inscription on foundation stones, cf. Rev. xxi. 14.

The first inscription is from the LXX of Num. xvi. 5, where (in the rebellion of Korah, Dathan, and Abiram) Moses says that God is about to show who are His true servants. So, means St. Paul, God will show it in the Church.

The second inscription does not correspond clearly to any passage in the O.T., but may be an allusion to Is. lii. 11, 'Depart ye, depart ye (ἀπόστητε), go ye out from thence, touch no unclean thing'—where those about to return from the exile are warned to separate themselves from all the iniquity of Babylon.

20-21. The meaning is that in the Church there are bound to spring up men like Hymenaeus and Philetus. Compare the teaching of the parable of the tares (St. Matt. xiii. 24) and the parable of the net which 'gathered of every kind' (*id.* 47). The comparison here is the multitude of vessels of different kinds needed in a household — some are of inferior material to start with, are more liable to be broken, and therefore serve commoner, less honourable uses. Of course the metaphor is not to be carried further, as *e.g.* by arguing that the vessels have no choice of their own material or use. St. Paul is only here emphasising the one point that men of very different spirituality and love of the truth will come into the Church. In the next verse (to the neglect of his metaphor) he makes it clear that the Christian can determine his own use, εἰς τιμήν.

21. ἐκκαθάρῃ ἑαυτὸν ἀπὸ τούτων, 'purify himself so as not to be one of these.'

ἡγιασμένον. See n. on 1 Tim. ii. 15.

εὔχρηστον, serviceable. The derivation of the word (as of the simple χρηστός) is from χράομαι.

22. As St. Paul goes on in 23 to suggest how Timothy is to bear himself towards the false teachings and disputations of which he has been speaking, the connection of 22 in thought, though not expressed, would seem to be, 'In order to deal with these men, you need in the first place to keep a very high standard of conduct and religion yourself.'

τὰς νεωτερικὰς ἐπιθυμίας. 'Youthful lusts' in the R.V. is not a happy rendering in modern English,

CH. II. 22-23.] SECOND EPISTLE TO TIMOTHY 87

σύνην, πίστιν, ἀγάπην, εἰρήνην, μετὰ τῶν ἐπικαλουμένων τὸν Κύριον ἐκ καθαρᾶς καρδίας. 23. τὰς δὲ μωρὰς καὶ ἀπαιδεύτους ζητήσεις παραιτοῦ, εἰδὼς ὅτι γεννῶσι μάχας.

because ἐπιθυμίαι (like 'lust' in older English) can cover the whole field of desire. By νεωτερικαὶ ἐπιθυμίαι St. Paul means all desires that make the special temptation of youth, not only sensual desires. He would include all the temptations of luxury and pleasure, pride in physical prowess, love of notoriety and position, the desire to display one's intellectual acuteness, love of variety and impatience of monotony. It is impossible to say whether St. Paul meant any special point in Timothy, but several passages in the Epistle suggest a warning against compromise, and the *desire to stand well with other people at too great a cost* is certainly a νεωτερικὴ ἐπιθυμία. For Timothy's age see 1 Tim. iv. 12, but one can be youthful without being young.

δικαιοσύνην, in the most general sense of 'right conduct,' such as God would commend.

ἀγάπην. See n. on 1 Tim. i. 5. It involves treating as brothers those towards whom one feels no particular affection.

μετὰ τῶν ἐπικαλουμένων, κ.τ.λ., to be taken closely with εἰρήνην—'the maintaining of peaceable relations with all who . . . ' in spite of personal feelings and the inclination to resent differences. The condition implied in ἐκ καθαρᾶς καρδίας (for the word see n. on 1 Tim. i. 5) implies the opposite duty of *not* always aiming at peaceable relations where sincerity of motive is doubtful and principle is at stake. There are some things worth quarrelling about; asserting oneself for personal reasons does not win respect, but asserting oneself for the cause or for others' sake does win respect. St. Paul's disagreement with St. Barnabas is a case in point.

23-26. How Timothy is to bear himself when brought into contact with the false speculations referred to. He is to avoid taking part in discussions about them, lest he should be led to strife which would lessen his authority as a teacher.

23. ἀπαιδεύτους, uneducated, ignorant, springing from ignorance. But παιδεύειν in the N.T. usually means *to discipline* (see n. on v. 25), and it is possible that the adjective here means 'undisciplined,' 'unrestrained.' An 'ignorant' argument is apt to be an 'undisciplined' argument also, because it raises questions without regard to *e.g.* the first principles of morality.

For the nature of the ζητήσεις, see n. on 1 Tim. i. 4 and iv. 3.

παραιτοῦ, ask to be excused.

24. The μάχεσθαι, like μάχας in 23, implies personal bitterness. St. Paul of course does not mean that the Christian is never to argue in the search for truth, but it is to be a 'pia et humilis inquisitio veritatis, parata semper doceri et per sanas patrum sententias studens ambulare' (*De Imitatione*).

24. δοῦλον δὲ Κυρίου οὐ δεῖ μάχεσθαι, ἀλλ' ἤπιον εἶναι πρὸς πάντας, διδακτικόν, ἀνεξίκακον, 25. ἐν πρᾳότητι παιδεύοντα τοὺς ἀντιδιατιθεμένους· μήποτε δῴη αὐτοῖς

δοῦλον Κυρίου. This phrase emphasises (1) the *permanence* of the tie; (2) the *completeness* of the service. 'Servant' expresses neither of these. 'Slave' is not a good rendering, because of the modern associations of the word. Perhaps the R.V. marg. 'bondservant' is as good a rendering as English supplies.

ἤπιος, soothing and gentle in bearing and manner, not overbearing or behaving so as to cause resentment.

διδακτικός, ready to teach and fit to teach—qualities which are not one and the same. On the one hand the διδακτικός would regard it as churlish not to wish to give another the benefit of any knowledge he possesses. On the other hand he tries to convey it in an acceptable way—not using sarcasm, not seeming to exalt himself, rather drawing knowledge from the pupil than exposing ignorance, and making much even of one word of truth contained in the answer given him ('Maluit videri invenisse bonos quam fecisse' —Tacitus). Even so the pupil will not always accept it at once, but some day what the teacher said will come back to the pupil's mind as *his own thought*, and then he will accept it. The teacher remembers also that 'neither hath God opened or will open all to one, that there may be a traffic in knowledge between the servants of God, for the planting both of love and humilitie.'

ἀνεξίκακον, able to put up patiently with evil—here referring specially to the flouts of opponents.

The kind of controversy to which St. Paul's words apply in modern times more often takes place in newspapers than in discussion face to face. It is mainly the personal touch in this that he would deprecate. Doubtless there are cases where the *man* must be attacked in order to expel him from authority which he uses unworthily. But as a rule it is a question of right or wrong arguments or interpretations. In such cases to prove an opponent a bad scholar or ignorant of history achieves only a negative result; to prove that he is inconsistent with his own past utterances may be a good 'debating point,' but is more negative still, because the greatest minds are those that grow and change; to suggest that he supports a reform because it will benefit himself or make things easier for himself, is to suggest what cannot be refuted and closes the door. In writing to the newspapers the ἤπιος avoids the suggestion of ignorance or insincerity, the διδακτικός marshals his facts but as far as possible leaves the conclusions to his opponent's intelligence, the ἀνεξίκακος passes without a word personalities written against himself. By expressing yourself with restraint you can be wonderfully effective.

25. **ἐν πρᾳότητι παιδεύοντα τοὺς ἀντιδιατιθεμένους,** disciplining those who oppose in a spirit of meekness. St. Luke (in Acts vii. 22, xxii. 3) is the only N.T. writer who uses

ὁ Θεὸς μετάνοιαν εἰς ἐπίγνωσιν ἀληθείας, 26. καὶ ἀνανήψωσιν ἐκ τῆς τοῦ διαβόλου παγίδος ἐζωγρημένοι ὑπ' αὐτοῦ εἰς τὸ ἐκείνου θέλημα.

παιδεύω in the simple sense of instructing. The usual use in Christian writings is that of *e.g.* Heb. xii. 6, 'Whom the Lord loveth he chasteneth' (παιδεύει)—as St. Augustine puts it, παιδεύειν is 'per molestias erudire.' ἀντιδιατιθεμένους means contentious or obstinate opposition. πραότης is the spirit of which ἤπιος (v. 24) expresses the outward manifestation—in discussion it is the spirit which remembers that we also may make mistakes and that almost every error in doctrine has come from *overstating a truth*.

25-26. **μήποτε δῴη, κ.τ.λ.**, 'If perchance (in the hope that) God may give,' etc. The Classical use of μή to express something that one *apprehends* and wishes to avoid gave rise to a use where it expresses that which one *surmises*, whether with or without the wish to avoid. In these cases 'perhaps' or 'if perhaps' is the best rendering. Cf. St. Luke iii. 15, διαλογιζομένων . . . μήποτε αὐτὸς εἴη ὁ Χριστός, 'whether haply he were the Christ.'

For T.R. δῷ R.V. has δῴη (a late form of Optative). W. H. have δῴη in text, δώῃ in marg. (a form of Ionic Subjunctive). The natural sequence and the Subjunctive ἀνανήψωσι are in favour of the Subjunctive form. Later Greek included a fair number of Ionic forms, and many occur in the dialect of modern Greek peasants.

ἐπίγνωσιν. See n. on iii. 7.

26. **καὶ ἀνανήψωσιν ἐκ τῆς τοῦ διαβόλου παγίδος**, 'and they should wake up sober out of the snare of the devil'—a double metaphor.

ἐζωγρημένοι ὑπ' αὐτοῦ εἰς τὸ ἐκείνου θέλημα. In interpreting this passage we may start from the certainty that the pronouns must refer to different persons. If the more emphatic pronoun had stood first (*i.e.* if the words were ἐζωγρημένοι ὑπ' ἐκείνου εἰς τὸ θέλημα αὐτοῦ) to refer them to the same person would have been possible, but as it stands we may rule out such a rendering as that of the A.V.

Assuming that the pronouns must refer to different persons, εἰς τὸ ἐκείνου θέλημα must mean 'to work the will of *God*.' But even so the following varieties have been considered possible:—

(1) 'Having been taken captive by the Lord's servant unto the will of God,' as R.V. text.

(2) 'Having been taken captive by the devil, unto the will of God' —taking εἰς τὸ ἐκείνου θέλημα with ἀνανήψωσιν. So R.V. marg.

(3) 'Having been taken captive by the devil according to the will of God,' *i.e.* by divine permission or 'so that the will of God may eventually be brought about'—*i.e.* God permits men to be in bondage to Satan for a time in order to work His ultimate end in them.

A slight point against (1) is that ζωγρηθέντες would in this case be more natural than ἐζωγρημένοι, but the Perfect is obviously possible in the sense 'becoming prisoners of the Lord's servant.'

Against (2) is the awkward order.

The seeming strangeness of the idea from our point of view is not a sufficient argument against (3). It is quite consistent with St. Paul's words elsewhere to think of men as temporarily brought under the power of Satan. See note on 1 Tim. i. 20.

In favour of (3) it may be urged (a) that ἐζωγρημένοι is a natural explanation of παγίδος; (b) that a Greek reading the passage without any preconceived idea as to what it *ought* to mean would take αὐτοῦ as referring to διαβόλου.

The balance of argument seems to favour (3), but εἰς τὸ ought not in any case to be translated 'in accordance with'—it properly means 'to bring about.'

CHAPTER III

1. Τοῦτο δὲ γίνωσκε, ὅτι ἐν ἐσχάταις ἡμέραις ἐνστήσονται καιροὶ χαλεποί. 2. ἔσονται γὰρ οἱ ἄνθρωποι

1-17. This chapter describes the way in which evil principle and evil conduct will spread in the 'last days,' and in face of them Timothy is (1) reminded once more of the Apostle's teaching and example (verses 10-11), (2) urged to hold fast all that his early training in the Scriptures had taught him (verses 14-17).

To St. Paul the 'last days' meant a time near at hand. Doubtless, as we see by comparison of the language of this Epistle with 1 Thess. iv. 15, 17, he modified his expectation of being alive himself when the Lord came; and in some cases he had to warn his disciples not to let the ordinary duties of life be disturbed by feverish anticipations (2 Thess. ii. 2). But passages may be quoted from his Epistles of all periods, showing that he shared the general idea of Christians as to an early return of our Lord, and that this affected to some extent his attitude towards *e.g.* social questions, without leading him to attempt any special forecast of the future. Cf. such passages as 1 Thess. iv. 15-17, v. 2-3, 2 Thess. ii. 2-3, Rom. xiii. 11-12, 1 Cor. vii. 29-31, Phil. iv. 5.

2. ἔσονται γὰρ οἱ ἄνθρωποι. . . .

In the list which follows we need not expect to find any special arrangement or division—St. Paul is writing a letter and not a treatise. But his beginning with φίλαυτοι, φιλάργυροι and ending with φιλήδονοι suggests the main thought, viz. that men will pervert the main aims of life and accept the dictation of their lower selves as to what is worth devoting life to. All the words that come in between suggest the insolent rejection of all restraint, of all claims which conflict with those lower selves — the claims of God, the claims of parents and natural affection, the claims of society. It is the perversion of mind and will on which St. Paul is laying stress, and he does not mention by name the more flagrant vices as we understand them. The reason for this is succinctly given in ἔχοντες μόρφωσιν εὐσεβείας—the perversion described is not inconsistent with the outward pretence of religion. We may go further and say that in the whole list there is not a quality for which men do not find excuses and fair names—love of self is 'self-realisation,' the discarding of claims is 'independence,' treason is 'diplomacy,' and even the τετυφωμένος is an intellectual 'original,' the ἀνόσιος a 'seeker for truth.'

φίλαυτοι, φιλάργυροι, ἀλαζόνες, ὑπερήφανοι, βλάσφημοι,

The use of the collective οἱ ἄνθρωποι is also to be observed. St. Paul is not saying 'there will be men of such and such a kind'—which would be true of any time—but 'men generally will be of such and such a kind.' He is characterising whole nations and generations, and implies that public opinion will accept a standard of morality and conduct of the kind described. There are at all times individuals who are φιλάργυροι, and so long as they are not approved by opinion generally the taint is limited. But St. Paul means that a time will come when the accumulation of wealth will become the dominant aim of public policy—'Everything, human and divine, sacrificed to the idol of public credit, and national bankruptcy the consequence' (Burke) —a time when responsibility and generosity will take a subordinate place as springs of action, when the homes men live in and their spiritual possibilities will count as nothing if they do not help the machine which raises the sum-total of wealth for the community. There will always be individuals who can be described as ἀνήμεροι, but St. Paul means to characterise an age in which brutal force is accepted for the arbitrament of all claims. Or again, a large section of mankind at all times will be weak before the attractions of pleasure and is φιλήδονος, but it is a different thing when a whole nation gets into the habit of accepting the amount of pleasure and ease to be secured as the natural criterion of the value of a particular kind of life or line of policy. In fact St. Paul is thinking throughout of the prevalent tone of a society which has lost all sense of moral values.

φίλαυτοι. This word means 'self-loving,' in the sense of seeking to make everything comfortable and easy for oneself—at the expense of other people, if necessary. The bad sense was the usual one, but it was capable of bearing a good sense, as Aristotle shows in a passage which comes as near as pagan philosophy could come to expressing the thought, 'Whosoever shall lose his life for my sake shall find it.' See *Ethics*, ix. 8. 4 : 'Those who use self-loving as a term of reproach apply the name to those who take more than their due of money and honour and bodily pleasures ; for the generality of men desire these things and set their hearts upon them as the best things in the world. . . . If what a man always set his heart upon were that he, rather than another, should do what is just or temperate or in any other way virtuous—if, in a word, he were always claiming the noble course of conduct, no one would call him self-loving, and no one would reproach him. And yet such a man would seem to be more truly self-loving. At least he takes for himself that which is noblest and most truly good, and gratifies the ruling power in himself, and in all things obeys it.'

The word φίλαυτος occurs nowhere else in the N.T., but it was doubtless from its use here and in Christian literature that when English wanted a word for 'selfishness' it first tried 'philauty.' It also tried 'suicism' and did not use 'selfish' till the 17th century. The first use of it noted in the New English Dictionary is in 1640—'A carnal selfe-ish spirit is very loathsome in things spiritual' Bridge

φιλάργυροι. One special and prominent manifestation of φιλαυτία. See note on 1 Tim. vi. 10. Of all forms of selfishness it bears the fairest excuse, because the necessities of life compel us to 'make money,' and the point at which it becomes avarice is not easily recognisable. 'As the baggage is to an army, so is Riches to Virtue. It cannot be spared, nor left behind, but it hindereth the march' (Bacon). The best criterion of what we are doing is its *effect on others*. St. John in Rev. xviii. 11-13, describing the way in which the great city piled up luxury and wealth for itself, ends by the climax 'traffic in the souls of men.' If my trade is in that which is wholly baneful it is φιλαργυρία. If it is in the necessities of life, but carried on under unfair conditions of profit, it is φιλαργυρία ('It is not linen you're wearing out, but human creatures' lives'). The dangers of avarice have of course been a commonplace with writers in all ages. For a worldly man's honest attempt to hit the mean, read Bacon's *Essay* 34 'Of Riches'—the best sentence in which is 'Seeke not proud riches, but such as thou mayest get justly, use soberly, distribute cheerefully, and leave contentedly.' For useful advice to a clergyman in these matters, read Herbert's chapter 26, *The Parson's Eye*. For an attempt to apply principle to business methods read Ruskin's *Unto This Last*. But it must not be thought that avarice is only the fault of the rich. Herbert's example of the man who 'hath wherewithal to buy a spade, and yet he chuseth rather to use his neighbour's' is capable of wide application. 'He will redeem a *penny* with his reputation and lose all his friends to boot' (Earle's *Microcosmography*).

ἀλαζόνες. Aristotle (*Ethics*, iv. 7) defines the ἀλαζών as a man who 'lays claim to things that men esteem without really having them at all, or lays claim to them to a greater degree than his possession of them warrants.' Hence 'bragging,' 'boastful.' The derivation is from ἀλάομαι (wander), the connection being through the wandering charlatans who made a living by professing wonder-working knowledge of one kind or another, *e.g.* the mendicants (called ἀγύρται), who as the devotees of some god professed ability to tell fortunes or to do injury, like later witches. St. Paul probably means by 'boastfulness' here the presumptuous confidence in one's power to control one's own destiny and impose one's will on others. We may compare St. James iv. 16, where the word is used of the man who says, 'To-morrow I will do so and so' instead of saying, 'If God will'; and 1 John ii. 16, where ἡ ἀλαζονία τοῦ βίου means the self-confident claim to regulate one's life according to one's own desires without regard to divine guidance. In the present passage therefore the word naturally leads those words which signify a false independence of all outside claims, whether divine or human. See note above.

ὑπερήφανοι, arrogant, haughty,

γονεῦσιν ἀπειθεῖς, ἀχάριστοι, ἀνόσιοι, 3. ἄστοργοι, ἄσπονδοι, διάβολοι, ἀκρατεῖς, ἀνήμεροι, ἀφιλάγαθοι, 4. προδόται, προπετεῖς, τετυφωμένοι, φιλήδονοι μᾶλλον

expressing in one's demeanour towards others that spirit of 'independence.' 'I ask nothing of you and I owe you nothing.' The derivation is from ὑπέρ and φαίνομαι, 'displaying oneself as above others.'

βλάσφημοι. For the origin of the word see n. on 1 Tim. i. 13. Here A.V. has *blasphemers*, R.V. *railers*. The passage in 1 Tim. (R.V. *blasphemer*) is the only other use of βλάσφημον in St. Paul. Where he uses the noun βλασφημία it is only in the sense of *railing*, but the verb βλασφημέω is freely used in both senses. There is therefore only the context to guide us, and this rather favours the R.V. rendering.

γονεῦσιν ἀπειθεῖς, disowning what among all races has been regarded as the most binding human claim.

ἀχάριστοι, 'unthankful' — the same spirit applied more widely—the unwillingness to admit oneself under obligation to any. Gratitude is not only the paying of a debt, but the riveting of affection and even a source of power, because the person to whom you show gratitude is made thereby responsible in a sense for what you are and has an acknowledged share in all that you achieve. St. Paul obviously regards ingratitude as more than gross manners, as a serious weakening of the ties that make human brotherhood possible.

ἀνόσιοι, 'rejecting the law of God.' See n. on 1 Tim. i. 9.

3. ἄστοργοι, 'refusing natural affection.'

ἄσπονδοι, 'admitting of no truce,'

'implacable.' The idea is of people who forgive nothing and give up nothing in order to render amity possible.

διάβολοι, 'slanderers,' who spread enmity more actively by speaking evil of persons and parties and imputing base motives.

ἀκρατεῖς, 'without control over passions.' Aristotle (*Eth.* vii.) says of the ἀκρατής that εἰδὼς ὅτι φαῦλα πράττει διὰ πάθος—he acts παρὰ τὴν προαίρεσιν καὶ τὴν διάνοιαν. The ἀκρατής is not so far gone down as to be blind to moral differences, but at the critical moment the temptation is more present to him than the vision of better things—his tragedy is that so often he 'wishes he could.'

ἀνήμεροι, properly of uncivilised, savage people. Here therefore it means the temper that rejects all the claims of social life in the widest sense—is inhospitable, treats poverty as an object of ridicule, refuses the shelter of one's house in storm or danger, goes by on the other side to avoid having to help a man in distress, exults in the bloodshed of a gladiatorial show, and in a wider sense believes that 'might is right.'

ἀφιλάγαθοι, 'not lovers of good,' whether good persons or good life; but the words in the context, both here and with φιλάγαθος in Titus i. 8, suggest that the primary reference is to love of good *persons*.

4. προδόται. Probably St. Paul is thinking primarily of traitors in the Church, *e.g.* men who to compass private ends laid information before

ἢ φιλόθεοι, 5. ἔχοντες μόρφωσιν εὐσεβείας τὴν δὲ δύναμιν αὐτῆς ἠρνημένοι· καὶ τούτους ἀποτρέπου. 6. ἐκ τούτων γάρ εἰσιν οἱ ἐνδύνοντες εἰς τὰς οἰκίας καὶ αἰχμαλωτίζοντες γυναικάρια σεσωρευμένα ἁμαρτίαις, ἀγόμενα ἐπιθυμίαις ποικίλαις, 7. πάντοτε μανθάνοντα καὶ μηδέ-

the Roman authorities, which compelled these to take cognisance of the fact that so and so was a Christian.

προπετεῖς, reckless, headstrong—letting no consideration stop them when they want to reach something. Such a man could describe himself as a 'man of action,' and is a good instance of the vice that would be a virtue if it were kept under the control of higher principle.

τετυφωμένοι. See n. on 1 Tim. iii. 6.

φιλήδονοι μᾶλλον ἢ φιλόθεοι describes summarily the underlying motive, and closes the description with what is practically a repetition of its opening word φίλαυτοι. ἡδονή is capable of the widest meaning, but in such a compound as φιλήδονος it means the pleasures that appeal to the senses.

5. **ἔχοντες μόρφωσιν εὐσεβείας**, 'having an appearance of religion,' or, better, 'affecting a form of religion.' See Lightfoot's excursus on σχῆμα and μορφή in Phil. ii. He defines μορφή in its original sense as 'comprising all those sensible qualities which, striking the eye, lead to the conviction that we see such and such a thing'—when contrasted with σχῆμα it is that which is intrinsic and essential ('form') as opposed to that which is accidental and outward ('figure,' 'fashion'). But with regard to the present passage he observes: 'In two passages where St. Paul speaks of an appearance

which is superficial and unreal, though not using σχῆμα, he still avoids μορφή as inappropriate and adopts μόρφωσις instead (Rom. ii. 20, 2 Tim. iii. 5). Here the termination denotes the aiming after or affecting the μορφή.'

τὴν δύναμιν αὐτῆς ἠρνημένοι, 'having renounced its power,' i.e. its authority and power to control the life, its 'reality' as opposed to semblance.

6. **οἱ ἐνδύνοντες**, 'who make their way into.' The word means naturally 'enter,' and derives any idea of 'creeping'—secretly and treacherously—rather from the context in any special case.

γυναικάρια—diminutive of γυνή—'little women,' and therefore, contemptuously, 'feeble women.'

σεσωρευμένα, 'covered with a heap of.' The metaphor suggests the idea of being so covered that they cannot struggle out or get to the light.

ἀγόμενα ἐπιθυμίαις ποικίλαις, 'led hither and thither by varying desires'—the excitement of new doctrine, the pleasure of feeling themselves important and being able to patronise men-teachers.

7. **πάντοτε μανθάνοντα**. The Apostle does not deny that they have a creditable zeal for learning, in a sense, but their desire for novelty leads it astray. Johnson's warning, that 'Those writers who lay on the watch for novelty could have little

ποτε εἰς ἐπίγνωσιν ἀληθείας ἐλθεῖν δυνάμενα. 8. ὃν τρόπον δὲ Ἰαννῆς καὶ Ἰαμβρῆς ἀντέστησαν Μωϋσεῖ, οὕτως καὶ οὗτοι ἀνθίστανται τῇ ἀληθείᾳ, ἄνθρωποι κατε-

hope of greatness,' is still more true of the search for truth in religion.

ἐπίγνωσιν may well here stand for the intensified sense 'further knowledge,' 'full knowledge,' the preposition adding this to the simple word.

6-7. The description in these verses is remarkable. As leaders of the corrupted character described in verses 2-5, St. Paul gives a prominent place, as we might expect from the rest of the letter, to those who disseminated false teaching. The cunning by which they sought to get a hold over women first made them more dangerous, and is another evidence of the growing importance of women in the Church. That women are more susceptible than men to the suggestions of their spiritual guides may or may not be a fault according to the degree of independence and reserve maintained. But the danger was well illustrated in the history of the Friars, against whom one of the chief accusations was that, being preferred by women as confessors, they often exercised an unfitting and mercenary influence over them. Chaucer illustrates this in several places.

St. Paul's description of such men as 'making captives' of these women 'laden with sins' may, however, suggest a rather different idea, viz. that the women were conscience-stricken and welcomed such teachers as professed an esoteric knowledge of the ways of penance and absolution. Their 'varying desires' may imply their seeking first one method and then another by which they hoped to exchange the panic of conscious sin for the consciousness of sin forgiven. The comparison of such teachers to the magicians in v. 8 suggests that this was the kind of hold they exercised.

8. Jannes and Jambres are doubtless the magicians who (Ex. vii. 11) prevented Pharaoh's believing Moses by imitating the signs which he gave. The names are those of Jewish tradition, which relates other facts about them. Cf. vii. 19 in the Fragments of a Zadokite Work (Charles's *Pseudepigrapha*): 'For aforetime arose Moses and Aaron through the Prince of the Lights. But Belial raised Jochanneh and his brother with his evil device.'

The comparison suggests that the false teachers referred to by St. Paul professed to have as much γνῶσις as the Apostle, and even more. We may certainly see in it, therefore, a reference to the beginning of the false teachings that eventually became known as 'Gnostic.' It is perhaps well to note that Ephesus was a home of magic—the art of conferring spiritual or bodily benefit by spells or charms.

οὕτω, *i.e.* by imitating and pretending to surpass the truth as taught by St. Paul.

κατεφθαρμένοι τὸν νοῦν. See n. on 1 Tim. vi. 5. For νοῦς compare such passages as Rom. vii. 23, where see Sanday and Headlam's note ('It is the rational part of conscience,

φθαρμένοι τὸν νοῦν, ἀδόκιμοι περὶ τὴν πίστιν. 9. ἀλλ' οὐ προκόψουσιν ἐπὶ πλεῖον· ἡ γὰρ ἄνοια αὐτῶν ἔκδηλος ἔσται πᾶσιν, ὡς καὶ ἡ ἐκείνων ἐγένετο. 10. σὺ δὲ παρηκολούθησάς μου τῇ διδασκαλίᾳ, τῇ ἀγωγῇ, τῇ προθέσει, τῇ πίστει, τῇ μακροθυμίᾳ, τῇ ἀγάπῃ, τῇ ὑπομονῇ, 11. τοῖς διωγμοῖς, τοῖς παθήμασιν, οἷά μοι ἐγένετο ἐν Ἀντιοχείᾳ, ἐν Ἰκονίῳ, ἐν Λύστροις, οἵους διωγμοὺς ὑπήνεγκα, καὶ ἐκ πάντων με ἐρρύσατο ὁ Κύριος. 12. καὶ πάντες δὲ οἱ θέλοντες εὐσεβῶς ζῆν ἐν Χριστῷ Ἰησοῦ διωχθήσονται. 13. πονηροὶ δὲ ἄνθρωποι καὶ γόητες προκόψουσιν ἐπὶ τὸ χεῖρον, πλανῶντες καὶ πλανώμενοι. 14. σὺ δὲ μένε ἐν

the faculty which decides between right and wrong.')

ἀδόκιμοι, rejected when a sound test is applied. Cf. ii. 15.

9. οὐ προκόψουσιν. Cf. ii. 16, but there the meaning is 'They will get more and more corrupt'; here the meaning is 'They will not secure a wider acceptance.'

ὡς ἡ ἐκείνων ἐγένετο, exposed by subsequent failure. See Ex. viii. 18.

10. παρηκολούθησας [παρηκολούθηκας]. For the word see n. on 1 Tim. iv. 6. The Aorist is the right reading here. It states a fact about the past, implies nothing about the present.

ἀγωγῇ, conduct; προθέσει, purpose; μακροθυμία, ὑπομονῇ — see notes on 1 Tim. i. 16 and 2 Tim. ii. 10.

ἀγάπῃ, note on 1 Tim. i. 5.

11. οἷα — οἵους. Take these as parallel: 'such sufferings as befell me—such persecutions as I endured.'

The reference to Antioch, Iconium, Lystra points to the events of Acts xiii. 14-xiv. 22. It was probably at this time that Timothy became a Christian, and we may assume that he knew all that had been happening to the Apostle.

12. Timothy probably heard these same words on the occasion referred to—it is a reminder of the teaching of Acts xiv. 22.

καὶ — δὲ. 'Yea, and all . . .'

13. πονηροί, actively evil, with a will to do mischief.

γόητες, impostors. The word (from γοάω, to wail) was properly applied to the chanters of spells — hence fraudulent pretenders.

προκόψουσιν, as in ii. 16, 'will get more and more corrupt.'

πλανῶντες καὶ πλανώμενοι. Observe the order. A man may be deceived first and then deceive others, but the reverse is possible. He keeps repeating the claims or teaching by which he hopes to impose on others (e.g. for purposes of gain or influence) until he comes at last to believe in his own claims and teaching. His victims help him to this by flattery and admiration—he can hardly go back on all that he has said without sacrificing his whole stock-in-trade. Arguments used to

οἷς ἔμαθες καὶ ἐπιστώθης, εἰδὼς παρὰ τίνων ἔμαθες,
15. καὶ ὅτι ἀπὸ βρέφους ἱερὰ γράμματα οἶδας τὰ δυνά-

defend a position of which one is not sure more often convince the arguer than those to whom the arguments are addressed. It is for this reason that one so often hears a perfectly sincere person say, 'I always feel so much more clear after I have talked it over with some one'—in which case more thought with oneself and less speech with others would probably be wise.

This consideration is of importance to many teachers who are certainly not willingly πλανῶντες, but who accept without thought much that is for the time being orthodox with their party or their society, and repeat it until it becomes part of themselves and they are neither intellectually nor morally strong enough to go back on it.

14. ἐπιστώθης, 'wast assured of,' i.e. 'didst accept with conviction.'

παρὰ τίνων [παρὰ τίνος]. The plu. is the right reading, and the reference is to Lois and Eunice as well as to St. Paul himself. The character of the teacher is an argument for his truth: 'God cannot be wanting to them in Doctrine to whom he is so gracious in Life.' But the special reference here is to parental teaching and example, and more especially to parental teaching in the Bible. Parents who neglect their share in this hardly realise perhaps that they are leaving to others all that is most solemn and thoughtful in their sons, and they are hurt when they find that those others know more about their sons than they know themselves. Such a son may turn to his parents in some kind of trouble, but in difficulties of another kind he will turn naturally to those who have shared the solemn side of his life and experience. For sharing this the Bible is the great key. Present-day difficulties with regard to the nature of inspiration are often urged as an excuse for leaving such things to the expert, but the difficulty, if such there be, should be faced by parent and son together. The Advent of our Lord as the Messiah—so different from the expected one—must have presented to Eunice just as great a difficulty in the interpretation of the Old Testament as any difficulty presented by modern reconsideration of the nature of Biblical inspiration. And yet St. Paul at sixty is able to say to a man of forty, 'Remember that it was from your mother you learnt it.'

15. ἱερὰ γράμματα, 'sacred writings.' The Old Testament books collectively are usually spoken of in the N.T. as αἱ γραφαί, but compare Rom. i. 2, ἐν γραφαῖς ἁγίαις. The word ἱερός is applied to anything with external consecration, whence τὸ ἱερόν of the temple-precincts and τὰ ἱερά of the 'sacred things,' 1 Cor. ix. 13 (the only other use of the Adjective in the N.T.). ἅγιος rather refers to the inner character of holiness. Hence either word could be used of the Scriptures.

We cannot, however, assume that even in St. Paul's time the Jew had a 'Bible' with finally closed canon recognised by all. The Law

μενά σε σοφίσαι εἰς σωτηρίαν διὰ πίστεως τῆς ἐν Χριστῷ Ἰησοῦ. 16. πᾶσα γραφὴ θεόπνευστος καὶ ὠφέλιμος πρὸς

and the Prophets (including Joshua, Judges, Samuel, Kings) seem to have been fully recognised in this sense before 200 B.C. The other books —the Hagiographa—gradually received such recognition in the two following centuries. The prologue of the Greek version of Ecclesiasticus (written about 125 B.C.) speaks of 'the Law itself and the Prophecies and the rest of the books.' But such a phrase is vague, and even in the first century A.D. it was disputed whether e.g. the book of Ecclesiastes was to be considered canonical. A final line seems not to have been drawn until the Synod of Jamnia about 90 A.D.

τὰ δυνάμενά σε σοφίσαι. This claim for the Old Testament is of course more than that we should read it 'for example of life'—it implies that now as in St. Paul's day the Old Testament leads us on to Christ, and shows us the whole plan by which mankind was made ready for the revelation of Christ. The words διὰ πίστεως τῆς ἐν Χριστῷ Ἰησοῦ should be taken with σοφίσαι —the Old Testament is to be read with the intelligence born of a personal faith in Christ. 'The scriptures are not understood but with the same Spirit that writ them.'

16. R.V., 'Every scripture inspired of God is also profitable for . . .,' but the margin admits the possibility of taking θεόπνευστος as part of the predicate. The former is probably right, because there was no occasion—least of all to Timothy —for declaring formally the inspiration of Scripture, which indeed was not questioned. There is also something incongruous in the combination of words, 'Every scripture is inspired of God and useful for . . .'

θεόπνευστος, 'given by divine inspiration.' The word is applied to dreams by Plutarch.

The rabbinical reverence for the exact word and letter of Scripture is an evidence of belief in a verbal and mechanical inspiration, and tended to extend such a belief. It is quite probable that St. Paul's teachers took such a view. But it is hardly possible to think that, *if the question had been raised as a theory or dogma*, St. Paul would have upheld such a view. It is from one point of view a matter of regret that in none of his extant writings is the theory of the subject touched upon. Where his quotations are not simply 'literary,' he uses passages from the Old Testament in their accepted sense and without ever seeming to question their literal accuracy or accepted application. But, on the other hand, he quotes the sense with a freedom which is inconceivable in a Hebrew scholar if he believed the Hebrew words to be words dictated by the Holy Spirit; and most of his quotations (about 70 out of 84) are from the Septuagint translation in preference to the Hebrew. The student should read the excursus on St. Paul's use of the O.T. at the end of chap. x. in Sanday and Headlam's *Romans*.

Any theory of inspiration which takes away the personality of the writer or makes him incapable of

διδασκαλίαν, πρὸς ἐλεγμόν, πρὸς ἐπανόρθωσιν, πρὸς παιδείαν τὴν ἐν δικαιοσύνῃ· 17. ἵνα ἄρτιος ᾖ ὁ τοῦ Θεοῦ ἄνθρωπος, πρὸς πᾶν ἔργον ἀγαθὸν ἐξηρτισμένος.

error is open in varying degrees to the same objection as the theory of verbal inspiration. Various theories have been formed, trying to keep something of the 'mechanical' view while avoiding some of its obvious difficulties. But the view widely held now lays stress on the inspiration of the person rather than on the inspiration of the book. If a man is more than others filled with divine grace and the enlightenment of the Holy Spirit he becomes in proportion more able to convey a revelation of truth without having his personal qualities merged in an overwhelming influence from without, and without being made incapable of error. For a summary on the subject see the article *Bible* in Hastings' Dictionary.

ἐλεγμόν [ἔλεγχον], 'reproof' (R.V.) or 'conviction.'

ἐπανόρθωσιν, 'correction' (R.V.)—perhaps rather 'recovery,' 'the bringing back into the right way.'

παιδείαν, 'discipline' (R.V. marg.).

The four words seem primarily to refer to our use of Scripture towards others, but not excluding the application to ourselves even of the discipline. What we apply to others we need to apply to ourselves at times.

17. ἄρτιος ... ἐξηρτισμένος, 'complete' . . . 'furnished completely' (R.V.). The words come from the stem ἀρ, the primary meaning of which was 'join'—from which come ἄριστος, ἀραρίσκω, ἄροτρον, ἀρετή. ἄρτιος therefore meant 'fitted with all its parts,' 'complete.' Perhaps 'fully equipped' is as exact an equivalent as we could find for ἐξηρτισμένος.

ὁ τοῦ Θεοῦ ἄνθρωπος. See n. on 1 Tim. vi. 11. The phrase, from its use of the prophets and messengers of God, has a special reference to the Christian minister, but is not here limited to him except in the sense in which every member has a ministry in the Church.

CHAPTER IV

1. ^aΔιαμαρτύρομαι ἐνώπιον τοῦ Θεοῦ καὶ Χριστοῦ Ἰησοῦ τοῦ μέλλοντος κρίνειν ζῶντας καὶ νεκρούς, καὶ τὴν ἐπιφάνειαν αὐτοῦ καὶ τὴν βασιλείαν ^bαὐτοῦ, 2. κήρυξον τὸν λόγον, ἐπίστηθι εὐκαίρως ἀκαίρως, ἔλεγξον, ἐπιτί-

^a Διαμαρτύρομαι   ^b αὐτοῦ·

'1-8. Final exhortation to earnestness, with mention of special reasons: (1) the growing tendency to unsound doctrine (3-4); (2) the probability that he will soon have to bear the burden without the Apostle's help (6-8).

1. διαμαρτύρομαι. See n. on 1 Tim. v. 21.

καὶ τὴν ἐπιφάνειαν. Undoubtedly the right reading is καὶ τὴν ἐπιφάνειαν (R.V. and W.H.) for T.R. κατὰ τὴν ἐπιφάνειαν. The Accusative expresses that by which one adjures, originating in the Accusative that naturally followed διαμαρτύρομαι in its literal sense of 'I call to witness.' Cf. Soph. O.C. 813: μαρτύρομαι τούσδ', οὐ σέ, 'I call these to witness, not thee.'

The ἐπιφάνεια means of course the second coming of our Lord, as in 1 Tim. vi. 14. In charging Timothy 'by this coming' the Apostle means to charge him to have the same earnestness now that he would necessarily have in the immediate presence of Christ. τὴν βασιλείαν αὐτοῦ, the whole manifestation of Christ's kingdom among men, including the ἐπιφάνεια.

The reading of the R.V. marg., 'I testify... both of his appearing and his kingdom,' would be justified by the N.T. use of διαμαρτύρομαι, e.g. Acts xx. 21, 24: διαμαρτυρόμενος τὴν εἰς Θεὸν μετάνοιαν—διαμαρτύρασθαι τὸ εὐαγγέλιον. But the context here (especially the words ἐνώπιον ... καὶ νεκρούς) is entirely against it.

2. κήρυξον, ἐπίστηθι, etc. As the actions implied are to be continued and repeated, we might have expected *Present* Imperatives. But the proper force of the Aorist is to signify the completion and conclusion of an action as a whole, and this is exactly what is emphasised here, as if the writer were saying, 'Preach the word right up to the coming of our Lord.' Cf. τὴν καλὴν παραθήκην φύλαξον in i. 14.

ἐπίστηθι. From meaning (1) stand by or near a thing, this word came to mean (2) fix one's mind or attention on, and so (3) be urgent, instant.

εὐκαίρως, ἀκαίρως, *i.e.* seizing every

μῆσον, παρακάλεσον, ἐν πάσῃ μακροθυμίᾳ καὶ διδαχῇ.

opportunity and risking the accusation of 'bad taste' by bringing in the subject when people do not want it. Of course St. Paul does not mean that the preacher is to be wanting in tact, but he does mean that he will miss half his opportunities if he limits himself to the set times. If a minister of Christ is a guest in a house where unworthy things are going on it may seem ἄκαιρον to take exception, but a quiet word with his host may be so εὔκαιρον that it may make him that host's confidant and confessor. We are far too much the slaves of 'times and seasons,' and to wait for a more convenient season often means that the word is never spoken at all. The 'out of season' depends more on the way in which a thing is done than on the time at which it is done. 'There is nothing spoken or done in the company where he is but comes under his test and censure. If it be well spoken or done, he takes occasion to commend and enlarge it; if ill, he presently lays hold of it lest the poison steal into some young and unwary spirits. ... But this he does discreetly, with mollifying and supplying words: This was not so well said as it might have been forborn; We cannot allow this; or else, If the thing will admit interpretation; Your meaning is not thus, but thus; or, So far indeed what you say is true and well said; but this will not stand. This is called *keeping God's watch*. ... Besides, if he perceive in company any discourse tending to ill, either by the wickedness or quarrelsomeness thereof, he either prevents it judiciously or breaks it off seasonably by some diversion. There is much preaching in friendliness' (George Herbert).

ἔλεγξον. The classical meaning of this word is to question with a view to convincing or convicting, and so 'to reprove.' R.V. text has 'reprove' here, marg. 'bring to the proof.' There does not seem to be any passage in the N.T. in which 'reprove' is inapplicable as a translation, though Dr. Armitage Robinson rightly points out that in Eph. v. 11, St. John iii. 20, 'expose' is rather better.

ἐπιτίμησον, 'rebuke'—implies more sharpness than 'reprove.'

μακροθυμίᾳ. See n. on 1 Tim. i. 16. Even rebuke must not be prompted by the sense of provocation and must aim at teaching. Otherwise 'you have reproved divers things worthy of reproof, but in a manner worthy to be reproved ... not with that gravity wherewith such faults ought to be reproved: like one puffed up and not like a mourner.' Rebuke from authority depends for its effect on its manner as much as on its rightness; if it robs the person of dignity and self-respect it has taken from him one of his best faculties for recovery. The object of rebuke should generally be 'to make a man feel what he remembers to have felt before, but with a great increase of sensibility.' In all such exercise of authority we need to remember the warning of the *De Imitatione*: 'Raro sine laesione conscientiae ad silentium redimus.' 'Possunt verba sonare *sed spiritum non conferunt*.'

3. ἔσται γὰρ καιρὸς ὅτε τῆς ὑγιαινούσης διδασκαλίας οὐκ ἀνέξονται, ἀλλὰ κατὰ τὰς ἐπιθυμίας τὰς ἰδίας ἑαυτοῖς ἐπισωρεύσουσι διδασκάλους κνηθόμενοι τὴν ἀκοήν, 4. καὶ ἀπὸ μὲν τῆς ἀληθείας τὴν ἀκοὴν ἀποστρέψουσιν, ἐπὶ δὲ τοὺς μύθους ἐκτραπήσονται. 5. σὺ δὲ νῆφε ἐν πᾶσι, κακοπάθησον, ἔργον ποίησον εὐαγγελιστοῦ, τὴν διακονίαν

3. ὑγιαινούσης. See n. on 1 Tim. i. 10.

3-4. The first stage described is the negative one of distaste for the truth as it has been presented to them. With some this comes because it makes too great demands on them—perhaps morally; with others it comes because it does not flatter their intellectual side sufficiently. But the most common cause is the consciousness that their religion so far has not done for them what they hoped for—they looked for some overwhelming power and it has not come. Instead of seeking the cause of this in himself, a man is inclined to blame something outside; the teaching he gets is not definite enough, the preaching is feeble and the preachers unspiritual, or the portion of the Church to which he belongs must be without authority and credentials if it exercises so little power. In the search, therefore, for something that will give him more spiritual feeling and consciousness of power he 'seeks other teachers.'

This is the second stage, because he now consciously places himself under the guidance of men chosen by himself. Though conscious of previous failure, he does not doubt that he is wise enough to choose his spiritual guides. Notice the emphasis on individual choice in the words τὰς ἰδίας—ἑαυτοῖς.

The last stage is described in verse 4. Hitherto he has kept up the appearance of being an impartial seeker after truth, has justified his action by the plea of 'eclecticism,' or the desire to 'hear all sides of the question.' Now he shows the peculiar animus of the pervert, and refuses even to listen to arguments in favour of what he formerly professed to believe. Fantastic μῦθοι have come to exercise a peculiar fascination over him and he surrenders himself to them.

For the μῦθοι see note on 1 Tim. i. 4. The way in which St. Paul speaks of them here implies a definite kind of wrong teaching, which Timothy would understand without further specification.

5. νῆφε, be alert and watchful against the danger. The metaphor is of course from the inability of the drunken man to guard against anything.

κακοπάθησον. Here the reference is to the hardships of ministerial toil.

εὐαγγελιστοῦ. Philip is called 'the evangelist' in Acts xxi. 8, and from what is said of him we should naturally conclude that the word was applied to one who went and preached Christ in new districts.

σου πληροφόρησον. 6. ἐγὼ γὰρ ἤδη σπένδομαι, καὶ ὁ καιρὸς τῆς ἐμῆς ἀναλύσεως ἐφέστηκε. 7. τὸν ἀγῶνα τὸν καλὸν ἠγώνισμαι, τὸν δρόμον τετέλεκα, τὴν πίστιν τετήρηκα· 8. λοιπὸν ἀπόκειταί μοι ὁ τῆς δικαιοσύνης στέφανος, ὃν ἀποδώσει μοι ὁ Κύριος ἐν ἐκείνῃ τῇ ἡμέρᾳ, ὁ δίκαιος κριτής· οὐ μόνον δὲ ἐμοί, ἀλλὰ καὶ πᾶσι τοῖς ἠγαπηκόσι τὴν ἐπιφάνειαν αὐτοῦ.

The word also occurs in Eph. iv. 11, and this, like the present passage, is quite in harmony with such an understanding of the word. Here Timothy is urged not only to build up but also to win more souls for Christ. He is not called an evangelist—in one sense that was not his main work at Ephesus—but he is told to 'do the work of an evangelist.' See Introd., p. xv. An official position in the Church must not engross us so completely with its regular duties to the members as to make us lose all missionary spirit to those that are outside. The evangelist is not an official—there is no evidence that there was an 'order' of evangelists.

τὴν διακονίαν, quite general for any 'ministry,' 'service.' Cf. 1 Tim. i. 12.

πληροφόρησον, 'fulfil,' as in St. Luke i. 1. The word has other meanings, e.g. in Rom. xv. 13 ('fill'), Rom. iv. 21 ('fully assure'), Col. iv. 12 (where see Lightfoot's note), but the meaning here is certainly 'fulfil.'

6. The second reason for St. Paul's exhortation. See n. on verse 1.

σπένδομαι. Cf. Phil. ii. 17. The giving up of life is compared to a drink-offering or libation offered to God. Lightfoot compares Seneca's words when he was dying (Tac. *Ann.*, xv. 64): 'Respergens proximos servorum addita voce, libare se liquorem illum Jovi liberatori.'

ἀναλύσεως. The word ἀναλύω was used of the loosing of a ship from its moorings, and so 'departure' in any sense.

7. τὸν ἀγῶνα τὸν καλὸν ἠγώνισμαι, never daunted by opposition.

τὸν δρόμον τετέλεκα, never flagging through weariness.

τὴν πίστιν τετήρηκα, never careless as a watchman.

8. ὁ τῆς δικαιοσύνης στέφανος, the crown of victory due to righteousness. Alford well quotes Pope Coelestinus: 'Dei tanta est erga omnes homines bonitas ut eorum velit esse merita quae sunt ipsius dona.' The commonest use of στέφανος was for the wreath given as a prize at the games, and doubtless the metaphor here is from that.

τοῖς ἠγαπηκόσι τὴν ἐπιφάνειαν αὐτοῦ. As R.V., 'that have loved His appearing.' We need not confine the last word to the second Advent of Christ.

9. Σπούδασον ἐλθεῖν πρός με ταχέως· 10. Δημᾶς γάρ με ἐγκατέλιπεν, ἀγαπήσας τὸν νῦν αἰῶνα, καὶ ἐπορεύθη

9-18. **Personal matters. Timothy is summoned because St. Paul is left almost alone.**

10. Demas was with St. Paul in his first imprisonment (Col. iv. 14, Philemon 24). Notice that when comparing others with Timothy in Ph. ii. 20-21, St. Paul uses a similar expression οἱ πάντες γὰρ τὰ ἑαυτῶν ζητοῦσιν, and it is possible that Demas is included in this condemnation.

We need not assume that ἀγαπήσας τὸν νῦν αἰῶνα implies more than fear of persecution and desire for safety. To stay at Rome in the height of Neronian persecution required more than ordinary courage. The excuse that 'I can do no good by staying' was ready to hand, and we may call to mind the legend that St. Peter himself was induced to leave Rome and was turned back by the vision of Christ. Nevertheless, the departure of Demas has caused him to be placed among the apostates in Christian tradition.

τὸν νῦν αἰῶνα, literally 'the present age.' αἰών is the same word as the Latin *aevum*, and denotes a period of time. As explained in n. on 1 Tim. i. 16, the Jew conceived of time as divided into a series of αἰῶνες, of which 'the age to come,' 'the Messianic age,' was opposed to 'the present age.' The latter phrase naturally therefore took on a moral significance, implying the life of the world as it is now with all its imperfect aims, and imperfect life as opposed to the life of perfection that was to come under the glory of Christ's rule. So that ὁ νῦν αἰών may be translated 'the present life,' 'the life of this world,' almost with the signification which we attach to the phrase 'worldly life.' Cf. Rom. xii. 2, 'Be not fashioned according to this world' (τῷ αἰῶνι τούτῳ).

In order to understand the position of St. Paul and his friends at Rome, the student should read a description of what occurred there after the great fire, especially Tac. *Ann.*, xv. 44: 'Neither the emperor's generous gifts nor the rites employed for propitiating the gods banished the suspicion that the fire had been deliberately ordered. Therefore to get rid of such reports Nero accused the people commonly called Christians who were hated for their abominable crimes, and he subjected these to the most exquisite tortures. The name had originated with Christus, who, in the reign of Tiberius, had suffered the death penalty by order of the procurator, Pontius Pilate. A dangerous superstition had thus been checked for the moment, but it broke out again, not only in Judaea, the country of its origin, but even in Rome itself, whither all things that are horrible and shameful find their way from all parts of the world, receiving a ready welcome there. Accordingly, in the first place those were arrested who admitted their crime, and then through their information great numbers were convicted, not so much of any part in firing the city as of

εἰς Θεσσαλονίκην, Κρήσκης εἰς Γαλατίαν, Τίτος εἰς Δαλματίαν· 11. Λουκᾶς ἐστι μόνος μετ' ἐμοῦ. Μάρκον

hostility to mankind in general. Their sufferings were turned into sport. Some were done to death clad in the skins of beasts and torn by hounds; many were crucified or burnt to death, and some, when daylight failed, served the purpose of an illumination in the nighttime. Nero lent his gardens for this spectacle and gave an exhibition in the circus, himself going among the common folk in the garb of a charioteer or riding on a car. Whence, though the accused were guilty and deserving of the severest punishment, the people began to pity them, as suffering not so much for the benefit of the state as for the satisfaction of one man's savage instincts.' See Introd., p. xi.

Κρήσκης . . . Τίτος. The verb with each is ἐπορεύθη, but ἀγαπήσας τὸν νῦν αἰῶνα is not carried on to them. All we can infer is that they went without being sent—this is almost implied by the contrast of ἀπέστειλα in v. 12.

Of Crescens we know nothing. Titus is not mentioned by name in the Acts. He was a Gentile, and it was in his case that the question of circumcision was raised (Gal. ii. 1, 3). He visited Corinth on St. Paul's behalf (2 Cor. xii. 18, etc). After St. Paul's first imprisonment he visited Crete with the Apostle and was left there (Titus i. 5). From the present verse we gather that he was with St. Paul during part of his second imprisonment but had now gone to Dalmatia, which was part of Illyricum, east of the Adriatic. See, further, Introd., p. xxi.

11. Of all St. Paul's companions St. Luke would seem to have been with him most constantly. So far as our evidence goes (and assuming that St. Luke is the author of the Acts) he joined him first at Troas during the second missionary journey, accompanied him to Philippi, joined him there on the third journey and remained with him till his arrival in Jerusalem, afterwards accompanying him to Rome (Acts xvi. 10-17, xx. 5-15, xxi. 1-18, xxvii. 1 to xxviii. 16). For his presence during the first imprisonment, cf. Col. iv. 14, Philemon 24. As he is now again with the Apostle, the companionship had been fairly constant for a space of about sixteen years and has sometimes been accounted for by the supposition that St. Paul had an infirmity which needed frequent medical attendance. From Col. iv. 14 we gather that St. Luke was a physician. This constant companionship doubtless influenced St. Luke's purpose and line of thought in the writing of his gospel.

The present verse is interesting on a minor point, as a warning against conjectures based on literary circumstantial evidence. If this verse had not been written it would almost certainly have been held by some that Luke and Titus were the same man, since there is nothing elsewhere inconsistent with such a theory and neither of them is mentioned by name in the Acts.

ἀναλαβὼν ἄγε μετὰ σεαυτοῦ· ἔστι γάρ μοι εὔχρηστος εἰς διακονίαν. 12. Τυχικὸν δὲ ἀπέστειλα εἰς Ἔφεσον. 13. τὸν φαιλόνην ὃν ἀπέλιπον ἐν Τρωάδι παρὰ Κάρπῳ ἐρχόμενος φέρε, καὶ τὰ βιβλία, μάλιστα τὰς μεμβράνας.

St. Mark's association with St. Paul began earlier than St. Luke's, when he accompanied the Apostle and Barnabas from Jerusalem to Antioch (Acts xii. 25), but he left them at Perga on the first missionary journey (Acts xiii. 13) under circumstances which led later on to an estrangement between Paul and Barnabas (Acts xv. 37). St. Mark does not appear again in St. Paul's life till the first imprisonment, about twelve years later, when he was with the Apostle (Col. iv. 10, Philemon 24). We cannot say whether St. Mark reached Rome before St. Paul's death in consequence of the summons of this verse, but tradition associates him rather with St. Peter at Rome (cf. 1 Pet. v. 13).

ἀναλαβών, taking up on the way. Cf. Acts xx. 13 for the word.

εὔχρηστος εἰς διακονίαν. A striking phrase when taken with Acts xv. 38: 'Paul thought not good to take with them him who withdrew from them from Pamphylia and went not with them to the work.' The formerly unworthy colleague has now the honour of being summoned as likely to be specially helpful in St. Paul's direst need and danger. And the Apostle has no doubt that he will come. It is hardly fanciful to suppose that St. Paul's sharpness on that former occasion had helped to build up the character of Mark. Their friendship was not broken, or at any rate had been renewed. Friendship is not conserved by acquiescing in a man's weakness but by siding with his best against his worst in spite of the danger of temporary estrangement.

12. Τυχικὸν δὲ ἀπέστειλα εἰς Ἔφεσον. As St. Paul is presumably writing to Ephesus (but see Introd., p. xi.), and Tychicus probably arrived there before the letter, it is natural to suppose that the emphasis is on ἀπέστειλα as opposed to ἐπορεύθη. St. Paul does not want Timothy to suspect Tychicus as one of those who had deserted him.

Tychicus was of the province of Asia, and one of St. Paul's companions on the journey to Jerusalem (Acts xx. 4). He is also mentioned as the bearer of the Epistles to the Ephesians and Colossians.

13. φελόνην or φαιλόνην, a Greek form of the Latin word *paenula*. It was a sleeveless cloak of thick cloth, sometimes with a cape—resembling an Inverness cloak.

ἐν Τρωάδι. St. Paul was in Troas Acts xx. 4, but probably he had been there more recently.

βιβλία — μεμβράνας. The former would be papyrus *rolls* (not in *book* shape), and literary works were always produced in this form till long after St. Paul's time. Any copy of the Scriptures that St. Paul possessed would be in this form. The parchments (*i.e.* skins prepared as a writing surface) were too expensive to be used in the production of

14. Ἀλέξανδρος ὁ χαλκεὺς πολλά μοι κακὰ ἐνεδείξατο·
ἀποδώσει αὐτῷ ὁ Κύριος κατὰ τὰ ἔργα αὐτοῦ· 15. ὃν καὶ
σὺ φυλάσσου, λίαν γὰρ ἀντέστη τοῖς ἡμετέροις λόγοις.
16. ἐν τῇ πρώτῃ μου ἀπολογίᾳ οὐδείς μοι παρεγένετο,

literary works of any length, and their common use was for accounts and notes; the writing on them could be washed out, so that they could be used again and again. These were sometimes made up in book shape. In noticing St. Paul's request the student will remember the comparative expensiveness of all books in his time. The papyrus writing material was made from the pith of the Egyptian reed of that name. Though the possibility of making a writing surface of rag material was an early discovery, it was not at all common in Europe till the time of the invention of printing, and even then every sheet had to be made separately by hand until the nineteenth century. It is, of course, the use of wood-pulp for rag that finally made paper so cheap.

14. The name Alexander was too common for us to be certain of any identification—either with the Jewish representative in Acts xix. 33 or with the Alexander of 1 Tim. i. 20. Χαλκεύς means a worker in any metal, and the present Alexander was obviously at Ephesus.

πολλά . . . ἐνεδείξατο, 'did me much wrong'—something additional to the opposition referred to in v. 15.

ἀποδώσει is the correct reading for T.R. ἀποδῴη.

16. It is not possible to describe with any certainty the conditions of St. Paul's trial, especially because there were two systems of criminal jurisdiction working at Rome in Nero's time. On the one hand, there was the old system of *quaestiones perpetuae* still in full working order. On the other hand, through the practically universal authority of the princeps any criminal case could now be brought before him or a judge nominated by him, and under this system the criminal jurisdiction in Rome and for 100 miles round was specially delegated to the *praefectus urbi*. As we do not know the nature of the charges brought against St. Paul, it is only possible to surmise that they were such as would probably cause him to be brought before an imperial court. The phrase πάντα τὰ ἔθνη suggests that a great concourse was present at the trial, and we may imagine it as taking place in a large hall of the basilica shape. The phrase ἐν τῇ πρώτῃ μου ἀπολογίᾳ probably refers to the practice, when two charges were brought against a prisoner, of hearing each separately.

οὐδείς μοι παρεγένετο. Of course St. Paul could have a *patronus* to speak for him if he wished, but in addition to the patronus, whom we should call 'counsel for the defence,' it had always been customary to allow a prisoner to produce *advocati*, persons of weight likely to impress the court, who stood by him in the court, giving him the countenance of their public support and their testimony as to his character, and

ἀλλὰ πάντες με ἐγκατέλιπον· μὴ αὐτοῖς λογισθείη. 17. ὁ δὲ Κύριός μοι παρέστη, καὶ ἐνεδυνάμωσέ με, ἵνα δι' ἐμοῦ τὸ κήρυγμα πληροφορηθῇ, καὶ ἀκούσῃ πάντα τὰ ἔθνη· καὶ ἐρρύσθην ἐκ στόματος λέοντος. 18. ῥύσεταί με ὁ Κύριος ἀπὸ παντὸς ἔργου πονηροῦ, καὶ σώσει εἰς τὴν βασιλείαν αὐτοῦ τὴν ἐπουράνιον· ᾧ ἡ δόξα εἰς τοὺς αἰῶνας τῶν αἰώνων. ἀμήν.

19. Ἄσπασαι Πρίσκαν καὶ Ἀκύλαν, καὶ τὸν Ὀνησιφόρου

on occasion helping the conduct of his case by their suggestions. The fact that the word *advocatus* was coming to be used as synonymous with *patronus* probably shows that the position of the *advocati* was becoming a more legal one. But St. Paul seems to imply here that nobody had the courage to come forward and stand by his side as an advocatus. It is possible that a person who so came forward must be a Roman citizen; but in any case we may infer that the charge against St. Paul was a very dangerous one.

17. ὁ δὲ Κύριός μοι παρέστη. Where no man came forward St. Paul sees, as it were, a vision of Christ coming forward as his *advocatus* into the part of the court reserved for the prisoner. Perhaps the thought also occurred to St. Paul that the Greek word for *advocatus* was παράκλητος, the name applied to the Holy Spirit in St. John's writings (translated Comforter in our version, but more correctly Advocate), and that the Holy Spirit is described as in a sense our champion before assemblies of men : 'When he is come, he will reprove the world of sin and of righteous-ness and of judgment' (St. John xvi. 8).

ἐνεδυνάμωσε. 'When they deliver you up, be not anxious how or what ye shall speak : for it shall be given you in that hour what ye shall speak. For it is not ye that speak, but the Spirit of your Father that speaketh in you' (St. Matt. x. 19-20).

ἵνα ... τὸ κήρυγμα πληροφορηθῇ. The prisoner arraigned the world. The Apostle is more concerned with the opportunity of spreading the word than with the danger to his own life.

ἐκ στόματος λέοντος, a metaphor for a great danger as in Ps. xxi. 21. But Alford (arguing from the following mention of πᾶν ἔργον πονηρόν) thinks it means the devil, into whose power the Apostle would have fallen if he had failed through weakness to make a good confession.

18. The mention of deliverance from physical danger makes the Apostle think of deliverance from the greater spiritual danger. Cf. the words of the Lord's Prayer, ῥῦσαι ἡμᾶς ἀπὸ τοῦ πονηροῦ (St. Matt. vi. 13).

19. Aquila was a Jew of Pontus. His wife Prisca (or Priscilla) may

οἶκον. 20. Ἔραστος ἔμεινεν ἐν Κορίνθῳ· Τρόφιμον δὲ ἀπέλιπον ἐν Μιλήτῳ ἀσθενοῦντα. 21. σπούδασον πρὸ χειμῶνος ἐλθεῖν. ἀσπάζεταί σε Εὔβουλος, καὶ Πούδης, καὶ Λῖνος, καὶ Κλαυδία, καὶ οἱ ἀδελφοὶ πάντες. 22. Ὁ Κύριος μετὰ τοῦ πνεύματός σου. ἡ χάρις μεθ᾽ ὑμῶν.

have been of good Roman family. Expelled from Rome with the Jews in 52 A.D. they met St. Paul at Corinth, entertained him there (Acts xviii. 2-3), and went with him to Ephesus (v. 18), where they taught Apollos (v. 26). In Rom. xvi. 3 we read of their being at Rome again, with their house a place of assembly for Christians. The present verse shows that they had returned to Ephesus. These travels would suggest that Aquila was a merchant, and Acts xviii. 3 states that he was a tentmaker. The occurrence of both names in a cemetery at Rome connected with the Acilia gens suggests that Aquila was a freedman of that family. See further the excursus in Sanday and Headlam's *Romans*, xvi. 4.

For Onesiphorus see i. 16.

20. Erastus is perhaps the same as the 'treasurer' of Corinth mentioned in Rom. xvi. 23.

Trophimus was an Ephesian who had accompanied St. Paul to Jerusalem (Acts xx. 4) and was the occasion of the attack upon him because he was suspected of having taken him, though a Gentile, into the inner court of the temple precincts (Acts xxi. 29).

21. Of Eubulus we know nothing. Pudens and Claudia are, of course, common Roman names. For theories which identify them with characters in Martial and make Claudia a British woman of high rank, see Hastings' *Dictionary of the Bible*. Linus is reasonably identified with the first bishop of Rome (as stated by Eusebius).

Η ΠΡΟΣ ΤΙΤΟΝ ΕΠΙΣΤΟΛΗ

ΠΑΥΛΟΥ

CHAPTER I

1. Παῦλος δοῦλος Θεοῦ ἀπόστολος δὲ Ἰησοῦ Χριστοῦ, κατὰ πίστιν ἐκλεκτῶν Θεοῦ καὶ ἐπίγνωσιν ἀληθείας τῆς κατ᾽ εὐσέβειαν, 2. ἐπ᾽ ἐλπίδι ζωῆς αἰωνίου, ἣν ἐπηγγείλατο ὁ ἀψευδὴς Θεὸς πρὸ χρόνων αἰωνίων, 3. ἐφανέρωσε

1-4. The greeting.

1. For the designation Παῦλος ἀπόστολος, see n. on 1 Tim. i. 1; for the word ἐκλεκτῶν, 2 Tim. ii. 10; ἐπίγνωσιν, 1 Tim. ii. 4; εὐσέβειαν,

δοῦλος Θεοῦ. The phrase in this exact form as a superscription occurs only here, but compare the δοῦλος Ἰησοῦ Χριστοῦ of Rom. i. 1—also Phil. i. 1, James i. 1. As implying *completeness* and *permanence* of the service (see n. on 2 Tim. ii. 24) δοῦλος Θεοῦ was applicable even by heathen to the votary of a particular god. Compare the way in which it is used by the woman with a spirit of divination in Acts xvi. 17.

κατὰ πίστιν. The preposition should be taken in the same sense as in κατ᾽ ἐπαγγελίαν ζωῆς in 2 Tim. i. 1, viz. 'for the furtherance of.'

2. ἐπ᾽ ἐλπίδι, 'in the hope of.' The classical use of ἐπί to express *conditions* enabled it to express any accompanying circumstances which qualified or limited a fact. Cf. Rom. viii. 20, 'Creation was subjected to vanity, ἐπ᾽ ἐλπίδι.' The phrase here naturally attaches itself to κατὰ πίστιν . . . καὶ ἐπίγνωσιν ἀληθείας.

ζωῆς αἰωνίου. See n. on 1 Tim. i. 16.

ἐπηγγείλατο. This is a good instance of the distinction between ἐπαγγέλλομαι (promise freely) and ὑπισχνοῦμαι (which could be used of a promise made as a kind of bargain on conditions), because God is here represented as having made this promise to man *from all eternity*. For πρὸ χρόνων αἰωνίων see n. on 2 Tim. i. 9 and 1 Tim. i. 16.

ἀψευδής, only here in the N.T.

δὲ καιροῖς ἰδίοις τὸν λόγον αὐτοῦ ἐν κηρύγματι ὃ ἐπιστεύθην ἐγὼ κατ' ἐπιταγὴν τοῦ σωτῆρος ἡμῶν Θεοῦ, 4. Τίτῳ γνησίῳ τέκνῳ κατὰ κοινὴν πίστιν· χάρις καὶ εἰρήνη ἀπὸ Θεοῦ πατρὸς καὶ Χριστοῦ Ἰησοῦ τοῦ σωτῆρος ἡμῶν. 5. Τούτου χάριν ἀπέλιπόν σε ἐν Κρήτῃ, ἵνα τὰ λείποντα ἐπιδιορθώσῃ, καὶ καταστήσῃς κατὰ πόλιν πρεσβυτέρους, ὡς ἐγώ σοι διεταξάμην· 6. εἴ τις ἐστὶν ἀνέγκλητος, μιᾶς

3. **καιροῖς ἰδίοις**, as in 1 Tim. vi. 15, 'at His own appointed time.' But R.V. marg. 'in its own seasons' is possible, *i.e.* 'when the fulness of time came.'

τὸν λόγον αὐτοῦ. This substitution of a different object in the second clause of a relative sentence is quite classical.

For the thought cf. Rom. xvi. 25, μυστηρίου χρόνοις αἰωνίοις σεσιγημένου φανερωθέντος δὲ νῦν. God's purpose had been the same from all eternity, but no study of history or philosophy had enabled man to see it in its working before the revelation in Christ.

4. **γνησίῳ τέκνῳ, χάρις, εἰρήνη**. See n. on 1 Tim. i. 2.

5-9. The reason for leaving Titus in Crete—to complete the arrangements made by St. Paul and especially to appoint πρεσβύτεροι in each city.

For the occasion see Introd., p. xi. For the meaning of πρεσβύτεροι see note on 1 Tim. iii. 1. With regard to their appointment, as there explained, Titus is simply exercising the Apostle's authority as his delegate. To regard him as exercising *episcopal* authority over all Crete is doubtless true in fact, but to apply the name Bishop to him (at any rate at this time) is incorrect, and probably it is equally incorrect to regard him as holding any definite office for the purpose—his authority is due to his representing the Apostle for the time being. Notice that St. Paul uses πρεσβυτέρους (v. 5) and ἐπίσκοπον (v. 7) of the same ministry, just as the Ephesian πρεσβύτεροι in Acts xx. 17 are called ἐπίσκοποι in xx. 28.

5. **τὰ λείποντα**, the things lacking, *i.e.* what St. Paul had not been able to attend to.

κατὰ πόλιν. We gather from this that the Church had already spread in Crete, and that the Apostle had perhaps spent a considerable period there.

6. The description of the character required for a πρεσβύτερος must be compared with that in 1 Tim. iii. 1-7. The points emphasised are almost identical, though the actual phraseology is only identical in five—the variation being indeed rather striking in two letters written so near together. 1 Tim. iii. 6, 7 adds two points not expressly given here, viz. (1) μὴ νεόφυτον; (2) δεῖ μαρτυρίαν καλὴν ἔχειν ἀπὸ τῶν ἔξωθεν.

μιᾶς γυναικὸς ἀνήρ, etc. See n. on 1 Tim. iii. 2.

γυναικὸς ἀνήρ, τέκνα ἔχων πιστά, μὴ ἐν κατηγορίᾳ ἀσωτίας ἢ ἀνυπότακτα. 7. δεῖ γὰρ τὸν ἐπίσκοπον ἀνέγκλητον εἶναι, ὡς Θεοῦ οἰκονόμον, μὴ αὐθάδη, μὴ ὀργίλον,

ἀσωτία. From meaning wasteful expenditure (ὑπερβολὴ περὶ χρήματα—Aristotle) this word came to mean profligacy in a general sense. The reason why this in the sons debars the fathers from office in the Church is given in 1 Tim. iii. 5. Cf. 'The parson is very exact in the governing of his House, making it a Copie and Model for his Parish' (see Herbert's *Priest to the Temple*, ch. x.).

7. οἰκονόμον, over the household of God, and therefore he must not be one who has failed in his own household. The duties of a steward were (1) to control the other servants, (2) to expend and distribute as required. Cf. 1 Cor. iv. 1 for this comparison of ministers as 'stewards of the mysteries of God,' *i.e.* set to distribute to others the truth of the Gospel.

αὐθάδη, literally *self-pleasing* (αὐτός and stem of ἥδομαι), and therefore *stubborn, self-willed*. The best of men and best of clergymen are apt to show this fault—it is the bad side of a virtue that great men must have, viz. the readiness to shoulder responsibility. It seems to them hard to give full weight to the advice of others who neither do the work nor bear the consequences. Hence the complaint that often a parish is an autocracy and parish meetings only register things previously settled. 'He is called *parson*, persona, because by his person, the Church, which is an invisible body, is represented; and he is in himself a body corporate, in order to protect and defend the rights of the Church which he personates' (Blackstone). This legal view carried into the administration of ordinary parish affairs and regulation of the services has its natural result in causing the laity to stand aside. 'He that seeketh to be eminent among able men hath a great task; but that is ever good for the public. But he that plots to be the only figure among ciphers is the decay of a whole age' (Bacon, Essay on *Ambition*).

ὀργίλον, quick to anger. Aristotle says of οἱ ὀργίλοι, 'They are quickly angered and with the wrong people and for wrong causes and more than is justifiable; but they cease from anger quickly, which is an excellent point in them.' Anger in itself is not a vice; like ridicule, contempt, sarcasm, it is a weapon, but one that must be sparingly used and only to express what we call moral indignation, not to resent personal injury to ourselves. It must therefore be the outcome of a deliberate act of judgment, and *quickness* to anger is inconsistent with this. 'It is the best remedy to win time,' says Bacon in his Essay on *Anger*, but most of his suggestions in that essay are too worldly. In the priest there is a special reason for restraining even justifiable anger. It cannot be expected that the other person will instantly see that it is justifiable, and, whereas two ordinary men who have hurt one another can keep apart till time softens their

H

μὴ πάροινον, μὴ πλήκτην, μὴ αἰσχροκερδῆ, 8. ἀλλὰ φιλόξενον, φιλάγαθον, σώφρονα, δίκαιον, ὅσιον, ἐγκρατῆ, 9. ἀντεχόμενον τοῦ κατὰ τὴν διδαχὴν πιστοῦ λόγου, ἵνα δυνατὸς ᾖ καὶ παρακαλεῖν ἐν τῇ διδασκαλίᾳ τῇ ὑγιαινούσῃ καὶ τοὺς ἀντιλέγοντας ἐλέγχειν.

views, the tie between priest and disciple is one that does not permit a breach even for a single day. The loss of self-respect in the victim of an angry admonition is apt to create a lasting shyness—he feels that the only dignity left him is to keep out of your sight altogether.

See some further remarks in Mayor's excursus on 'Slow to Wrath' in St. James i. 19. Also see the n. on ἐπιείκεια in 1 Tim. iii. 3.

μὴ πάροινον, μὴ πλήκτην, as in 1 Tim. iii. 3.

μὴ αἰσχροκερδῆ. See n. on 1 Tim. iii. 8.

8. φιλόξενον, σώφρονα, as in 1 Tim. iii. 2.

φιλάγαθον. See n. on 2 Tim. iii. 4.

δίκαιον, in the ordinary un-theological sense of being just in all one's dealings. The three words ὅσιον, δίκαιον, σώφρονα come very near to 'godly, righteous and sober life,' i.e. fulfilling one's duty to God, to one's neighbour and to oneself. For ὅσιον see n. on 1 Tim. iii. 8.

ἐγκρατῆ, exercising self-control wherever there is a temptation to indulgence — not necessarily an ascetic, though some men find it necessary to be ascetic if they would be ἐγκρατεῖς, on the principle that

'I trust nor hand nor eye nor heart nor brain
To stop betimes: they all get drunk alike.
The *first* step I am master not to take.'
—BROWNING.

It means making only lawful use of the pleasures of life, not following them but *using* them. Aristotle says ὁ ἐγκρατής, εἰδὼς ὅτι φαῦλαι αἱ ἐπιθυμίαι, οὐκ ἀκολουθεῖ διὰ τὸν λόγον. Compare n. on ἀκρατής in 2 Tim. iii. 3.

9. ἀντεχόμενον . . . λόγου, R.V. 'holding to the faithful word which is according to the teaching.'

ἵνα δυνατὸς ᾖ καὶ παρακαλεῖν . . . καὶ ἐλέγχειν. He cannot exercise the authority of his ministry with such faults as those referred to—'the ordinary sort of people will wrest the defects of the man upon the profession.'

ὑγιαινούσῃ. See n. on 1 Tim. i. 10.

10-16. **The nature of the opposition likely to be met with in Crete.**

Here the danger is specified as mainly Jewish; for the bearing of which on the more general expression of 1 Tim. i. 4 see note on that passage. Jews were very numerous in Crete. St. Paul's reference is of course to those of them who had professed Christianity, but rather as a reformed kind of Judaism than as a revelation for the whole world. The danger therefore was not simply that their Christianity was imperfect, but that in Crete as elsewhere they represented St. Paul's doctrine as an imperfect form of Christianity which had neglected its Jewish basis. The

10. Εἰσὶ γὰρ πολλοὶ ἀνυπότακτοι, ματαιολόγοι καὶ φρεναπάται, μάλιστα οἱ ἐκ περιτομῆς, 11. οὓς δεῖ ἐπιστομίζειν· οἵτινες ὅλους οἴκους ἀνατρέπουσι διδάσκοντες ἃ μὴ δεῖ αἰσχροῦ κέρδους χάριν. 12. εἶπέ τις ἐξ αὐτῶν ἴδιος αὐτῶν προφήτης, Κρῆτες ἀεὶ ψεῦσται, κακὰ θηρία, γαστέρες ἀργαί. 13. ἡ μαρτυρία αὕτη ἐστὶν ἀληθής. δι' ἣν αἰτίαν ἔλεγχε αὐτοὺς ἀποτόμως, ἵνα ὑγιαίνωσιν ἐν τῇ πίστει, 14. μὴ προσέχοντες Ἰουδαϊκοῖς μύθοις καὶ ἐντολαῖς ἀνθρώπων ἀποστρεφομένων τὴν ἀλήθειαν. 15. πάντα καθαρὰ τοῖς καθαροῖς· τοῖς δὲ μεμιασμένοις καὶ

attempt to impose their own 'more complete' Christianity on Gentiles is doubtless what is referred to in ὅλους οἴκους ἀνατρέπουσι. See Introd., p. xxiii.

10. ἀνυπότακτοι, refusing to submit to any authority either in matters of faith or in matters of administration.

ματαιολόγοι. See n. on 1 Tim. i. 6.

φρεναπάται. The word does not occur before St. Paul. Cf. Gal. vi. 3.

οἱ ἐκ περιτομῆς. The phrase could of course include all Jews, but had come to be used expressly of the Judaic party in the Church. Cf. such a passage as Acts xi. 2.

11. ὅλους οἴκους ἀνατρέπουσι, subvert whole families by their teaching. See above.

αἰσχροῦ κέρδους χάριν. Cf. 1 Tim. vi. 5, νομιζόντων πορισμὸν εἶναι τὴν εὐσέβειαν. In what way they made profit is not clear. Possibly offering a form of teaching that fascinated the superstitious and credulous, they claimed maintenance by the Church. But it is more likely that by professing powers of exorcism, and of magical healing by incantations and spells, they charged fees for their services—διδάσκοντες ἃ μὴ δεῖ points to this. A certain type of mind will pay more for a mascot than for religious teaching.

12. The saying is attributed to Epimenides, a Cretan bard and sage who lived about 600 B.C. Much related of him is mythical, but he was summoned to Athens during a plague to purify the city. Probably he wrote in verse oracles and purificatory incantations, but many other poems were attributed to him. The Cretans seem to have borne a bad reputation continuously for lying and doing anything for gain. The latter may be referred to in κακὰ θηρία, ravening beasts. γαστέρες ἀργαί (lazy bellies) implies gluttonous eating without working for it.

14. Ἰουδαϊκοῖς μύθοις. See notes on 1 Tim. i. 4, iv. 3.

15. πάντα καθαρὰ τοῖς καθαροῖς. The prevailing use of καθαρός in the LXX is for ceremonial cleanness, and in the N.T. it signifies the purity of heart of which this was a symbol. In the present phrase St. Paul is obviously giving an answer to the

ἀπίστοις οὐδὲν καθαρόν, ἀλλὰ μεμίανται αὐτῶν καὶ ὁ νοῦς καὶ ἡ συνείδησις. 16. Θεὸν ὁμολογοῦσιν εἰδέναι, τοῖς δὲ ἔργοις ἀρνοῦνται, βδελυκτοὶ ὄντες καὶ ἀπειθεῖς καὶ πρὸς πᾶν ἔργον ἀγαθὸν ἀδόκιμοι.

false teaching referred to in the preceding verse, which must therefore have included the prohibition of some kinds of food, etc., as in 1 Tim. iv. 3. In Rom. xiv. St. Paul's teaching on the subject is given more at length. Cf. St. Mark vii. 18-19, with its concluding words, '(This he said) making all meats clean' (καθαρίζων).

The saying 'To the pure all things are pure' has become proverbial, and has sometimes been applied dangerously for the justification of any indulgence that one can defend by argument without the safeguards that St. Paul's teaching elsewhere supplies. *E.g.* it has sometimes been used to exalt the right of private judgment without sufficient regard to (1) the advantage of *unity* even in what some would regard as immaterial; (2) the claims which other consciences (regarded by us as weaker) have upon our help and forbearance and example. Certain things may be quite right for me in the nature of things because I can limit myself, but if as an employer of labour I am responsible for the lives of others it may be necessary for me to be able to say, 'I never do it myself.' St. Paul means that all things are pure to those who can receive them as the gift of God with no doubt in their hearts, but they cannot so receive them if it involves a breach of either (1) or (2). Even in matters of religious observance it may be more pleasing to God sometimes that we should forgo what we prefer and think most helpful, than that we should insist on it to the offence of others or even to the hurt of their feelings.

μεμιασμένοις, the opposite of καθαροῖς, defiled by base motives.

ὁ νοῦς can include the conscience, but is somewhat wider; it means all faculty of moral judgment, whether of their own conduct or of others' conduct or of principles considered in the abstract.

συνείδησις. See n. on 1 Tim. i. 5.

16. ἀρνοῦνται. Cf. 1 Tim. v. 8.

βδελυκτοί. This adjective, like the noun βδέλυγμα (derived from βδελύσσομαι, to feel a loathing for), expresses in the O.T. that which is an *abomination* in the sight of God, *e.g.* an idol or offering to an idol. For instance, in the phrase 'abomination of desolation,' it probably refers to the setting up of the image of Zeus in the temple of God. Here, therefore, it expresses men who are utterly reprobate in God's judgment.

πρὸς πᾶν ἔργον ἀγαθὸν ἀδόκιμοι, as regards every good work rejected. When faced with any opportunity of good work they fail to stand the test that it brings of their real motives. The literal meaning of ἀδόκιμος is failing to pass the test, like a metal being assayed. The use of *reprobate* in the English version is due to the word in the Vulgate, and means 'tested and rejected.'

It is impossible to read the above verses 10-16 without realising that there must have been more corruption involved in the false teaching than is allowed for in the explanation so far given. All attempt to characterise it further may be vain unless further knowledge is forthcoming, but even assuming an organised attempt to subvert the apostolic authority, to impose much Jewish ceremonialism with regard to food and purifications on Gentile converts, it hardly accounts for the vehemence of St. Paul's language. αἰσχροῦ κέρδους χάριν may be explained as above, and v. 12 may be accounted for by its literary character, but μεμιασμένοι, βδελυκτοί, πρὸς πᾶν ἔργον ἀγαθὸν ἀδόκιμοι are very strong expressions, implying degradation in morals, heathenism in religion, so far developed as to be beyond restoration. Ceremonialism and superstition of the Jewish type of course struck at the root of the 'law of liberty' and would make St. Paul's teaching vain, but it may be that in the opposition referred to there was much more of what we describe as antinomianism. From such indications as we get it is clear that this might be involved in any philosophical theory of the essential evil of matter, involving, as this did with some, the corollary that what was done in the body was of no spiritual account. See n. on 1 Tim. iv. 3.

CHAPTER II

1. Σὺ δὲ λάλει ἃ πρέπει τῇ ὑγιαινούσῃ διδασκαλίᾳ· 2. πρεσβύτας νηφαλίους εἶναι, σεμνούς, σώφρονας, ὑγιαίνοντας τῇ πίστει, τῇ ἀγάπῃ, τῇ ὑπομονῇ· 3. πρεσβύτιδας ὡσαύτως ἐν καταστήματι ἱεροπρεπεῖς, μὴ διαβόλους, μηδὲ οἴνῳ πολλῷ δεδουλωμένας, καλοδιδασκάλους, 4. ἵνα σωφρονίζωσι τὰς νέας φιλάνδρους εἶναι, φιλοτέκνους, 5. σώφρονας, ἁγνάς, οἰκουργούς, ἀγαθάς, ὑποτασσομένας

1-15. 'Give every class in the Church the teaching that is fitting: (1) the older men (v. 2), (2) the women (vv. 3-5), (3) the younger men (v. 6), setting them also an example in thyself (vv. 7-8), (4) slaves also (vv. 9-10), according to the teaching of the grace of God (vv. 11-12), and the hope set before us' (vv. 13-14).

1. ὑγιαινούσῃ. N. on 1 Tim. i. 10.
2. νηφαλίους. N. on 1 Tim. iii. 2; σεμνούς, 1 Tim. ii. 2, iii. 4; σώφρονας, 1 Tim. ii. 9; ἀγάπῃ, 1 Tim. i. 5; ὑπομονῇ, 2 Tim. ii. 10.
3. ἐν καταστήματι ἱεροπρεπεῖς, R.V. 'reverent in demeanour.' κατάστημα meant 'condition' or 'state' with regard to anything, just as the verb (πολέμιον καταστῆναι, ἐς φόβον καταστῆναι) indicates coming into a certain condition. Its use for *bearing* or *demeanour* or (L. and S.) *dress* is later. ἱεροπρεπής means 'befitting holy things' or befitting a sacred profession. St. Paul does not mean, of course, that this Puritan touch in outward bearing added anything to essential holiness; but to bear outwardly the mark of Christian prevented many embarrassing situations and invitations in a mixed Greek society. In such cases courtesy demands that one should bear an outward mark of profession—it is not only a question of having the courage of convictions. This principle applies to the wearing of a distinctive clerical dress. Some people are too impatient of anything that is merely 'outward' as in itself insignificant.

καλοδιδασκάλους, 'teachers of good'—a word not quoted elsewhere.

5. ἁγνάς, chaste in thought as in body. This word is used predominantly as opposed to sensual sins, though sometimes it has a wider meaning. It is of course to be

τοῖς ἰδίοις ἀνδράσιν, ἵνα μὴ ὁ λόγος τοῦ Θεοῦ βλασφημῆται· 6. τοὺς νεωτέρους ὡσαύτως παρακάλει σωφρονεῖν· 7. περὶ πάντα σεαυτὸν παρεχόμενος τύπον καλῶν ἔργων, ἐν τῇ διδασκαλίᾳ ἀφθορίαν, σεμνότητα, 8. λόγον ὑγιῆ,

distinguished from ἅγιος, which, from first meaning *separated* or *consecrated* to God's service, implied all aspects of holiness that befits such service.

οἰκουργούς, workers at home—a word first found here. T.R. has οἰκουρούς.

ἵνα μὴ ... βλασφημῆται, 'that the word of God be not injuriously spoken of.' See n. on 1 Tim. i. 13. The comparatively prominent place which women began to take in the Church presented a very real danger. It would hinder the Word if they allowed themselves a publicity or freedom beyond that of other self-respecting Greek women. St. Paul lays stress therefore mainly on the domestic virtues. Cf. n. on 1 Tim. ii. 11.

7. τύπον. See n. on 1 Tim. iv. 12.

ἀφθορίαν, another word found here for the first time. By 'uncorruptness' in teaching is probably meant keeping to the single motive of presenting truth, not trying to please or to make the truth easy. 'Stat super haec mutabilia sapiens et bene doctus in spiritu, non attendens quid in se sentiat vel qua parte flet ventus instabilitatis, sed ut tota intentio mentis eius ad debitum et optimum proficiat finem' (*De Imitatione*). There is a temptation 'to make truth easy' by the choice of subjects on which we most frequently dwell, by avoiding certain subjects, by choosing the philosophical aspects of a question, by dealing with certain religious questions from the point of view of the open-minded critic and certain moral questions from the point of view of the man of the world. If you are mainly a philosopher, or mainly a critic, or mainly a man of the world, you cannot perhaps help yourself, but then it is a question whether you ought to pretend to teach *with authority* in the Church, for which purpose a man must know what he believes, and make his words match his belief. Such methods as those described will win attention from certain types of mind, more especially when they seem to aim at reducing within 'practical' limits the uncompromising teaching of Christ. Cicero found fault with Cato—'dicit enim tamquam in Platonis πολιτείᾳ, non tamquam in Romuli faece, sententiam.' The man who teaches with authority in the Church must always speak as ἐν Χριστοῦ πολιτείᾳ.

σεμνότητα. See n. on 1 Tim. ii. 2.

8. λόγον, here of speech in general, not of preaching the Word only. λόγον ὑγιῆ therefore means a 'healthy tone,' whether in set discourse or in informal conversation. Conversation is made unhealthy not only by false and injurious speaking but by personalities, by frivolity of topics, by wit out of season, by pessimism.

ἀκατάγνωστον, ἵνα ὁ ἐξ ἐναντίας ἐντραπῇ μηδὲν ἔχων λέγειν περὶ ἡμῶν φαῦλον· 9. δούλους ἰδίοις δεσπόταις ὑποτάσσεσθαι, ἐν πᾶσιν εὐαρέστους εἶναι, μὴ ἀντιλέγοντας, 10. μὴ νοσφιζομένους, ἀλλὰ πᾶσαν πίστιν ἐνδεικνυμένους ἀγαθήν, ἵνα τὴν διδασκαλίαν τὴν τοῦ σωτῆρος ἡμῶν Θεοῦ κοσμῶσιν ἐν πᾶσιν. 11. ἐπεφάνη

ὁ ἐξ ἐναντίας, any adversary; here any one who is on the watch for a handle against the Christian profession.

φαῦλον. This word had originally meant 'worthless,' 'bad of its kind,' 'inferior,' as you would speak of *e.g.* a bad (φαῦλος) painter. In N.T. Greek it hardly differs from κακός.

9. ὑποτάσσεσθαι. 'Exhort' is of course understood from the preceding sentence (v. 6).

For n. on St. Paul's attitude to slavery see 1 Tim. vi. 1.

The μὴ ἀντιλέγοντας here is an illustration of what is there said of the comparative lightness of some forms of domestic slavery among the ancients, such a thing as ἀντιλέγειν between master and slave being inconceivable in our ideas of slavery. Slaves could become not only trusted but familiar members of the household, allowed much freedom of speech, cared for in old age.

10. κοσμῶσιν. From meaning (1) to arrange, set in order, this word meant (2) to adorn (in the literal sense), and (3) to bring honour or credit to in the sense in which Thucydides says αἱ τῶνδε ἀρεταὶ ἐκόσμησαν (τὴν πόλιν). The phrase here is striking: those lowest in the social scale are able not only to obey the teaching, but to add to its beauty by the commendation of their lives. There are none so poor in ability or so much despised by men that they cannot do God service in this way. The lesson is the same as that which the sculptor Rossi meant to teach when he was asked to carve a figure to bear the holy-water stoup in the Church of St. Anastasia at Verona and chose as his model for the purpose his deformed and hunchbacked son. The word κοσμέω is in a sense the strongest that could be used. Many people accept and practise the Gospel teaching without adorning it —faults of bearing and manner rob an otherwise excellent life of its commending power. To be just and generous is good, but to be just and generous with the right word and the right look is a point beyond.

11. See n. on v. 1. The following verses give the religious ground, so to speak, of the preceding practical precepts. It is as if St. Paul said, 'It must not be thought that these homely virtues have nothing to do with our religion—rather it is in these things that the saving grace of God manifests itself in our common lives.' His words are a protest against the tendency not to apply religious motive to the petty details of the daily round. 'For the least thing there is a judgment,' and in every detail of life we can 'adorn'

γὰρ ἡ χάρις τοῦ Θεοῦ σωτήριος πᾶσιν ἀνθρώποις,
12. παιδεύουσα ἡμᾶς, ἵνα ἀρνησάμενοι τὴν ἀσέβειαν καὶ τὰς κοσμικὰς ἐπιθυμίας σωφρόνως καὶ δικαίως καὶ εὐσεβῶς ζήσωμεν ἐν τῷ νῦν αἰῶνι, 13. προσδεχόμενοι τὴν μακαρίαν ἐλπίδα καὶ ἐπιφάνειαν τῆς δόξης τοῦ μεγάλου Θεοῦ καὶ σωτῆρος ἡμῶν Ἰησοῦ Χριστοῦ, 14. ὃς ἔδωκεν ἑαυτὸν ὑπὲρ ἡμῶν, ἵνα λυτρώσηται ἡμᾶς ἀπὸ

the doctrine which we profess. 'Nothing is little in God's service: if it once have the honour of that Name, it grows great instantly.'

ἡ χάρις. See n. on 1 Tim. i. 2.

12. παιδεύουσα. Here perhaps 'teaching,' but the usual N.T. meaning of 'disciplining' is not out of place. See n. on 2 Tim. ii. 25. The saving grace of God is that which introduces discipline into our lives, and without it we are simply following the line of least resistance from day to day.

ἵνα, in its full final sense, 'to the intent that we may...,' not simply 'teaching us that...'

ἀρνησάμενοι, 'disowning,' i.e. refusing allegiance to.

κοσμικάς, belonging to this material world, desires that are natural to those absorbed in its life. Cf. Heb. ix. 1, τὸ ἅγιον κοσμικόν, 'sanctuary of this world.'

σωφρόνως, δικαίως, εὐσεβῶς. See n. on δίκαιον in i. 8.

τῷ νῦν αἰῶνι. For the combined temporal and ethical meaning of this phrase see n. on 2 Tim. iv. 10.

13. 'The blessed hope and appearing of the glory...' Take both

ἐλπίδα and ἐπιφάνειαν with τῆς δόξης, which must certainly not be taken as in the A.V., 'glorious appearing.'

τοῦ μεγάλου Θεοῦ καὶ σωτῆρος ἡμῶν Ἰησοῦ Χριστοῦ. Take as in R.V. text, 'Of our great God and Saviour Jesus Christ.' This is certainly the way in which an ordinary Greek reader would have taken it, coming to it without any preconceived ideas of the theological fitness of the expressions, and therefore cogent reasons must be shown before we assume that St. Paul meant anything else. If an Athenian spoke of ὁ μέγας στρατηγὸς καὶ σωτὴρ ἡμῶν Δημοσθένης, no one would imagine that he was speaking of two persons. But the student may consult a long note on the subject in Alford, who comes to a different conclusion. He rightly remarks that in either way of taking it the divinity of our Lord is strongly emphasised, in the one case (as above) by statement, in the other case (R.V. marg.) by implication.

14. λυτρώσηται. See n. on ἀντίλυτρον in 1 Tim. ii. 6, which makes it clear that the words could retain the full meaning of 'ransom,' though it is clear from other passages that the metaphor of a price paid was

πάσης ἀνομίας, καὶ καθαρίσῃ ἑαυτῷ λαὸν περιούσιον, ζηλωτὴν καλῶν ἔργων.

15. Ταῦτα λάλει, καὶ παρακάλει καὶ ἔλεγχε μετὰ πάσης ἐπιταγῆς. μηδείς σου περιφρονείτω.

sometimes lost in the general sense of 'deliver.'

λαὸν περιούσιον. Deut. xiv. 2, καὶ σὲ ἐξελέξατο Κύριος ὁ θεός σου γενέσθαι σε λαὸν αὐτῷ περιούσιον ἀπὸ πάντων τῶν ἐθνῶν. This (with some other passages in which the same phrase occurs in the LXX) makes it clear that περιούσιος means 'as his own possession,' 'peculiar.' As the word does not occur in secular literature, it might otherwise have been possible to connect it with the meaning 'excel' borne by περίειμι.

The A.V. rendering *peculiar* is, of course, the adjective of the Latin *peculium*, which meant specially the private property allowed to a slave by his master though not recognised by law. Hence the adjective means 'as his own special possession.' Cf. Davenant, *Man's the Master*, iv. 1, 'Now even all peculiar fields are turned to common roads.'

15. μετὰ πάσης ἐπιταγῆς, 'with all authority,' making it a matter of *injunction*, not of advice merely or argument or persuasion. The following μηδείς σου περιφρονείτω means that he is not to minish ought of his authority as the delegate of the Apostle, nor to be weak and hesitating, as if these precepts were still a matter of question.

CHAPTER III

1. Ὑπομίμνησκε αὐτοὺς ἀρχαῖς ἐξουσίαις ὑποτάσσεσθαι, πειθαρχεῖν, πρὸς πᾶν ἔργον ἀγαθὸν ἑτοίμους εἶναι, 2. μηδένα βλασφημεῖν, ἀμάχους εἶναι, ἐπιεικεῖς, πᾶσαν ἐνδεικνυμένους πραότητα πρὸς πάντας ἀνθρώπους. 3. ἦμεν γάρ ποτε καὶ ἡμεῖς ἀνόητοι, ἀπειθεῖς, πλανώμενοι, δουλεύοντες ἐπιθυμίαις καὶ ἡδοναῖς ποικίλαις, ἐν κακίᾳ καὶ φθόνῳ διάγοντες, στυγητοί, μισοῦντες ἀλλήλους.

1-11. Precepts for conduct of believers towards the outer world (1-2), remembering that we ourselves were once subject to the same passions (3), and that only through the gift of God did we escape from them (4-7). Therefore above all things must believers set an example of good works (8), and avoid futile contentions about doctrine (9). A man who persists in false doctrine must be separated from our fellowship (10-11).

1. The best reading omits καί before ἐξουσίαις. ἐξουσία, the most general word for authority of all kinds, properly abstract, but used like our 'authorities' for 'those in authority.' For the precept see n. on 1 Tim. ii. 1.

2. βλασφημεῖν, speak injuriously of. See n. on 2 Tim. iii. 2.

ἐπιεικεῖς. See n. on 1 Tim. iii. 3. πραότητα, n. on 2 Tim. ii. 25.

3. ἀνόητοι, 'without understanding'—here especially meaning without understanding of the true ends of life and the things worth fighting for.

στυγητοί, hated or hateful. Only here in the N.T.

In this verse St. Paul is giving former evil life as a reason for special zeal in the good life urged in verses 1-2, and this on two grounds. The first is the natural instinct of a man conscious of having done wrong to try to make up for it—though we cannot thereby make God our debtor, the spirit of it is acceptable to Him. The bravest deeds in battle have often been done by men anxious to wipe out the discredit of some former cowardice. The other reason is that having been so bad ourselves, we can sympathise patiently with those who are still bad. It is helpful to lesser men to contemplate from what material many of the saints were made. That St. Paul should include himself (ἦμεν γάρ) in the hard words of this verse is at first surprising, but it is easily paralleled in his other writings (Rom. vii. 24, 1 Cor. ix. 27),

4. ὅτε δὲ ἡ χρηστότης καὶ ἡ φιλανθρωπία ἐπεφάνη τοῦ σωτῆρος ἡμῶν Θεοῦ, 5. οὐκ ἐξ ἔργων τῶν ἐν δικαιοσύνῃ ἃ ἐποιήσαμεν ἡμεῖς ἀλλὰ κατὰ τὸ αὐτοῦ ἔλεος ἔσωσεν ἡμᾶς διὰ λουτροῦ παλιγγενεσίας καὶ ἀνακαινώσεως Πνεύ-

and with his estimate of qualities, good and evil, there is probably no word in the verse that he could not apply literally to something in his earlier life.

4. **χρηστότης**. The word χρηστός is the adjective of χράομαι, and meant first *serviceable*. Hence it came to mean *good* in a great variety of senses. But its original signification made it imply of persons especially *the disposition to be good*, and so *goodness of heart* or *kindness*.

φιλανθρωπία between men is humanity or courteous behaviour. Here it is best translated as in R.V. 'love toward man.'

5. **κατά**, in pursuance of.

ἔσωσεν. Salvation is here spoken of as a thing accomplished once for all at the beginning of the Christian life. See n. on the word in 2 Tim. i. 9.

διὰ λουτροῦ παλιγγενεσίας. The word λουτρόν means 'washing,' and there is no clear instance of its use for the vessel of washing or purification. See Armitage Robinson's note on Eph. v. 26. It is therefore difficult to see why the R.V. allowed 'laver' in its margin.

The word παλιγγενεσία occurs only once besides in the N.T., viz. Matt. xix. 28, and there it is used of the 'renewal of all things' at the coming of Christ in glory (cf. Acts iii. 21). As regards the *word* therefore the present passage stands alone, but the idea of the new birth involved is expressed frequently and in various ways. The great passage is the conversation with Nicodemus in St. John iii. 3 f.: 'Except a man be born again he cannot see the kingdom of God.' 'Except a man be born of water and the Spirit he cannot enter into the kingdom of God.' But in St. Paul's Epistles compare the following: Rom. vi. 4 f., 'We were buried therefore with him through baptism·into death: that like as Christ was raised from the dead through the glory of God the Father, so we also might walk in newness of life.' 2 Cor. v. 17, 'If any man is in Christ he is a new creature (καινὴ κτίσις).' Eph. ii. 4-6, 'But God ... even when we were dead through our trespasses quickened us together with Christ ... and raised us up with him.' iv. 24, 'Put on the new man, which after God hath been created in righteousness and holiness of truth.' Col. iii. 9-10, 'Ye have put off the old man with his doings, and have put on the new man which is being renewed unto knowledge after the image of him that created him.' Gal. ii. 20, 'I have been crucified with Christ; yet I live; and yet no longer I but Christ liveth in me.' Cf. also 1. Pet. i. 23, 'Having been begotten again, not of corruptible seed, but of incorruptible, through the word of God, which liveth and abideth.'

The change then that is referred

EPISTLE TO TITUS

ματος Ἁγίου, 6. οὗ ἐξέχεεν ἐφ' ἡμᾶς πλουσίως διὰ Ἰησοῦ Χριστοῦ τοῦ σωτῆρος ἡμῶν, 7. ἵνα δικαιωθέντες

to in all these passages and in others is so great that it can be spoken of as a new birth, as the making of a 'new man,' a 'new creation.' In all of them it is connected with the beginning of the Christian life, and in all of them it is the divine act in that beginning—it is not the human condition of repentance or faith that is spoken of as bringing about the 'new creation,' but the divine gift. We may speak of that divine gift in various terms, as being the bestowal of a new nature or a new faculty, as being the gift of God's Holy Spirit, or as being the gift of union with Christ. These terms are all true when rightly defined, but the main fact is that it is a gift of God which makes possible what without it is impossible. That which it thus makes possible is life in which our will is identified with the will of God, in which the will of God is the 'major premiss' under which all the detailed actions of life must be brought.

The association of this great gift with Baptism has been a stumbling-block to many. They would have the human will bear a greater conscious part in the winning of so great a thing. But this is partly because they think of the gift as necessarily an overmastering and decisive power. Instead of which it is better to think of it as a seed in us that has to grow. The power in us can be neglected, enfeebled, kept latent—and where this has been so it needs to be claimed again by what we speak of as Conversion.

The power was there and the covenant of forgiveness was there, but the soul needed to realise and use what it had.

ἀνακαινώσεως Πνεύματος Ἁγίου. The R.V. text takes this as dependent, like παλιγγενεσίας, on λουτροῦ, and therefore of the renewing of our nature in Baptism. In the margin it takes it as governed directly by διά, and therefore presumably of the whole process of our renewal or sanctification by the Holy Spirit. Either is possible, but the other passages where this word or ἀνακαινόω is used are in favour of the latter: 2 Cor. iv. 16, 'Our inward man is renewed day by day.' Col. iii. 10, 'The new man which is being renewed unto knowledge.' Rom. xii. 2, 'Be ye transformed by the renewing of your mind.'

7. δικαιωθέντες, 'having been declared righteous,' 'having been accepted as righteous.' The word δικαιόω refers to the action of a judge in declaring a man 'not guilty,' and is St. Paul's regular word for expressing God's free act of forgiveness and reconciliation made possible through the atoning sacrifice of Christ, and realised by the individual through faith in Christ. δικαιωθέντες therefore is here to be referred to the beginning of the Christian life. See Romans iii. 21-26 and the whole treatment of the subject in that epistle, for which the student should consult Sanday and Headlam's notes

τῇ ἐκείνου χάριτι κληρονόμοι γενηθῶμεν κατ' ἐλπίδα ζωῆς αἰωνίου. 8. πιστὸς ὁ λόγος, καὶ περὶ τούτων βούλομαί σε διαβεβαιοῦσθαι, ἵνα φροντίζωσι καλῶν ἔργων προΐ

on the word δικαιόω and the doctrine of justification.

τῇ ἐκείνου χάριτι. ἐκείνου naturally refers to the more remote noun, and is therefore to be taken here as referring to Θεοῦ, not to Ἰησοῦ Χριστοῦ.

κληρονόμοι γενηθῶμεν. The figure whereby the possession of Christian privileges is spoken of as an 'inheritance' is undoubtedly to be traced to Jewish habits of thought. The inheritance of the Holy Land was the seal of their being the covenant people, and as their ideas became more spiritualised those who were to have a part in the blessings of the Messianic reign could be spoken of as 'inheriting the kingdom.' In St. Paul's language the inheritance can include all the blessings of faith, whether already possessed or looked forward to, and he adds to the force of the thought by associating it with his teaching as to our sonship of God. Rom. viii. 16-17, 'The Spirit himself beareth witness with our spirit, that we are children of God: And if children, then heirs ; heirs of God and joint-heirs with Christ.' So Gal. iv. 7. The commonest expansion of the phrase is 'to inherit the kingdom,' as in 1 Cor. vi. 9, etc., but compare 1 Cor. xv. 50, τὴν ἀφθαρσίαν κληρονομεῖ: Heb. i. 14, κληρονομεῖν σωτηρίαν: vi. 12, κληρονομούντων τὰς ἐπαγγελίας : 1 Pet. iii. 9, ἵνα εὐλογίαν κληρονομήσητε : Heb. ix. 15, τὴν ἐπαγγελίαν τῆς αἰωνίου κληρονομίας : 1 Pet. i. 4, εἰς

κληρονομίαν ἄφθαρτον καὶ ἀμίαντον καὶ ἀμάραντον, τετηρημένην ἐν οὐρανοῖς εἰς ὑμᾶς.

ζωῆς αἰωνίου. See n. on 1 Tim. i. 16. The Genitive here may be taken either with ἐλπίδα (R.V. text) or with κληρονόμοι (R.V. marg.). The natural order of the Greek and the occurrence of the same phrase in i. 2 are in favour of the former.

Verses 5-7 contain much of St. Paul's characteristic teaching. Man's salvation is dependent on no works that he can perform but on the free gift of God, who saves us by giving us a new birth in Baptism, wherein the guilt of sinfulness is washed from us and life as a 'new man' is made possible ; then renews our nature progressively to sanctification by the help of His Holy Spirit ; so that, having been thus accepted by Him as righteous, we may enter into our full inheritance as sons in pursuance (realisation) of the hope set before us of everlasting life.

8. For the connection of thought see note above, v. 1.

πιστὸς ὁ λόγος here naturally refers to the preceding words. See n. on 1 Tim. iii. 1.

διαβεβαιοῦσθαι (as in 1 Tim. i. 7), to affirm strongly, to express thyself with all conviction and emphasis.

προΐστασθαι. From meaning 'to be at the head of' the word was used for 'govern,' 'manage' in any sense, but retaining generally the idea of *taking the lead* in a matter.

σταϲθαι οἱ πεπιϲτευκότεϲ Θεῷ. ταῦτά ἐϲτι καλὰ καὶ ὠφέλιμα τοῖϲ ἀνθρώποιϲ· 9. μωρὰϲ δὲ ζητήϲειϲ καὶ γενεαλογίαϲ καὶ ἔρειϲ καὶ μάχαϲ νομικὰϲ περιΐϲταϲο· εἰϲὶ γὰρ ἀνωφελεῖϲ καὶ μάταιοι. 10. αἱρετικὸν ἄνθρωπον μετὰ μίαν καὶ δευτέραν νουθεϲίαν παραιτοῦ, 11. εἰδὼϲ

Perhaps R.V. 'maintain' is as good a translation as we can get here. The καλῶν ἔργων is most naturally referred to the honourable conduct in life which St. Paul has been emphasising in verses 1-2. In some doubt as to this, the Revisers allowed in the margin 'profess honest occupations,' which was undoubtedly a necessary precept, as many of the usual occupations (*e.g.* the making of images and every other trade necessarily connected with heathen things) would compromise the Christian profession.

oἱ πεπιϲτευκότεϲ Θεῷ, R.V. 'they which have believed God.' But in Acts xviii. 8 it translates (text) ἐπίϲτευϲε τῷ Κυρίῳ, 'believed in the Lord.' The most common N.T. construction with πιϲτεύειν was εἰϲ; the most common classical construction was the Dative. The attempt to maintain a regular distinction between them is hardly justified, though the exact equivalent of 'to believe the words of' would always require the Dative.

9. As opposed to sound and upright life in one's proper vocation, the love of disputation for its own sake (a characteristic vice of Greeks, who looked upon it as cultivating the higher faculties) is condemned.

For γενεαλογίαϲ and the subject see n. on 1 Tim. i. 4.

περιΐϲταϲο. Cf. 2 Tim. ii. 16.

νομικάϲ, having to do with (Jewish) law.

μάταιοι. See n. on 1 Tim. i. 6.

10. αἱρετικόν, an adjective occurring only here. The word αἵρεϲιϲ meant literally a *choosing*, and so came to be used of the choosing of one's own principles or philosophy—hence of a party or sect. It is used in the Acts of the Sadducees and Pharisees, and (from the Jewish point of view) of Christianity (xxiv. 14). It was not from the first meaning of the word, but from its natural use of any party or school which marked itself off from the 'orthodox,' that it came to bear a bad meaning—'heresy.' Here the word αἱρετικόν means any one who was factious in maintaining his special views, and *factious* (R.V. marg.) is the best rendering. Titus is told to 'avoid' such a one; no more severe course is enjoined in this case, but such men were to be kept aloof from the Church as far as possible, and it was to be made plain that they did not represent the teaching of the Church. Their influence was to be minimised, and in no way were they to be associated with the work. It is not necessary to read into this passage the meaning of 1 Tim. iv. 2. St. Paul was perhaps here dealing with a less serious danger, and trusted to the fact that the man was 'self-condemned.' Cf. 'When after many admonitions any continues to be

ὅτι ἐξέστραπται ὁ τοιοῦτος καὶ ἁμαρτάνει ὢν αὐτοκατάκριτος.

12. Ὅταν πέμψω Ἀρτεμᾶν πρός σε ἢ Τυχικόν, σπούδασον ἐλθεῖν πρός με εἰς Νικόπολιν· ἐκεῖ γὰρ κέκρικα παραχειμάσαι. 13. Ζηνᾶν τὸν νομικὸν καὶ Ἀπολλὼ σπουδαίως

refractory, yet he gives him not over, but *is long before he proceed to disinheriting*' (*Priest to the Temple*, ch. xvi.).

12-15. Personal matters and salutation.

12. Artemas is not known except from this passage. For Tychicus see n. on 2 Tim. iv. 12.

The only Nicopolis of any importance was the city on the coast of Epirus. It was founded artificially by Augustus to celebrate the victory of Actium, B.C. 31, and it stood on the site occupied by his camp before the battle. It had games, fisheries, and some commerce. It was destroyed by the Goths and rebuilt by Justinian, but its importance passed to Prevesa, five miles away. The choice of this place to spend a winter in suggests that St. Paul meant now to add Epirus to the provinces in which he had founded the Church. But we do not know that he ever reached the place, and it is mere conjecture from the present passage that it marked the limit of his last journey and that he was arrested there.

13. Zenas is not mentioned elsewhere. νομικός could of course mean 'learned in law,' from the secular point of view, but here it almost certainly means a Jewish scribe, who from the literary point of view could be called a γραμματεύς,

from his skill as a jurist νομικός, and as a teacher of the law νομοδιδάσκαλος. It is interesting to find him in company with Apollos, who is also described as ἀνὴρ λόγιος, δυνατὸς ὢν ἐν ταῖς γραφαῖς (Acts xviii. 24). They were presumably two of the learned men among the early converts. For Apollos see Acts xviii. and 1 Corinthians. He was an Alexandrian Jew whom Priscilla and Aquila found teaching an imperfect knowledge of Christ at Ephesus. When he had become a full Christian he went to Corinth, and obtained such influence there that a party of special adherents used his name against St. Paul. It has been maintained that Apollos was the author of the Epistle to the Hebrews.

πρόπεμψον, 'set on their way,' 'forward them in their journey.'

14. The words καλῶν ἔργων προίστασθαι must be taken in the sense in which they occur in v. 8. If the first of the two meanings there suggested is the right one, we must take it here to mean 'maintain good works with a view to supplying such needs,' *i.e.* needs such as those of Zenas and Apollos, implied in πρόπεμψον ἵνα μηδὲν αὐτοῖς λείπῃ. If the second meaning is the right one it could mean 'keep to honourable occupations to supply (their own) needs.' The following ἵνα μὴ ὦσιν ἄκαρποι is more natural with

πρόπεμψον, ἵνα μηδὲν αὐτοῖς λείπῃ. 14. μανθανέτωσαν δὲ καὶ οἱ ἡμέτεροι καλῶν ἔργων προΐστασθαι εἰς τὰς ἀναγκαίας χρείας, ἵνα μὴ ὦσιν ἄκαρποι.
15. Ἀσπάζονταί σε οἱ μετ' ἐμοῦ πάντες. ἄσπασαι τοὺς φιλοῦντας ἡμᾶς ἐν πίστει.
Ἡ χάρις μετὰ πάντων ὑμῶν.

the former ('that they may help on the good work'), but possible with the latter, because the maintenance of their principles in business was essential to their having an influence on pagan surroundings.

οἱ ἡμέτεροι is naturally taken of 'our own disciples in Crete.' But καί implies that they are contrasted with somebody. Alford says with Titus, because he is the actual subject of πρόπεμψον. But it is perhaps more natural to take it as a comparison with Zenas and Apollos— 'as these men are giving themselves to the work, so let our disciples also learn from them to...'

15. ἄσπασαι τοὺς φιλοῦντας ἡμᾶς ἐν πίστει. Notice that this is a form of salutation not used elsewhere by St. Paul.

INDEX TO INTRODUCTION AND NOTES

N.B.—In the following references :
A stands for the First Epistle to Timothy.
B stands for the Second Epistle to Timothy.
C stands for the Epistle to Titus.

GREEK

ἀγαθοεργέω, A. VI. 18.
ἀγάπη, A. I. 5, B. I. 7.
ἄγγελοι, A. III. 16, V. 21.
ἁγιασμός, A. II. 15.
ἅγιος, A. II. 15, C. II. 5.
ἁγνεία, A. V. 1.
ἁγνός, A. V. 22, C. II. 5.
ἀγωνίζομαι, A. IV. 10.
ἀδόκιμος, B. III. 8, C. I. 16.
ἀθανασία, A. VI. 16.
αἰδώς, A. II. 9.
αἵρεσις, αἱρετικός, C. III. 10.
αἰσχροκερδής, A. III. 8.
αἰών, A. I. 16, 17.
  τὸν νῦν αἰῶνα, A. VI. 17, B. IV. 10.
αἰώνιος, A. I. 16.
  πρὸ χρόνων αἰωνίων, B. I. 9.
ἀκαίρως, B. IV. 2.
ἀκρατής, B. III. 3.
ἀλαζών, B. III. 2.
ἀλήθειαν λέγω, οὐ ψεύδομαι, A. II. 7.
ἁμαρτωλός, A. I. 9.
ἀμήν, A. I. 17.
ἀνάγνωσις, ἀναγινώσκω, A. IV. 13.
ἀναζωπυρέω, B. I. 6.
ἀνακαίνωσις Πνεύματος Ἁγίου, C. III. 5.
ἀνάλυσις, B. IV. 6.

ἀνανήφω, B. II. 26.
ἀναστροφή, A. IV. 12.
ἀνδραποδιστής, A. I. 10.
ἀνεξίκακος, B. II. 24.
ἀνεπίληπτος, A. III. 2, VI. 14.
ἀνήμερος, B. III. 3.
ἀνήρ, ἄνθρωπος, A. II. 8.
ἄνθρωπος Θεοῦ, A. VI. 11, B. III. 17.
ἀνόητος, C. III. 3.
ἄνομος, A. I. 9.
ἀνόσιος, A. I. 9.
ἀντιθέσεις, A. VI. 20.
ἀντιλαμβάνομαι, A. VI. 2.
ἀντιλέγω, C. II. 9.
ἀντίλυτρον, A. II. 6.
ἀνυπόκριτος, A. I. 5, B. I. 5.
ἀνυπότακτος, A. I. 9, C. I. 10.
ἄξιος ὁ ἐργάτης τοῦ μισθοῦ, A. V. 18.
ἀπαίδευτος, B. II. 23.
ἅπαξ λεγόμενα in Pastoral Epistles, Introd. xxx.
ἀπέχεσθαι βρωμάτων, A. IV. 3.
ἀποδοχή, A. I. 15.
ἀποθησαυρίζω, A. VI. 18.
ἀπόστολος, A. I. 1.
ἀπωθέω, A. I. 19.
ἀργαὶ μανθάνουσι, A. V. 13.
ἀρκέω, A. VI. 8.

ἀρνοῦμαι, A. v. 8.
ἄρτιος, B. iii. 17.
ἀσέβεια, ἀσεβής, A. i. 9, B. ii. 16.
ἄσπιλος, A. vi. 14.
ἄσπονδος, B. iii. 3.
ἄστοργος, B. iii. 3.
ἀστοχέω, A. i. 6.
ἀσωτία, C. i. 6.
αὐθάδης, C. i. 7.
αὐθεντέω, A. ii. 12.
αὐτάρκεια, A. vi. 6.
ἀφθαρσία, A. vi. 16, B. i. 10.
ἀφθορία, C. ii. 7.
ἀφιλάγαθος, B. iii. 3.
ἀφιλάργυρος, B. iii. 3.
ἀχάριστος, B. iii. 2.
ἀψευδής, C. i. 2.

βαθμός, A. iii. 13.
βαρέω, A. v. 16.
βασιλεύς (used of God), A. i. 17.
   (of the Roman Emperor), A. ii. 1.
βδελυκτός, C. 1. 16.
βέβηλος, A. i. 9, B. ii. 16.
βιβλία, B. iv. 13.
βίος, A. i. 16.
βλασφημέω, B. iii. 2.
βλασφημία, A. i. 13, vi. 4.
βλάσφημος, A. i. 13, B. iii. 2.
βοῦν ἀλοῶντα οὐ φιμώσεις, A. v. 18.
βυθίζω, A. vi. 9.

γάγγραινα, B. ii. 17.
γαστέρες ἀργαί, C. i. 12.
γενεαλογίαι, A. i. 4, C. iii. 9.
γνήσιος, A. i. 2.
γόητες, B. iii. 13.
γραμματεύς, C. iii. 13.
γραφαὶ ἅγιαι, B. iii. 15.
γραώδης, A. iv. 7.
γυμνάζω, A. iv. 7.
γυναικάρια, B. iii. 6.

δαιμόνια, A. iv. 1.

δειλία, B. i. 7.
δέησις, A. ii. 1, B. i. 3.
δέσμιος (τοῦ Κυρίου), B. i. 8.
διά (of time, circumstances), A. ii. 15.
διὰ πολλῶν μαρτύρων, B. ii. 2.
διαβεβαιοῦμαι, A. i. 7, C. iii. 8.
διάβολος, A. i. 20, B. ii. 26.
διάβολοι, A. iii. 11, B. iii. 3.
διακονία, A. i. 12.
διάκονος, A. iii. 8.
   (of women), Introd. xxxi, A. iii. 11.
διαλογισμός, A. ii. 8.
διαμαρτύρομαι, A. v. 21, B. iv. 1.
διαπαρατριβαί, A. vi. 5.
διδακτικός, B. ii. 24.
διδάσκαλος ἐθνῶν, A. ii. 7; cf. B. i. 11.
διεφθαρμένων τὸν νοῦν, A. vi. 5; cf. B. iii. 8.
διηκόνησε, B. i. 18.
δίκαιος, C. i. 8.
δικαιοσύνη, A. vi. 11, B. ii. 22.
δικαιόω, C. iii. 7.
δίλογος, A. iii. 8.
δοκιμάζω, A. iii. 10.
δόκιμος, B. ii. 15.
δόξα, A. i. 11, C. ii. 13.
δοῦλοι (ὑπὸ ζυγόν), A. vi. 1.
δοῦλος Θεοῦ, C. i. 1.
δοῦλος Κυρίου, B. ii. 24.
δύναμις, B. i. 7.
δῷ, δῴη, δώῃ, B. ii. 25.

ἐγκρατής, C. i. 8.
ἑδραίωμα, A. iii. 15.
ἐζωγρημένοι ὑπ' αὐτοῦ κ.τ.λ., B. ii. 26.
εἰρήνη (in greeting), A. i. 2.
εἰς (purpose), B. ii. 26.
ἔκγονα, A. v. 4.
ἐκζητήσεις, A. i. 4.
ἐκκλησία, A. iii. 15.

INDEX

ἐκλεκτοί, B. ii. 10.
ἐκλεκτῶν ἀγγέλων, A. v. 21.
ἐκ σπέρματος Δαβίδ, B. ii. 8.
ἐλεγμός, B. iii. 16.
ἐλέγχω, B. iv. 2.
ἔλεος (in greeting), A. i. 2.
ἐλπίς, A. i. 1.
ἐν (instrument, cause, sphere, etc.), A. i. 18, ii. 7, iv. 2, B. i. 1.
ἐνδυναμοῦμαι, B. ii. 1.
ἐνδύνω, B. iii. 6.
ἐνοικέω, B. i. 5.
ἑνὸς ἀνδρὸς γυνή, A. v. 9.
ἔντευξις, A. ii. 1.
ἐντολή, A. vi. 14.
ἐντρέφω, A. iv. 6.
ἐξηρτισμένος, B. iii. 17.
ἐξουσία, C. iii. 1.
ἐπαγγελίαν ζωῆς, A. iv. 8.
ἐπαγγέλλομαι, A. ii. 10, C. i. 2.
ἐπαίροντας χεῖρας, A. ii. 8.
ἐπακολουθέω, A. v. 24.
ἐπανόρθωσις, B. iii. 16.
ἐπ' ἐλπίδι, C. i. 2.
ἐπί (result, etc.), B. ii. 14.
ἐπίγνωσις, A. ii. 4, B. iii. 7, Introd. xxix.
ἐπιεικής, A. iii. 3.
ἐπιθυμία, B. ii. 22.
ἐπιμένω, A. iv. 16.
ἐπισκοπή, A. iii. 1.
ἐπίσκοπος, A. iii. 1, iv. 14, C. i. 5.
ἐπιταγή, C. ii. 15.
ἐπιτιμάω, B. iv. 2.
ἐπιφάνεια, A. vi. 14, B. i. 10, iv. 1.
ἔσχαται ἡμέραι, B. iii. 1.
ἑτεροδιδασκαλέω, A. i. 3, vi. 3.
εὐαγγέλιον, A. i. 11.
εὐαγγελιστής, B. iv. 5, Introd. xv.
εὐκαίρως, ἀκαίρως, B. iv. 2.
εὐμετάδοτος, A. vi. 18.
εὐσέβεια, A. ii. 2, vi. 11, Introd. xxix.

εὐχαριστία, A. ii. 1.
εὔχρηστος, B. ii. 21.
ἐφίσταμαι, B. iv. 2.
ἕως (with Pres. Ind.), A. iv. 13.

ζωγρέω, B. ii. 26.
ζωή, A. i. 16, iv. 8.
ζωὴ αἰώνιος, A. i. 16.
ζωογονέω, A. vi. 13.
ζῶσα τέθνηκε, A. v. 6.

ἡδονή, φιλήδονος, B. iii. 4.
ἤπιος, B. ii. 24.
ἤρεμος, A. ii. 2.
ἡσυχία, ἐν ἡσυχίᾳ, A. ii. 11.
ἡσύχιος, A. ii. 2.

θεμέλιος, A. vi. 19, B. ii. 19.
θεόπνευστος, B. iii. 16.
θλίβω, A. v. 10.

ἴδιος, A. vi. 1.
ἱερὰ γράμματα, B. iii. 15.
ἱεροπρεπής, C. ii. 3.
ἱερός, A. i. 9, B. iii. 15.
Ἰησοῦ Χριστοῦ, A. i. 1.

καθαρός, A. i. 5, C. i. 15.
καιροῖς ἰδίοις, A. ii. 6, vi. 15, C. i. 3.
κακὰ θηρία, C. i. 12.
κακοῦργος, B. ii. 9.
καλέω, B. i. 9.
καλοδιδάσκαλος, C. ii. 3.
καλός, A. iv. 6, vi. 12, Introd. xxix.
καλῶν ἔργων προΐστασθαι, C. iii. 8, 14.
καρδία, A. i. 5.
κατά (purpose), B. i. 1, C. i. 1.
καταλέγω, A. v. 9.
καταργέω, B. i. 10.
κατάστημα, C. ii. 3.
καταστρηνιάω, A. v. 11.
καταστροφή, B. ii. 14.

καταφρονέω, A. IV. 12.
καυτηριάζω, A. IV. 2.
κενός, A. I. 6.
κενοφωνίαι, A. VI. 20, B. II. 16.
κληρονόμος, C. III. 7.
κλῆσις, B. I. 9.
κοινωνικός, A. VI. 18.
κοπιάω, A. IV. 10, v. 17, B. II. 6.
κόπος, A. IV. 10.
κοσμέω, C. II. 10.
κοσμικός, C. II. 12.
κόσμιος, A. III. 2.
κρῖμα τοῦ διαβόλου, A. III. 6.
κωλυόντων γαμεῖν, A. IV. 3.

λατρεύω, B. I. 3.
λογομαχίαι, A. VI. 4.
λόγον ὑγιῆ, C. II. 8.
λουτροῦ παλιγγενεσίας, C. III. 5.
λυτρόω, C. II. 14.

μακάριος, A. VI. 15.
μακάριος Θεός, A. I. 11 ; cf. VI. 15.
μακροθυμία, A. I. 16, B. IV. 2.
μανθάνω (construction), A. v. 13.
μαρτύριον, A. II. 6.
μαρτύριον τοῦ Κυρίου, B. I. 8.
μαρτύρομαι, A. v. 21.
ματαιολογία, μάταιος, A. I. 6.
μάχεσθαι, μάχαι, B. II. 24.
μεμβράνα, B. IV. 13.
μεμιασμένος, C. I. 15.
μεσίτης, A. II. 5.
μή (with participles), A. I. 7.
('if perchance'), B. II. 25.
μιᾶς γυναικὸς ἄνδρα, A. III. 2.
μνεία, B. I. 3.
μορφή, μόρφωσις, B. III. 5.
μῦθοι, A. I. 4, B. IV. 4, C. I. 14.
μυστήριον, A. III. 9, 16, Introd. xxix.

νεόφυτος, A. III. 6.
νεωτερικὰς ἐπιθυμίας, B. II. 22.

νηφάλιος, A. III. 2.
νήφω, B. IV. 5.
νομή, B. II. 17.
νομικός, C. III. 13.
νομίμως, A. I. 8, B. II. 5.
νομοδιδάσκαλοι, A. I. 7, C. III. 13.
νοσῶν, A. VI. 4.
νοῦς, B. III. 8, C. I. 15.

ξενοδοχέω, A. v. 10.

ὅ (wherefore), A. VI. 7.
οἴδαμεν, A. I. 8.
οἱ ἐκ περιτομῆς, C. I. 10.
οἰκεῖοι, A. v. 8.
οἰκονομίαν Θεοῦ, A. I. 4.
οἰκονόμος, C. I. 7.
οἶκος Θεοῦ, A. III. 15.
οἰκουργός, C. II. 5.
ὁμολογίαν (τὴν καλήν), A. VI. 12.
ὀργίλος, C. I. 7.
ὀρθοτομέω, B. II. 15.
ὅσιος, A. I. 9, II. 8, C. I. 8.

παγίς, A. VI. 9, B. II. 26.
παιδεύω, A. I. 20, B. II. 23, 25, C. II. 12.
παλιγγενεσία, C. III. 5.
πάντα καθαρὰ τοῖς καθαροῖς, C. I. 12.
παράβασις, A. II. 14.
παραγγελία, παραγγέλλω, A. I. 5.
παραγίνομαι, B. IV. 16.
παραδιατριβαί, A. VI. 5.
παραθήκη, A. VI. 20, B. I. 12, 14, Introd. xxx.
παραιτοῦμαι, A. IV. 7, v. 11.
παράκλησις, A. IV. 13.
παράκλητος, B. IV. 17.
παρακολουθέω, A. IV. 6.
παρατίθεμαι, A. I. 18.
παρέδωκα τῷ Σατανᾷ, A. I. 20.
πάροινος, A. III. 3.
πᾶσα γραφὴ θεόπνευστος, B. III. 16.

INDEX

Παῦλος (name), A. I. 1.
πειρασμός, A. VI. 9.
περίεργοι, A. V. 13.
περιΐσταμαι, B. II. 16.
περιούσιος (λαός), C. II. 14.
πιστεύω (construction), C. III. 8.
πιστὸς ὁ λόγος, A. I. 15, III. 1, IV. 9, B. II. 11, C. III. 8, Introd. xxix.
πλανῶντες καὶ πλανώμενοι, B. III. 13.
πλέγματα, A. II. 9.
πλήκτης, A. III. 3.
πληροφορέω, B. IV. 5.
πνεύμασι πλάνοις, A. IV. 1.
πονηρός, B. III. 13.
πορισμός (ἡ εὐσέβεια), A. VI. 6.
πραγματεῖαι (αἱ τοῦ βίου π.), B. II. 4.
πρᾳότης, B. II. 25.
πραϋπάθεια, A. VI. 11.
πρεσβυτέριον, A. IV. 14.
πρεσβύτεροι, A. III. 1, IV. 14, C. I. 5.
   (accusations against), A. V. 19, 20.
   (appointment of), A. III. 1, IV. 14, C. I. 5.
   (character of), A. III. 1, C. I. 6.
   (payment of), A. V. 17.
πρεσβύτερος ('an older man'), A. V. 1.
προάγω, A. I. 18.
πρόδηλος, A. V. 24.
προδότης, B. III. 4.
πρόθεσις, B. I. 9.
προΐστασθαι (καλῶν ἔργων), C. III. 8, 14.
προκόπτω, B. II. 16.
πρόκριμα, A. V. 21.
προπέμπω, C. III. 13.
προπετής, B. III. 4.
προσέρχομαι, A. VI. 3.
προσευχή, A. II. 1.
πρόσκλισις, A. V. 21.
πρὸς ὀλίγον, A. IV. 8.
προφῆται, προφητεία, A. I. 18, IV. 14.
προφήτης (of Epimenides), C. I. 12.

ῥητῶς, A. IV. 1.
ῥίζα πάντων τῶν κακῶν (ἡ φιλαργυρία), A. VI. 10.

Σατανᾶς, A. I. 20.
σεμνός, σεμνότης, A. II. 2, III. 4.
σκεπάσματα, A. VI. 8.
σκεύη εἰς τιμήν, B. II. 20.
σπαταλάω, A. V. 6.
σπένδομαι, B. IV. 6.
στέφανος (τῆς δικαιοσύνης), B. IV. 8.
στόμα λέοντος, B. IV. 17.
στυγητός, C. III. 3.
στῦλος καὶ ἑδραίωμα, A. III. 15.
συγκακοπαθέω, B. I. 8, II. 3.
συνείδησις, A. I. 5.
σύνεσις, B. II. 7.
σφραγίς, B. II. 19.
σχῆμα, B. III. 5.
σώζω, σωτηρία, B. I. 9.
σωρεύω, B. III. 6.
σωτὴρ πάντων ἀνθρώπων, A. IV. 10.
σωφρονισμός, B. I. 7.
σωφροσύνη, A. II. 9.
σώφρων, C. I. 8.

τεκνογονία, A. II. 15.
τέκνον, A. I. 2.
τεκνοτροφέω, A. V. 10.
τέλος, A. I. 5.
τίς (for relative), A. I. 7.
τύπος, A. IV. 12.
τυφόω, A. III. 6, VI. 4, B. III. 4.

ὑβριστής, A. I. 13.
ὑγιαίνω, A. I. 10, VI. 3, Introd. xxix.
ὑγιής, C. II. 8.
ὑπερήφανος, B. III. 2.
ὑπερπλεονάζω, A. I. 14.
ὑπόμνησις, B. I. 5.
ὑπομονή, ὑπομένω, A. VI. 11, B. II. 10.
ὑπόνοιαι, A. VI. 4.
ὑποτίθεμαι, A. IV. 6.

ὑποτύπωσις, A. I. 16, B. I. 13.
ὑστέροις καιροῖς, A. IV. 1.
ὑψηλοφρονέω, A. VI. 17.

φαιλόνης, φελόνης, B. IV. 13.
φαῦλος, C. II. 8.
φιλανθρωπία, C. III. 4.
φιλαργυρία, φιλάργυρος, A. VI. 10, B. III. 2.
φίλαυτος, B. III. 2.
φιλήδονος, B. III. 4.
φιλόξενος, A. III. 2.
φλύαρος, A. V. 13.
φρεναπάτης, C. I. 10.
φύλαξον (τὴν παραθήκην), B. I. 14.

φωτίζω, B. I. 10.

χαλκεύς, B. IV. 14.
χάριν ἔχω, B. I. 3.
χάρις, A. I. 2.
χάρισμα, A. IV. 14, B. I. 6.
χῆραι, A. v. 3.
χρηστότης, C. III. 14.
Χριστοῦ Ἰησοῦ, A. I. 1.
χρυσίον, A. II. 9.

ψεύστης, A. I. 10.

ὡσαύτως, A. II. 9.
ὤφθη ἀγγέλοις, A. III. 16.

INDEX TO INTRODUCTION AND NOTES

ENGLISH

abstinence from foods	A. IV. 3, C. I. 15.
'adorn the doctrine'	C. II. 10.
advocatus	B. IV. 16, 17.
aeons (Gnostic)	A. IV. 3, I. 4.
Alexander	A. I. 20, B. IV. 14.
amen	A. I. 17.
anacoluthon	A. I. 3.
angels	A. III. 16, V. 21.
anger	C. I. 7.
anonymous accusations	A. V. 19.
antinomianism	C. I. 16.
Aorist tense	A. IV. 6, B. III. 10.
imperative	B. IV. 2.
Apollos	C. III. 13.
apostle	A. I. 1.
apostolic and sub-apostolic writings	Introd. xxiv.
Aquila	B. IV. 19.
argument—dangers of	A. VI. 4, 5, B. III. 13.
arrogance	B. III. 2.
Artemas	C. III. 12.
article (translation in English)	A. I. 18.
asceticism	A. IV. 3, V. 23.
athlete as example	B. II. 5.
authority—qualities for	B. I. 7.
autocracy in the parish	C. I. 7.

Baptism	C. III. 5.
baptismal profession	A. VI. 12.
Bible—study and inspiration	B. III. 14-16.
bishops—meaning of ἐπίσκοποι	A. III. 1 (see ref. πρεσβύτεροι).
„ responsibility of ordaining power	A. V. 22.
„ authority of Timothy and Titus	A. III. 1, C. I. 5.
boastfulness	B. III. 2.
books	B. II. 14, IV. 13.
'call,' 'calling'	B. I. 9.
canon of Old Testament	B. III. 15.
„ New Testament—growth of	Introd. xxiv.
„ Muratorian canon	Introd. xxv.
„ Marcion's list	Introd. xxvii.
canticles	A. III. 16, B. II. 11.
'charge'	A. V. 7.
'charity'	A. I. 5.
choice of helpers	A. V. 22-25.
choice of one's own teachers	B. IV. 3.
Church—Greek words for	A. III. 15.
church workers	A. V. 11.
circumcision of Gentiles	Introd. xv.
„ of Timothy	Introd. xv.
„ in the case of Titus	Introd. xxi.
Claudia	B. IV. 21.
commercial morality	B. III. 2.
compromise, danger at Ephesus	B. II. 14, Introd. xix.
conscience	A. I. 5, IV. 2.
contentment	A. VI. 6.
controversy, methods of	B. II. 24.
conversation	A. IV. 12, C. II. 8.
Corinth, Timothy at	Introd. xvi.

INDEX

Corinth, visits of Titus	Introd. xxii.
Corinthians, Epistles to	Introd. xvi, xxi.
covetousness	A. III. 3, 8, VI. 10, B. III. 2.
creeds	A. III. 16.
Crescens	B. IV. 10.
Cretans, character of	Introd. xxiii, C. I. 12.
Crete, heresy in	C. I. 10-16.
„ Church and Titus in	Introd. xxii, C. I. 5, 10-16.
deacon, character and work	A. III. 8, 9.
deaconesses	Introd. xxxi, A. III. 11.
death, of none effect through Christ	B. I. 10.
deception of self and others	B. III. 13.
'deliver to Satan'	A. I. 20.
Demas	B. IV. 10.
desertion of St. Paul	B. I. 15, IV. 10.
detachment from worldly affairs	B. II. 4.
devil, power of	A. I. 20, B. II. 26.
devils, 'doctrines of devils'	A. IV. 1.
Didache, the 'Teaching of the XII Apostles'	A. I. 1.
discipline of others	B. I. 7, II. 25.
„ of self	B. II. 5.
divinity of our Lord	C. II. 13.
doxology	A. I. 17, VI. 15.
drinking wine	A. III. 3.
elders ($\pi\rho\epsilon\sigma\beta\acute{u}\tau\epsilon\rho oi$)	A. III. 1, IV. 14; see $\pi\rho\epsilon\sigma\beta\acute{u}\tau\epsilon\rho oi$.
„ Jewish	A. III. 1, IV. 14.
emotionalism	A. V. 11.
Ephesus, history and trade	Introd. xvii.

Ephesus, religion at . . . Introd. xviii.
„ Church and heresies . . Introd. xix, xxxiii.
„ Timothy's authority at . Introd. xx, A. I. 4.
Epimenides . . . . . C. I. 12.
episcopal authority . . . . A. III. 1; cf. C. I. 5.
„ ordaining power . . A. v. 22.
Erastus . . . . . . B. IV. 20.
Essenes . . . . . . A. IV. 3.
eternal life . . . . . A. I. 16.
Eunice . . . . . . Introd. xiii, B. III. 14.
evangelist . . . . . B. IV. 5, Introd. xv.
evil spirits . . . . . A. I. 20, IV. 1.

factiousness . . . . . C. III. 10.
'faithful is the saying' . . . A. I. 15, III. 1, IV. 9,
          C. III. 8.
false teachers . . . . . B. III. 7, 13.
farmer as example . . . . B. II. 6.
fasting . . . . . . A. IV. 3, v. 23.
friendship . . . . . B. IV. 11.

gain sought by religious profession   A. VI. 5, C. I. 11.
Gnostic heresies . . . . A. I. 4, IV. 3, VI. 20,
          B. III. 8, Introd. xxvii.
„ literature . . . . Introd. xxviii.
governments, St. Paul's attitude to   A. II. 1.
'grace before meat' . . . A. IV. 4.
gratitude . . . . . B. III. 2.
Greek (application of name) . . Introd. xiii.
greetings in Epistles . . . A. I. 1, C. III. 15.
'guard the deposit' . . . B. I. 14.

hardship, suffering . . . . B. I. 8, II. 3.
health affecting conduct . . . A. v. 23.

INDEX

'heirs,' 'inheritance'	C. III. 7.
heresies at Ephesus	A. I. 4, IV. 3, VI. 20, B. II. 7, III. 8, Introd. xix.
„ in Crete	C. I. 10-16.
heresy, heretic (meaning of word)	C. III. 10.
Hermogenes	B. I. 15.
holy (Greek words for)	A. II. 8, 15, B. III. 15.
hospitality	A. III. 2, V. 10.
Hymenaeus	A. I. 20, B. II. 17.
hymns	A. III. 16, B. II. 11.
ignorance as an excuse	A. I. 13.
imprisonment of St. Paul, first	Introd. ix.
„ „ second	Introd. xi, B. I. 16, IV. 9 fol.
independence, true and false	A. VI. 6, B. III. 2.
ingratitude	B. III. 2.
inspiration of Scripture	B. III. 16.
intellect, pride of	A. VI. 4, 5.
„ guided by the Spirit	B. I. 14.
Jannes and Jambres	B. III. 8.
Jewish asceticism	A. IV. 3.
„ heresies and speculations	A. I. 4, IV. 3, C. I. 10, 16.
„ names	A. I. 1.
„ sects	A. IV. 3.
judgment of character	A. V. 24.
justification	C. III. 7.
Laodiceans, spurious letter to	Introd. xxv, xxviii.
'last days'	B. III. 1.
law, purpose of	A. I. 8.
lawyer	C. III. 13.

laying on of hands	A. IV. 14.
learning, the wrong kind	A. V. 13, B. III. 7, IV. 3.
Linus	B. IV. 21.
liturgical phrases	A. III. 16, VI. 15, B. II 11.
Lois	B. III. 14.
love (Greek words for)	A. I. 5.
lusts, 'youthful lusts'	B. II. 22.
lying, St. Paul's estimate of	A. I. 10.
„ pagan and Christian view of	A. III. 8.
Lystra	Introd. xiii.
magic at Ephesus	Introd. xviii.
'man of God'	A. VI. 11.
Marcion	Introd. xxvii.
Mark	B. IV. 11.
marriage	A. III. 2. IV. 3, V. 11, 14.
„ between Jews and Gentiles	Introd. xiv.
„ second marriage	A. III. 2, V. 11, 14.
„ divorce	A. III. 2.
martyrdom of St. Paul	Introd. xii.
mediator, Christ as	A. II. 5.
ministry, development of	A. III. 1, Introd. xxxi.
„ precepts for	B. II. 3-6.
„ payment of	A. V. 17.
„ maintenance of	B. II. 4.
„ judgment of ministers	A. V. 19.
„ gifts of, and danger of neglect	B. I. 6, 7.

(See also ref. ἐπίσκοποι, πρεσβύτεροι, διάκονοι, προφῆται, εὐαγγελιστής.)

INDEX

money, love of	A. III. 3, 8, VI. 10, B. III. 2.
Montanism	A. I. 18, IV. 1.
morals of Roman world	A. I. 19.
Muratorian fragment	Introd. x, xxiv.
mysteries	A. III. 9, 16.
'myths'	A. I. 4, B. IV. 4, C. I. 14.
names, Jewish	A. I. 1.
'nephews' (A.V.)	A. V. 4.
Nero, persecution under	Introd. ix, xi, B. IV. 10.
'new birth'	C. III. 5.
newspaper controversy	B. II. 24.
Nicopolis	C. III. 12, Introd. x.
older men, treatment of	A. V. 1.
Old Testament, canon and use of	B. III. 15, 16.
Onesiphorus	B. I. 16, IV. 19.
oral teaching	B. II. 14.
ordination	A. I. 18, III. 1, IV. 14; B. I. 6, 7, II. 2.
„ of Timothy	The above and Introd. xiv.
„ gifts at	A. IV. 14, B. I. 6.
outward form of religion	B. III. 5.
outward marks of profession	C. II. 3.
parchments	B. IV. 13.
parents, duty to	A. V. 4, B. III. 2.
„ religion of	B. I. 3.
parental teaching	B. III. 14.
'parson'	C. I. 7.

'partaker of other men's sins'	A. v. 22.
partiality	A. v. 22.
patience	A. i. 16, B. ii. 10.
Paul (the name)	A. i. 1.
payment of ministry	A. v. 17, Introd. xxxi.
peaceable disposition	B. ii. 22.
'peculiar'	C. ii. 14.
Perfect tense	A. ii. 14, iv. 10, B. ii. 8.
persecution under Nero	Introd. ix, xi, B. iv. 10.
perverts	B. iv. 3.
philosophy, influence of	A. i. 4, iv. 3, B. ii. 14, Introd. xix, xxxiii.
phraseology of Pastoral Epistles	Introd. xxix.
Phygelus	B. i. 15.
pleasure, love of	B. iii. 4.
polygamy	A. iii. 2.
prayer (Greek words for)	A. ii. 1.
,, usage in the Church	A. ii. 1, 8.
,, at meals	A. iv. 5.
preaching	C. ii. 7.
pride of intellect	A. vi. 4, 5.
priests	See ref. πρεσβύτεροι.
Prisca	B. iv. 19.
private judgment, limitations of	C. i. 15.
'profane'	A. i. 9.
professions, wrong	C. iii. 8, 14.
prophecy, prophets in the Church	A. i. 18, iv. 1, 14.
public opinion, corruption of	B. iii. 2.
Pudens	B. iv. 21.
pure, 'to the pure all things are pure'	C. i. 15.
reading	A. iv. 13.

INDEX

reason guided by the Spirit	B. I. 14.
rebuke in public	A. V. 20.
„ methods of	B. IV. 2.
redemption	A. II. 6.
regeneration	C. III. 5.
'reprobate'	C. I. 16.
responsibility for choice of helpers	A. V. 22.
resurrection of Christ, encouragement from	B. II. 7.
„ denial of	B. II. 18.
riches, dangers of	A. VI. 9, 10, 17, B. III. 2.
roll of widows	A. V. 3, 9, 11.
Roman empire, St. Paul's attitude to	A. II. 1.
Rome, persecution at	Introd. xi, B. IV. 10.
„ St. Paul at	Introd. ix, xi; cf. B. IV. 9 fol.
sanctification	C. III. 5.
Satan	A. I. 20; cf. B. II. 26.
Saul (the name)	A. I. 1.
save, salvation	B. I. 9, A. IV. 10.
Scriptures, inspiration and use of	B. III. 15, 16.
seal-inscriptions	B. II. 19.
season, 'in season and out of season'	B. IV. 2.
second Advent, expectations of	A. VI. 14, B. III. 1.
self-control	B. III. 3, C. I. 8.
self-deception	B. III. 13.
selfishness	B. III. 2.
self-willed	C. I. 7.
shame of the cross	B. I. 8.
slavery	A. VI. 1, 2, C. II. 9, 10.
soldier as example	B. II. 2-4.
speaking evil	A. VI. 4, B. III. 2.

spirits of evil	A. I. 20, IV. 1.
spiritual utterances	A. I. 18, IV. 1, 14.
spurious literature	Introd. xxv, xxviii, xxxiv.
strength of character	B. I. 7, II. 1.
study of the clergy	A. IV. 7.
suspicion	A. VI. 4.
Tatian	Introd. xxvii.
teaching, qualities for	B. II. 24, C. II. 7.
,, discontent with sound teaching	B. IV. 3.
'Teaching of the XII Apostles'	A. I. 1.
thanksgiving	A. II. 1, IV. 4.
'thorn in the flesh'	A. I. 20.
trades possible for Christians	C. III. 8, 14.
training of clergy	A. IV. 7.
trials at Rome	B. IV. 16.
'trivial round'—its importance	C. II. 11.
Trophimus	B. IV. 20.
truth, pagan and Christian ideas of	A. III. 8; cf. I. 10.
Tychicus	B. IV. 12.
'vessels to honour'	B. II. 20.
vocation to religious work	A. V. 11.
vows of celibacy	A. V. 11.
'washing the feet'	A. V. 10.
wealth, dangers of	A. VI. 6-9, 10, 17, B. III. 2.
widows	A. V. 3, 9, 11.
wine	A. III. 3, V. 23.
women, place in the Church	A. II. 11, III. 11, V. 3, 9, 11, C. II. 5.

women, apparel	A. II. 9, C. II. 3.
„ subjection of	A. II. 13.
„ idle gossip	A. V. 13.
„ under false teachers	B. III. 7.

(See also *widows, marriage*.)

words, importance of	A. VI. 4.
work of clergy	A. IV. 10, V. 17.
works of piety and humility	A. V. 10.
young men in authority	A. III. 6, IV. 12.
„ 'youthful lusts'	B. II. 22.
Zenas	C. III. 13.

www.ingramcontent.com/pod-product-compliance
Lightning Source LLC
Chambersburg PA
CBHW051059160426
43193CB00010B/1243